THE AGEING COUNTRYSIDE

The Growing Older Population of Rural England

Edited by Professor Philip Lowe and Lydia Speakman

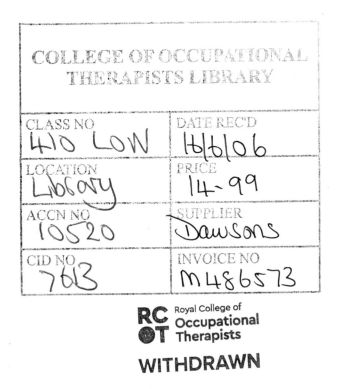

Published by Age Concern England
1268 London Road
London SW16 4ER

© 2006 Age Concern England

First published 2006

A catalogue record for this book is available
from the British Library

ISBN-13: 978-0-86242-414-5

ISBN-10: 0-86242-414-3

Whilst the information contained in this book is
believed to be true and accurate at the time of going
to press, neither Age Concern England nor the author
can accept any legal responsibility or liability for any
errors or omissions that may be made. Please note that
while the agencies or products mentioned in this book
are known to Age Concern, inclusion here does not
constitute a recommendation by Age Concern for a
particular product, agency or service.

Every effort has been made to contact and obtain
permission from the authors and/or copyright holders
of the works from which contributors have quoted. We
are very grateful to the authors and copyright holders
from whose works we have quoted and acknowledge
here their contribution to research in the field. Source
acknowledgments are placed in the text. Any omissions
of detail about sources which are brought to our
attention will be rectified should the book be reprinted
or revised in the future.

Copy-editor Karin Fancett
Production Leonie Farmer
Cover design Nigel Soper

Design and typesetting: www.Intertype.com
Printed in Great Britain by Bell & Bain Ltd, Glasgow

Contents

Foreword

As this book very clearly demonstrates, the ageing of rural England will be of profound importance to its economic and social future.

Demographic ageing is a long-term dynamic that our countryside areas hold in common with the rest of the UK and indeed the rest of Europe. Within England, and in other states, this dynamic is particularly important for rural areas because the impact of a combination of demographic factors means that the countryside is ageing more quickly and more extensively than elsewhere.

The implications of ageing are profound, reaching into all areas of our lives. It is important that we look at the full range of its impacts – on rural economies, within rural communities and on rural services. If we restrict our view we will not respond adequately to the opportunities it presents and address challenges fully and effectively.

It is also a dynamic which is under-researched. The editors of this book and the chapter authors have worked hard to present a strong evidence base about the pattern and the impact of rural ageing – delving into both qualitative and quantitative sources to present a rich picture. Their work exposes the inadequacy of the evidence base, an issue which must be addressed quickly and comprehensively if we are to respond effectively.

Finally, we must explode the myths and the rhetoric which underpin the pervasive stereotypes about the negative consequences of rural ageing. Whatever else they may be, neither our rural areas nor our older people are passive, dependent, undynamic or outdated. Both are complex, changing and diverse and their productive contribution to our national life goes unrecognised. Working in rural England, and working with the context of our emerging demography, requires a clear understanding of the current and future situation and the development of approaches which work with this reality.

It is important that those of us who care deeply for the future of rural England, and for the future welfare of its people and the cohesion of its communities, look carefully at, and respond to, the ageing of the countryside. This book provides a firm foundation for that process and we welcome its arrival and thank all who have contributed.

Gordon Lishman
Director General
Age Concern England

Stuart Burgess
Chairman
Commission for Rural Communities

About the authors

Philip Lowe is Director of the Rural Economy and Land Use (RELU) Programme of the UK Research Councils. He has been a leading figure in the development of the field of rural economy. In 1992, he founded the Centre for Rural Economy at the University of Newcastle upon Tyne, where he holds the Duke of Northumberland Chair of Rural Economy. He has played a key role in rural policy development at the national and European levels and in the North of England. He is currently a Board member of the Commission for Rural Communities and Chair of the Market Towns Advisory Forum. He was awarded the OBE in 2003 for his contribution to the rural economy.

Lydia Speakman works as a freelance consultant specialising in countryside and rural issues. She has worked for a range of organisations, including the Countryside Agency, local authorities, Age Concern England and Regional Development Agencies, undertaking research on various rural issues such as transport, countryside access, rural services and the rural economy.

Tony Champion is Emeritus Professor of Population Geography at Newcastle University. He has over 30 years' experience of studying migration and residential mobility, including looking at its determinants and its implications for population profiles and planning policies. His most recent research projects have looked at the evidence base on frequent movers (for the Social Exclusion Unit), the role of migration in changing the socio-demographic profile of British cities and their neighbourhoods (for theJoseph Rowntree Foundation), patterns of migration and population change in English cities (for ODPM's State of the Cities Report 2005) and demographic aspects of the viability and self-containment of areas of all scales from street to national (for ODPM's New Horizons programme).

John Shepherd is Professor of Geography at Birkbeck University of London, where he has taught and researched since 1975. In 2004 he became Director of the Defra Rural Evidence Research Centre (RERC), a multi-disciplinary consortium of six university departments that carries out independent research for Defra to support policy making. In 2003/04 he led the team that developed the new rural/urban definition of England and Wales and recently created the new rural classification of local authorities and primary care organisations of England. His own research for the RERC is led by the need to identify the main patterns of social and economic diversity across rural England that guide strategic policy making while also identifying localities for the detailed qualitative studies to support the delivery of services.

Irene Hardill is Professor of Economic Geography at The Graduate School, College of Business, Law and Social Sciences, Nottingham Trent University. Her research interests embrace demography and ageing, the juggling of paid and unpaid work (unpaid caring activity as well as voluntary action) and household decision making. Recent research has been sponsored by Age Concern, the Regions for All Ages programme and ESRC. Her publications include *Gender, Migration and the Dual Career Household* (Routledge, 2002) and the *Regional Strategies and Demographic Ageing: Age Proofing Toolkit*. She is a co-convenor of the Regional Studies Association Working Group on Demography and Ageing.

Dr Alana Gilbert is a post-doctoral research economist at The Macaulay Institute. Her research interests lie primarily in econometric analysis using large-scale data sets. To date she has applied her quantitative skills to the examination of a range of topics including the rural/urban wage gap, issues facing older people living in rural areas, business reactions to the foot and mouth disease outbreak, and farm incomes in Scotland.

Dr Lorna Philip is a lecturer in the Department of Geography and Environment at the University of Aberdeen. Her main area of research interest is rural socio-economic development, with a particular focus on social exclusion in rural communities. Recent research includes the completion of a Scoping Study of Older People in rural Scotland. She is currently working on a project investigating the role of formal organisations, social networks and civic participation among older people in rural Scotland.

Professor Mark Shucksmith is Professor of Planning at the University of Newcastle upon Tyne, and was until recently Professor of Land Economy and Director of the Arkleton Centre for Rural Development Research at the University of Aberdeen, and Co-Director of the Scottish Centre for Research on Social Justice. He is First Vice-President of the International Rural Sociological Association for 2004–08, and is Programme Adviser to the Joseph Rowntree Foundation 'Action in Rural Areas' programme. He is a Board member of the Countryside Agency and is a member of the Affordable Rural Housing Commission. He has provided advice to governments and agencies in several countries, and has led research for the EU, Scottish Executive, Defra, Joseph Rowntree Foundation, ESRC, Countryside Agency and many others.

Anne Green is a Principal Research Fellow at the Institute for Employment Research, University of Warwick. She has a background in geography and works primarily on spatial dimensions of economic, social and demographic change and on local and regional labour market issues, encompassing rural and urban areas. Her research interests include the geography of employment and non-employment, migration and commuting, and urban/rural/regional development. She has undertaken research for the Department of Works and Pensions, the Joseph Rowntree Foundation, the Countryside Agency and the ODPM.

Richard Baker is a National Development Manager for Age Concern England and is responsible for the development and co-ordination of Age Concern's work in the areas of regional policy, rural affairs and productive ageing. He leads Regions for All Ages, a collaborative programme between ACE and the English Regions Network, promoting awareness of the implications of ageing for regional policy within Europe and the UK. He has also worked with Defra, the Countryside Agency and others to extend knowledge about the demographic ageing of rural areas. He is a Board member of PRIME, an initiative promoting self-employment for older people, and a Trustee of the Employers Forum on Age, a business-led organisation promoting age diversity in employment. He is a Visiting Fellow at both the Centre for Rural Economy at the University of Newcastle and the Policy Oriented Social Sciences Research Group at Nottingham Trent University.

Nick Le Mesurier is Research Fellow at the University of Birmingham. He has undertaken numerous service evaluation projects for older people in a variety of joint health/social services/voluntary sector settings. He is the author of *The Hidden Store: Older People's Contributions to Rural Communities,* which was commissioned by Age Concern England and published in March 2003.

Mark Bevan is a Research Fellow in the Centre for Housing Policy, University of York. He has maintained a keen interest in housing issues in rural areas throughout his career, which originally stemmed from doctoral research on affordable housing and housing needs in rural East Suffolk. Other research has examined a number of different aspects of housing in rural areas, including the private rented sector, the role of social housing, the housing and support needs of older people, the impact of second and holiday homes on rural communities, and rural homelessness.

Karen Croucher is a research fellow at the Centre for Housing Policy, University of York, with a long-standing interest in housing and care for later life. She is currently lead researcher on a comparative evaluation of models of housing with care for later life (funded by the Joseph Rowntree Foundation) and was also one of the lead researchers on the evaluation of Hartrigg Oaks. Recent projects include an evaluation of the housing and support needs of older people in rural areas (funded by the Countryside Agency/Housing Corporation) and a systematic review of the evidence of the effectiveness of assistive technologies in helping people with dementia remain in their own homes (for the ESRC).

Acknowledgements

Producing this book has been a collaborative effort between editors and authors. Age Concern England and the Countryside Agency have backed the project from the start. One of our authors, Nick Le Mesurier, gave invaluable advice in the early shaping of the scope and direction of the volume. Helen Thomson, Ken Roy, Andy Rudd and Nicola Lloyd of the Commission for Rural Communities kindly commented on drafts and helped with statistics.

Leonie Farmer of Age Concern Publishing has ably seen the text through to publication. To all these we are grateful. To Richard Baker of Age Concern England we owe especial gratitude, for inspiring the project and guiding it throughout.

Philip Lowe
Lydia Speakman

Chapter 1
The greying countryside

Philip Lowe and Lydia Speakman

Introduction

'Ageing' has become a powerful factor shaping rural areas. In rural England, two-fifths of the population is over 50, a quarter is over 60 and 1 in 12 is over 75, and these proportions are growing. The process we have termed the 'greying countryside' is having profound and wide-ranging effects not only on the social fabric of rural areas but also on the functioning of the rural economy. In fact, our whole society is ageing, but the proportion of older people is considerably greater in rural than in urban areas through the interaction of ageing with the effects of in- and out-migration. In England, the median age of a rural resident is 42 while that of an urban resident is 36.

Rural areas are thus at the cutting edge of a major social transition, offering an important reference point for policy makers and analysts in understanding the broader implications of demographic ageing. As two of our authors, Champion and Shepherd (Chapter 2), remark, rural England is 'acting as the pioneer in the nation's population ageing'. In doing so, the greying countryside also challenges received assumptions – about both older lives and rural living.

Indeed, this book takes on two notions – 'ageing' and 'the countryside' – that are steeped in mutually reinforcing stereotypes. In our society, both carry connotations of repose, disengagement and detachment. In combination, they achieve their apotheosis in the notion of 'retirement to the countryside' – a state of inactivity, as it were, in a place of inactivity. Older people who have moved to rural areas do themselves speak of having 'escaped the rat race' (Halfacree, 1994). However, despite popular perceptions and aspirations to the contrary, retirement in-migration makes only a minor contribution to the greying countryside. Moreover, images of rural areas as places of retreat and of later life (what many people used to refer to as 'old age') as a time of withdrawal are less and less suited to the contemporary realities of the rural economy and older people's lifestyles. A key purpose of this book, therefore, is to tackle the myths and outdated prejudices that too often obscure public policy debates on ageing in the countryside.

The dynamics of the greying countryside are complex and changing. In recent decades the rural economy has been transformed from an agrarian to a service-based economy (Countryside Agency, 2003). At the same time, the new generations who have acceded to middle and older age fully expect to enjoy longer and more active lives than their parents. Disproportionately, they live or have come to live in rural areas, and their needs and demands have become predominant influences on rural public and commercial services.

This book brings together a collection of essays by prominent specialists, each one addressing a different facet of the greying countryside. Together they portray the diverse ways in which older lives and rural living are changing. They seek to understand how the transitions that people make in later life are shaped by, and in turn shape, rural contexts. The overall purpose is to highlight some of the dominant trends and processes, and to identify key challenges that the ageing countryside raises for society.

Demographic ageing

'Demographic ageing' is a phrase used to describe the changing age profile of the population, in which older age groups come to outnumber younger ones. The broad shaping factors behind this trend – increased longevity and a falling birth rate – represent welcome advances in well-being and personal choice for the many, brought about by improvements in medicine, education and material wealth through the last century. It is happening in most advanced societies. In the UK in 1997 the average 65 year old man was expected to live to age 83, but his counterpart in 2015 is projected to live to age 90 (Continuous Mortality Investigation, 2005). At present, there are about 16.4 million people over the age of 50 in England, which is a third of the population.

Figure 1.1 Age profile of urban and rural England

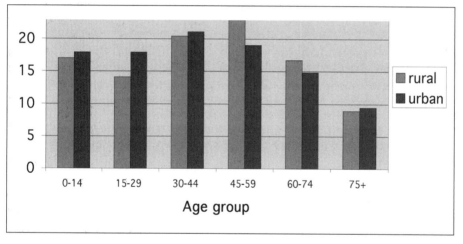

Source: Office for National Statistics 2001 Census

Although now a well-established process, demographic ageing of the population is not a smooth trend but progresses through peaks and troughs largely reflecting past fluctuations in the birth rate. Over the next 20 years, it will be the turn of the baby boom generation to reach older age. In the post-war period there were, in fact, two baby booms – one in the mid to late 1940s, and another, much bigger one, between the mid 1950s and early 1970s. As Figure 1.1 demonstrates, together they mean that there is a large bulge in the population of people who are currently aged 30–60. As the baby boomers age, so the proportion of older people in the population will increase considerably in the early decades of this century. The effect will be heightened by the much smaller size of the successor cohorts – those born in the 1970s and 1980s.

While they are thus set to accelerate the demographic ageing of the population, it may be expected that the baby boomers will coincidently change the character of older living (Huber and Skidmore, 2003). Although ageing involves inevitable transitions, people bring their own expectations and responses to the process. The post-war generation has grown up through an era of unprecedented affluence and sweeping social change that has transformed the family, work, civil society and the welfare state beyond recognition. This generation was in the vanguard of consumerism and the spread of libertarian ideas. It will bring to older age attitudes and values that are more socially liberal, more individualistic and less deferential than those of its parents' generation. The baby boomers are thus likely to challenge many of the accepted tenets and boundaries of older living. Through a rhetoric of choice and opportunity, they will make later life ('old age') their own. In doing so, they will be abetted by advances in health, prosperity and technology that are widening the horizons of older living.

Across the globe, older people are concentrated in rural areas, and such areas are generally characterised by an ageing population (Wenger, 2001). In developing countries, this is the outcome of selective depopulation of young people flocking to the cities. What is different about England and other post-industrial societies is that rural areas are repopulating and are doing so selectively with older age groups, such that the rural population is ageing but growing at the same time (see Chapter 2).

The distinctive aspect is therefore the direct link to counter-urbanisation that has dominated internal migration patterns in England since the 1960s (Boyle and Halfacree, 1998), and is caused by:

- commuting patterns – the great growth of the commuter hinterlands around all the conurbations, but especially across the south and south-east of England;

- work-driven migration – the movement of people and jobs to smaller centres and to rural areas, and from the north to the south;

- retirement-related moves – most strongly from the south-east, especially to rural and coastal settlements in south-western and eastern England.

Commentators often associate the greying of the countryside with retirement migration. However, only around 10 per cent of rural in-migrants are retired (Countryside Agency, 2004b). The more significant migration flows are, on the one hand, the loss of younger age groups and, on the other hand, the in-migration of young families and middle-aged people. The largest rural population gains are of people in their 30s and 40s and their children. However, the children often move away when they grow up. It is thus the adult in-migrants ageing in situ that are contributing most to the burgeoning older population of rural areas, and will continue to do so over the coming decades.

The consequence of counter-urbanisation is much higher rates of growth for rural districts.[1] Although rural districts contribute just over a third of England's population they accounted for well over half of the total population increase in the decade 1993–2003. These trends are affecting all regions of England, although middle-aged people have tended to move into more accessible rural areas, while older people have gravitated towards more remote and coastal areas (Champion, 1996, page 16). The counties with disproportionately high numbers of people of pensionable age include Dorset and Devon, Surrey and Sussex, Norfolk and

---

1   The classification of rural areas and local authority districts is discussed in Chapter 2.

Suffolk, Lancashire and Cumbria, North Yorkshire and Northumberland (Warnes and McInerney, 2004).

Looking forward, England's population is expected to grow by 5.5 million up to 2028. The bulk of the growth – 5.3 million – will be attributable to the increase in the number of people over 60, and most of that increase will occur in rural districts (Chapter 2). In general, the ageing trend is more accentuated the more rural the district – in other words, the greater the proportion of a district's population living in rural settlements the older it will tend to be now and the more it will age over the next 25 years. Indeed, over this period, while the median age for the populations of rural districts will rise towards 50, districts such as Berwick-upon-Tweed, West Somerset, North Norfolk, East Lindsey, West Dorset and South Lakeland are set to have three out of five of their residents aged over 50. The largest percentage growths are going to occur in the older age categories – people in their 60s, 70s and 80s. For very old people – those aged 85 and over – the numbers are projected to almost treble in the next 25 years (Chapter 2).

The boundaries of later life

The growing proportion of older people is portrayed by commentators as a looming and potentially crippling threat to our society. Such reactions betray a deep-seated ageism. That is not to deny that there are real challenges for pensions and welfare systems that are based on the principle that those in work contribute to those in retirement or in need of social and health care. However, more general notions of an increasing burden of dependency – captured in such terms as the dependency ratio – are quite misleading. For most people, longevity entails additional years of active life, not of dependency (Mullan, 2000). That should be seen not only as a personal benefit, but also as a potential benefit to the wider society, in terms of the social and economic contribution that active older people can make. Indeed, the effective functioning of families, households, communities and local economies is coming more and more to depend on their contribution. This is particularly the case in rural areas with strongly ageing populations.

Yet stereotypes of older people that are deeply rooted in social attitudes and public practices circumscribe their lives and the contribution they can make to society. Particularly potent notions are those historically rooted ones that see the termination of the working life as a decisive break marking a withdrawal into inactivity and dependency. For most people prior to the twentieth century, post-employment support would have been precarious, reliant on the family or the workhouse, and so work would have to continue until health collapsed. When the state pension was introduced in 1908, on a means tested basis for those over 70, it was intended to provide a short respite before the onset of dependency and death (Carnegie Trust, 1993). Although the situation has changed considerably since then, the state retirement pension is still associated with dependency and impending demise. There is a tendency thus to speak of older people as 'they' whom 'we' have to support (Laslett, 1989).

A detailed study of how older people in rural areas actually live their lives was carried out by Clare Wenger (1992). Over a period of 11 years, she researched the social networks of 500 people aged over 65. Far from being a homogeneous group of dependent people, she found that the majority continued to lead their social and domestic lives as usual. Many more were likely to give help than to receive it, and many continued to help adult children and grandchildren. Her study in particular underlined the interdependence of the generations.

If 'old age' is no longer the brief interlude between a full working life and death, what is it and what are its boundaries? Greater longevity is pushing at the outer boundaries of 'old age' and bolstering increased life expectancies. In general, the additional years of life are active ones, rather than the prolongation of morbidity.

Indeed, we are seeing a compression of morbidity as people live longer and stay healthier. Someone aged 50 today faces the prospect of as much active life ahead of them as the working life behind them (Marmot et al, 2003). Moreover, on average, rural residents live longer and have better levels of health than their urban counterparts (Countryside Agency, 2004b).

The inner boundary of what people consider as later life ('old age') has also been changing. Over the last 30 years there has been a remarkable blurring of the timing for older people exiting the labour market. Thus, whereas in the 1960s just 1 in 20 men in their late 50s and 1 in 8 men in their early 60s were economically inactive, the equivalent figures for the mid 1990s were 1 in 4 and 1 in 2 respectively (Chapter 5). Coincidentally, more and more middle-aged women have been seeking formal employment, leading in particular to a large increase in part-time employment. Levels of economic activity between the sexes have thus been converging in the 50s age range. It has also become the norm for people, whichever their gender, to retire from work in their mid/late 50s or early 60s. Indeed, one-half of men and a third of women retire before reaching the state pension age (Disney et al, 1997).

The move into retirement too is not the dramatic and predetermined rupture it once was. Through early retirement, but also part-time, self and casual employment, more and more people are managing their own, often gradual, withdrawal from the labour market. Some are precipitated to take such steps by redundancy, ill health or the efforts of firms to downsize or outsource, but others have the resources and opportunities to choose to retire partially or early. Likewise, while for some the consequence is a shortening of the working life, for others it may involve discrete or indefinite prolongation of work.

Crucially, though, when they do leave behind full-time employment, few people regard themselves as entering later life ('old age'). Indeed, as life expectancy has increased, so the popular perception of when later life ('old age') begins has also receded. In a recent public opinion survey, 1 in 3 adults said they would not consider someone to be old until they reached the age of 70. The survey found that as people get older they delay the age that they think of as getting old. Of those surveyed, 1 in 4 optimistically said that youth 'never ends' (Abrams, 2005).

The ancient adage that you are only as old as you feel has perhaps never been more true. We therefore do not adopt any categorical position in this book on when later life begins. Purely for purposes of statistical analysis we present data in a number of chapters on people over the age of 50. Although this is a quite arbitrary choice, we hope that for most of those included it captures the period when they make most of the key decisions, choices and transitions that structure their later life. However, to give one counter example, it may be that many of those who in their 40s move to a rural area are making decisions about where they want to live permanently, and are therefore destined to become part of the greying countryside.

The divisions of later life

For those aged 50 or more, our data analysis often breaks down the older population into 5, 10 or 15 year age bands. Again this is done purely for the purposes of statistical analysis and implies no underlying categorisation or claims that age is a fundamental determinant of behaviour, attitudes or needs. As Baker and Speakman maintain, 'from the point of view of the individual, age is a very weak identifier compared with other characteristics such as gender and race, or even state of health … As an indicator of preference or need, a specific age or narrow age bands are less and less likely to describe an increasingly diverse population' (Chapter 6).

More useful in understanding different patterns of behaviour and needs in older age is the identification of major transitions that people typically experience in later life, including:

- family-life transitions, such as moving through parenting, caring for one's own parents, grand-parenting, or loss of a partner;

- transitions from work to retirement, encompassing semi-retirement and voluntary roles;

- health transitions ranging from lifetime changes such as the menopause through to significant loss of physical or mental capacity.

Not everyone experiences these transitions and certainly not in the same sequence, and the age at which people do encounter them varies considerably. Consequently, a focus on transitions is helpful both in clarifying the distinctive needs of different older groups and in illuminating the choices and constraints facing people as they grow older.

Migration to the countryside provides an additional and distinctively rural overlay to these other transitions. Many of those who are moving to rural areas in the middle years of their ife are doing so as they negotiate important family-life and work-related transitions (see Chapter 3). They may be recent empty-nesters and therefore no longer tied to school catchments and want to downsize their accommodation and maybe unlock some capital. Frequently they will also be downsizing their economic activity (Stockdale and Findlay, 2001). A job-related move for one partner may necessitate a shift to part-time employment or full-time homemaking for the other partner, usually the woman. Other shifts out of full-time employment for those moving to rural areas include partial retirement, self-employment and even setting up a small business (Findlay et al, 1999). Often, therefore, time and energy are also unlocked, either deliberately or incidentally, and can be channelled into other roles including caring and volunteering ones, as well as into leisure activities. As Hardill (Chapter 3) remarks: 'Migrating to the countryside is the result of far-reaching and interlinked mid-life decisions about rearranging household, family and work relations. The change of house and scene is also a change of direction chosen to fit the household to what is seen as the next stage in their lives.'

In-migrants thus project certain functions on to their chosen residential location, related to their stage of life and desired lifestyles. Such expectations, as well as their extra-local connections, set them apart from established residents (Boyle and Halfacree, 1998). While there may be benefits for local communities and economies from this influx, it often sets up a local/incomer divide which may be a source of tension and social exclusion, as established residents are marginalised by or forced to adapt to the pressures counter-urbanisation brings. The effects of migration are thus to throw together in rural locations people with different life experiences, resources and expectations, ranging from the mobile, the affluent and the well-connected, to the poor and those who are locally reliant or dependent. People therefore often encounter the transitions of older age in sharply different circumstances, even though living in the same or similar rural localities.

Indeed, a characteristic feature of older age groups is their diversity. This is attributable to the fact that the distinct life courses people have pursued have cumulative effects that tend to magnify the consequences of their class, gender or health status through life. Wenger's work highlighted a number of basic distinctions that she found among the older rural population, and these emerge as clear themes throughout the rest of this book:

- those who have always lived in the countryside, and those who have moved from urban areas;
- those who lead active lives, and those whose independence has been curtailed by frailty or ill health;
- those dependent on the state pension, and those with contributory pensions, savings and a substantial income.

Undeniably, age itself levels some aspects of these divides. Whatever their background or origins, older people within a locality share a certain commitment to the place where they live. They demonstrate this in many ways ranging from support for local voluntary organisations to use of local shops and services. But for many the identification with place is more emotional and psychological – this is where they have chosen to spend their remaining days. There is thus a sort of investment of the self in the locality, which finds its expression, according to a recent study of ageing in place, in an 'enormous commitment to and capacity for involvement in community' (Godfrey et al, 2004).

Of course, as people's horizons shrink this focus on the locality becomes more intense. In Chapter 8, Bevan and Croucher report on older people's concerns about where they live and the importance to them particularly of 'transport, support services and other types of infrastructure that facilitate independence'. To remain independent they may need a variety of informal, as well as formal, supporting services. Living in a rural area is considerably easier for those who can afford to run a car, buy private healthcare or pay for domestic or gardening help. However, with their smaller and dispersed populations, rural areas are intrinsically more difficult to provide with local or home-based services. Thus, with public or commercial services more expensive or less available, rural residents are much more thrown back on what they can do for themselves, as individuals, households or communities. Moreover, with families often too far away to offer much in the way of day-to-day support (Ermisch, 2004), many rural older people come to rely on friends and neighbours and local community institutions not only for assistance with small household tasks, shopping or transport but also for general social contact and support.

Declining mobility, through frailty, disability or inability to drive, may heighten this reliance for some. The local solidarity of older people, though, has its limitations and is not for everyone (Wenger, 1992). Hardill records that some of the late middle-aged rural in-migrants whom she interviewed anticipated having to move again 'when their resources, supports and skills for independent living decline, especially if they are unable to drive a car, tend the garden or manage the stairs' (Chapter 3). Champion and Shepherd also detect a significant net movement of people aged over 75 from villages and the dispersed countryside and into rural towns (Chapter 2).

Inevitably, frailty, ill health and bereavement take their toll on the oldest old people. Given their greater longevity, women make up two-thirds of those aged over 75 and half of them live alone. The Melton Mowbray Ageing Project is tracking the lives of this age group (Jagger et al, 2001; Jagger, 2004). Of those in this survey, 17 per cent could be classified as very lonely and over 50 per cent as moderately lonely. Some felt they did not have as much social contact as they would have liked, but for more (almost a third) the issue was that they had friends or family that they would like to see more. Almost a fifth of those aged 75 and over sometimes felt that life was not worth living, but four-fifths did not, and they retained a positive outlook on life.

The economic potential of older people

Participation in the labour market profoundly structures the experience of working life, and withdrawal from the labour market is a crucial stage in the ageing process, which in turn structures people's trajectories into later life. There is great diversity in the degree of choice that people are able to exercise over the manner and timing of their exit from the labour market.

Anne Green's analysis in Chapter 5 reveals how rural labour markets are responding to the growing numbers of older workers. Rural districts are shown to have higher employment rates and this is particularly so for older age groups and the more rural districts. In the age groups from 50 to 64 years, employment rates in rural districts are consistently at least 5 percentage points higher than in urban districts. This marked tendency for older rural residents to be in employment, moreover, is carried over into later exits from the labour market. Thus, whereas the majority of men in the 60–64 age group in urban districts have become economically inactive, the majority in rural districts remain economically active. More than a quarter of women in their early 60s in rural districts are also economically active. Employment rates fall sharply after the age of 65, but less so in rural districts, where 1 in 6 men in their late 60s and 1 in 12 in their early 70s are still economically active.

On the face of it, rural labour markets would appear to be adapting to the greying countryside. With a much older age profile to draw on and in particular a dearth of younger workers, it is important that rural areas make the most of their ageing workforce. This is certainly evident in the higher employment rates for older age groups and the later moves out of employment. Rural areas are thus in the lead in reversing the unsustainably high levels of early retirement seen nationally in the past 15 years.

Rural areas have been assisted in making these adjustments by both high demand factors and intrinsic features of rural labour markets. Over several decades there has been a gradual drift of employment from the conurbations and major cities to smaller settlements – what is sometimes called the urban–rural shift of employment – with employment growth in rural areas outpacing that in urban areas. At the same time, rural areas have been in the vanguard in the move towards more flexible forms of employment, including self-employment, part-time working, temporary working, home working and pluriactivity (multiple job holding).

These flexible forms of employment are more prevalent in rural districts, and for older people (Countryside Agency, 2003; Commission for Rural Communities, 2005a). Indeed, they account in large part for the later exit from the labour market of those living in rural districts, the majority of those working over the age of 60 being either part-time or self-employed, albeit differentiated by gender. Thus, for women, part-time employment plays a much more important role in transitions out of or continuing employment than in urban districts, and it is the predominant form of rural female employment for those aged over 55. For men, self-employment plays the equivalent part, and it is the predominant form of rural male employment for those aged over 65.

While self-employment and part-time employment are much more significant pathways between work and retirement in rural districts, two other pathways – unemployment and long-term sickness – are much less significant than in urban districts. Self and part-time employment are thus identified by rural agencies as components in flexible retirement strategies and in household income portfolios (Countryside Agency, 2003). To give just one example, a quarter of the rural self-employed are over 55 and half of them are in households with at least one pensioner. More generally, the greater prevalence of self-employment has been identified as a crucial driver of rural economies, both in terms of entrepreneurial activity and as a source of income and employment for a significant proportion of the rural workforce (Countryside Agency, 2003). Rural areas also support disproportionately more small businesses, many established by middle-aged in-migrants (Keeble et al, 1992; Centre for Rural Economy, 2000). Moreover, the evidence is that older people are more successful in starting a business than their younger counterparts (Cressy and Storey, 1995).

However, Anne Green (Chapter 5) sounds notes of caution. First of all, the rural economy has an over-representation of traditional sectors and occupations, including ones in decline, and an under-representation of knowledge sectors and occupations such as business services and professional occupations. This composition, alongside the small size of rural firms, militates against investment in skills. That raises concerns that some rural areas, particularly geographically isolated ones, may be at risk from the entrenchment of a 'low-skilled' equilibrium (in which local employers compete in low value-added markets and consequently demand a low-skill workforce).

Secondly, the much vaunted flexibility of rural labour markets may actually reflect a lack of choice and opportunity. Many enter part-time or self-employment reluctantly, out of necessity, when they find that other options are limited or unavailable. These forms of employment are also often associated with casual employment, low income and a lack of investment in training. But at the other end of the spectrum they include lucrative consultancy-type roles. The self-employed especially are a diverse group, encompassing the spectrum from the most vulnerable to the most successful within the rural workforce. The delayed exit from employment and into retirement may also be through necessity rather than choice. Incomes are lower in remoter rural areas, as is the proportion of people with contributory pensions. Working into very much later life is a necessity for some, simply to make ends meet.

Anne Green clearly demonstrates that people's past working lives foreshadow the transition they make from employment to retirement in later life. Individuals with the highest qualifications tend to have the greatest control over the timing and nature of these transitions. They are able to choose early retirement for positive reasons or remain in work after pensionable age, combining the benefits of employment and the flexibility of partial retirement. In contrast, those in low paid, lower skilled jobs are often greatly restricted in the way they move from full employment to retirement, which may pitch them permanently into poverty (see Chapter 4). There are a great many that would choose to go on working or to return to work, but are prevented from doing so by employment rules and pension regulations that impose a retirement age, as well as by employers' prejudices against older workers.

Household income and the power of the grey pound

The current generation of people of pensionable age who have recently retired are the most affluent to date thanks to a combination of occupational pension schemes, high levels of savings, and in many cases bequests from their parents. At the same time, the gap between rich and poor pensioners has increased significantly. While many more older people are financially comfortable and able to enjoy their lives, around a quarter of pensioners in private households exist on low incomes, defined as below 60 per cent of the median household income.

In general, the incidence of poverty in rural areas is somewhat lower than in urban areas, but this is not the case for older people. Older recipients of the state pension make up the largest group on low incomes in rural areas (Countryside Agency, 2000). Gilbert, Philip and Shucksmith demonstrate in Chapter 4 that there is a clear geographical dimension to income status in later life. Older people in more accessible rural areas are the most affluent while those in remoter rural areas are worst off. Income levels in remote rural areas are significantly lower than other areas, with 29 per cent of low income households containing someone over 60. Not surprisingly, older people tend to experience longer spells in poverty than younger people. Around 1 in 10 people receiving pensions in private households depend on the state pension benefits and when residents in care homes are included half of the older rural population rely solely on the state pension. Older people living alone in rural areas are particularly likely to experience poverty, and yet are less likely to take up welfare entitlements (Harrop and Palmer, 2002).

While there are thus pressing issues today to do with poverty among the rural older population, the situation also looks decidedly uncertain for those set to retire over coming decades. Indeed, pensions have become the biggest source of contemporary demographic concern. The recent UK crisis in money-purchase pension funds and the ending of many final salary schemes mean that continuing improvements to pensioner incomes from private schemes can no longer be guaranteed. The state continues to review its role in pension provision with an increasing emphasis on targeted rather than universal benefits. People thus face increasing pressures to take greater personal responsibility for their retirement. However, increasing longevity may overstretch the financial provisions that individuals do make. It could also have a significant impact upon intergenerational wealth transfers, as parents spend their accumulated wealth on their own extended retirement years. Many future retirees therefore face uncertainty about their level of retirement income.

Despite these future uncertainties, older people collectively make a significant contribution to the UK economy (Chapter 6). Annual expenditure by people aged over 50 amounts to 45 per cent of total household expenditure. This age group also owns 85 per cent of the country's wealth. Disposable incomes for people aged over 50 have been steadily growing, and most do not experience a sharp drop in their standard of living on retirement as this tends to coincide with the cessation of mortgage payments as well as work-related expenses. The older population therefore represents an increasingly significant market share for a wide range of goods and services, albeit one that has been largely ignored by business and advertising agencies who continue to chase the dwindling youth market.

In examining the older rural consumer in Chapter 6, Baker and Speakman point out that consumer patterns are more shaped by generational characteristics than by chronological age. Tomorrow's older people are likely to have different expenditure patterns compared with their parents' generation. This is illustrated in the growing adoption of communication technologies, such as mobile phones and internet usage, by people aged over 50. In meeting the demands of the older consumer, business needs to focus more on universal design and applicability, rather than on age-based stereotypes. Older people are increasingly likely to use their resources for their own benefit rather than pass it on as inheritance. They look for value for money and quality in a product or service, and wealthier older people are particularly prominent purchasers of leisure, health and educational services.

People's consumption habits and lifestyles in rural areas are crucially dependent on personal mobility. Car ownership levels are much higher in rural areas, including among older people, with 85 per cent of all rural households having access to one car or more (Office for National Statistics, 2001). The proportion of people over the age of 50 in rural households without a car is 14.7 per cent, which is half that for those in urban areas. Moreover, 41.5 per cent of older rural residents are in households with two or more cars (ONS 2001). While most rural residents are thus able to access retailers and services over a wide geographical area, older rural consumers do have a much higher propensity to shop locally. In order for rural retailers and businesses to maintain or even expand their customer base in response to the greying countryside, it is important that they do not simply provide for the poor and those without their own transport, but that they understand better the needs and preferences of older consumers in general. With rural lifestyles so heavily reliant on the continuing ability to drive and the affordability of running a car, factors which limit this mobility or force up its costs will have a major impact for individuals and households as well as for the wider rural economy.

Besides the personal spending of older people, there is the purchasing undertaken by the public and private sectors on their behalf. This includes work in the construction and care sectors to meet the requirements of those with changing housing and care needs. Regional Development Agencies are increasingly interested in the contribution of the public sector to peripheral economies. Expenditure on the provision of statutory health and social services in rural areas for older people is considerable, with a large proportion of that expenditure on labour. It is estimated that around 10 per cent of the rural workforce are employed in health and social services (Commission for Rural Communities, 2005a).

It is not only older rural residents that have the potential to support local economies but also those who visit the countryside. Baker and Speakman estimate that the older day visitor market to the countryside is worth over £5 billion per annum. The growth of interest in countryside recreation among older people keen to maintain their health offers many rural areas a growing market of 'older activity seekers', but if rural areas are to benefit from this growth the right type of facilities and services are required to encourage such visitors to spend money in the local economy.

The complex contribution that older people's income and expenditure make to the rural economy was illustrated by the impact of the 2001 foot and mouth crisis. With the countryside effectively closed as a disease-control measure, many older people stayed away from visiting rural areas. The loss of income to the tourism and leisure sector was estimated at £3 billion. The worst affected county was Cumbria, which alone lost an estimated £400 million in visitor income. However, the Cumbrian economy did not collapse during the crisis – indeed local employment was not affected (Bennett et al, 2002). This has in part been attributed to the £1 billion pension income that flows into households in the county and which ensured a continued level of consumer spending. Cumbria is one of a number of rural counties where non-waged income to households – including pensions, savings, dividends, business income and benefit payments – exceeds waged income. In such areas the rural economy vitally depends on the grey pound.

Contributing to the rural community

With roles no longer ascribed by formal labour market positions or family responsibilities, it is through the informal social networks in which they are embedded that older people express their identity and find useful roles. Social contact with family, friends and neighbours, and also with community groups, is important in enabling older people to remain independent, active and healthy (Wenger, 1992, 1994a, 1994b). Indeed, people who are socially integrated live longer, whereas socially isolated people are more likely to suffer illness and premature mortality (Chapter 7).

Older people in rural areas appear to have as much contact with their families as retired people in urban settings. They are more likely to belong to a voluntary organisation and be part of a religious group (Hoggart et al, 1995). In general, rural residents are much more likely than urban residents to say that people help each other. They are also more likely to engage in voluntary work (*State of the Countryside 2005*, Commission for Rural Communities, 2005, pages 61–63). These tendencies are more marked among older age groups: the National Survey of Voluntary Activity identified that 40 per cent of those aged 55–64, 45 per cent of the 65–74 age group and 35 per cent of those aged over 75 engage in some organised voluntary work (Office for National Statistics, 1997).

However, the image of close-knit rural communities, where everyone knows everyone else and neighbours are always there to lend a hand, is often a myth (Wenger, 1995). Conscious efforts have to be made, therefore, to build the networks of support that form such an important basis for community interaction. In Chapter 7 Le Mesurier analyses the scope for this using the concept of social capital which he defines, following Putnam, as including 'features of social organisations such as networks, norms, and social trust that facilitate co-ordination and co-operation for mutual benefit'. There is a great deal of evidence that older people, with time and inclination to socialise, to volunteer and to be neighbourly, are active builders of social capital. As Le Mesurier's says, older people provide much of the glue that binds rural communities together.

Voluntary organisations, which have built up relationships of trust with local communities and are sensitive to local issues and personalities, are ideally placed to help people to form links and identify needs which are not always apparent to service providers. Many local authorities now routinely contract out community services to voluntary agencies, and these and other health services are often reliant on this grass-roots approach using local volunteers, many of whom are older people. Examples include community transport schemes, mobile day centres, or meals on wheels services. Older people are also active in a wide range of other voluntary activities to improve their community or the environment, such as Local Heritage Initiatives and English Nature's volunteer warden scheme. Older people are known to volunteer for longer and to be more reliable than younger volunteers (Yates and Jochum, 2003).

Nevertheless, Le Mesurier warns that there are risks inherent in too great a reliance upon 'an ageing corps of people willing to devote time, energy and commitment to serving others in the community'. Voluntary organisations constantly have to be recruiting fresh volunteers and this is not an easy task. Services provided by volunteers may benefit from their informality and responsiveness, but they may also be quite variable. One locality may sustain a great deal of activity but another, with equal or more pressing needs, may sustain very little. Local authorities also have different attitudes towards the voluntary and community sectors, some being more supportive than others. The consequence is a considerable 'patchiness' in informal support services (Chapter 8).

Social change in rural communities impacts on social capital. Migration is the most ubiquitous factor, but with mixed effects. It can lead to communities becoming polarised between locals and newcomers. Outsiders, though, may bring fresh outlooks and a willingness to join in and volunteer. They also have extra-local connections, which may be useful to a community in promoting or defending local interests. The stereotype is the retired NIMBY protestor, and certainly counter-urbanisers are often prominent in rural preservation movements (Lowe et al, 2001). In the longer term, the relentless individualisation of our society, including the growing phenomenon of family break up, may further impact on the social capital of rural areas.

Services for older people

People living in rural areas are entitled to reasonable access to a range of nationally available services. That raises the issue of how to secure access in dispersed locations and specifically how to target those most in need, when often they are hard to identify as well as hard to reach. The majority of older people in rural areas are mobile and reasonably affluent and able to exercise choice over the services they use over extensive geographical areas. Many, though, are not so fortunate and must depend on local services that are often quite inadequate, and which have been undermined over time by the influx of more affluent and more mobile households into rural areas.

The growing number of older residents presents challenges to service providers. Older people in particular are often seen as most in need of services but may be least able to access them. Their needs may cover a range of services and, to provide maximum support, these services should be delivered in a coherent way. There is a tendency to pigeonhole older people's interests within social services departments. However, their lives embrace a wide range of service usage, from transport to housing, and from leisure to education. Indeed, with the greying countryside, commercial and public services generally – and not just those dedicated to care – will have to adjust to reflect the changing profile of the local population.

The point is emphasised by the population projections for rural districts presented in Chapter 2 (see Figure 2.7), which show that the numbers of people in all the age bands below 60 will be smaller in 2028 than now and will be much larger in all the age bands above 60. Much of the service and housing capacity currently oriented towards younger age groups will therefore become progressively surplus or ill-fitting for the population that it serves and should be re-oriented or adapted for older age groups. However, forward planning and housing allocations for rural areas pay little regard to the needs of either today's or tomorrow's older residents. For example, most rural new build is for family homes and executive housing.

The combination of distance and dispersion mean that the cost of supplying services is higher per capita in rural areas. Yet in England, unlike Wales and Scotland, the national resource allocations to local authorities and healthcare providers do not compensate for additional costs arising from rurality, nor is there any recognition of the impact of an ageing population on such budgets. At the same time, as Bevan and Croucher point out in Chapter 8, many local authorities traditionally spend less on social care and services and are more reluctant than urban authorities to increase local taxes.

The notion of ageing in place, particularly in one's own home, is attractive to most people. This is the philosophy behind Care in the Community and it implies that various supporting and preventative services be provided responsively at the local level and to people's homes. The Government's strategy 'Opportunity Age' makes the commitment that older people should be given 'the support they need to remain in their own home for as long as possible' (Department for Work and Pensions, 2005, para 37). Chapter 8 demonstrates the role of transport and low level support services such as gardening schemes, lunch clubs and lend-a-hand schemes in enabling older rural residents to thrive and remain independent. However, shortage of resources means that many rural authorities and their partners are unable to sustain community-based supports and services oriented towards the broader needs of the older population and are often concentrating instead on intervening when individuals suffer a crisis. This approach may be as short sighted as it is uncaring (Social Exclusion Unit, 2005). As Bevan and Croucher (Chapter 8) argue, the 'costs of delivering preventative services in rural areas need to be considered against the social and economic costs of individuals having to give up their own home'. Overall, older people in rural areas receive less help from social services to live at home than older people in urban areas (7.2 per cent against 11.1 per cent – Countryside Agency/Age Concern, 2005).

The other factor militating against ageing in place is the centralisation of essential services such as social care, GP surgeries, clinics and day care, as well as shops and commercial services. Not surprisingly, personal mobility, or lack of it, is a major concern for dispersed rural communities. Those without private transport can suffer real hardship. While all rural pensioners now have some form of concessionary bus scheme available to them, the take-up rate has fallen to less than a third, reflecting the paucity of public transport services, the increased availability of community transport and the growing number of people driving cars well into their 70s (Countryside Agency, 2003). Better service integration to reduce the need for older people to travel, combined with innovative schemes such as taxi-buses, can only be part of the solution. Many of Bevan and Croucher's respondents (see Chapter 8) regarded the ability to drive as a key factor in independent living. Such sentiments are likely to loom ever larger as those reaching later life take for granted their own personal mobility. In the future older people in rural areas are bound to be more vociferous in ensuring that their transport needs are better addressed.

Conclusions: towards a countryside for all ages

This book sets out some of the realities of the greying countryside. The marked trajectory towards an ageing population is inescapable. However, gloomy talk of doomsday scenarios – of the stagnation of society, of fiscal and pension crises, of the collapse of the welfare state – appear unwarranted. An older population presents challenges, but also opportunities, and we have sought to explore both aspects. What is undeniable is that rural areas are in the vanguard of demographic ageing, and they thus offer a testing ground not only for how the greying countryside should function but more generally how the greying society of the future could work. In this spirit, we set out below some of the key challenges – economic, social and communal – that the greying countryside presents for society.

Economic challenges: the retired countryside won't work

The Government has admitted that 'Older people are often overlooked in wider planning agendas because attention tends to be placed on people whom planners think are economically active' (ODPM/Department of Health, 2003). The development of rural economies such as those of Cumbria and Herefordshire, where the majority of the income to households does not come from employees' earnings, cannot afford to focus exclusively on efforts to raise the productivity of those in work. The conditions for self-employment and small businesses to thrive and for the local economy to maximise returns from the grey pound also require attention. However, developing separate programmes of support – for, say, rural employment, entrepreneurship and social inclusion – may not be the right approach if this cuts across the way many rural households actually make interlinked economic and social decisions. For example, after retirement rural residents increasingly supplement their pensions with part-time jobs or businesses; alternatively the security that a pension brings may allow another household member to work part-time or set up a business. A more holistic approach would recognise the different sources of household livelihoods (waged and unwaged) and the way household members use these to look after each other (Bennett and Phillipson, 2004).

The realities of the greying countryside – with the median age of the population of rural districts moving up towards 50 – necessitate that rural areas promote a substantial increase in the employment rate of people in their 50s and 60s. However, age discrimination remains a pervasive barrier to older workers' employment, despite Government initiatives such as the New Deal for those aged 50+. Although many people look forward to retirement and some would prefer to take early retirement, there are a great many who would choose to go on working but are prevented from doing so by outdated employment rules and occupational pension regulations or by age discrimination on the part of employers. A report for Age Concern England (Meadows and Volterra Consulting 2004) estimates that the national social, financial and economic costs of inactivity among older people who could and want to be working amount to £30 billion annually – up to a quarter of that would be accounted for by people living in rural areas. This is happening at a time when there is a growing shortage of labour and skills in a range of sectors including health and social services. People also need encouragement to make better plans for their retirement while still in the labour force. One obstacle to be overcome is that many underestimate how much longer they are likely to live (Marmot et al, 2003). In addition, means must be found to release the vitality and resources of older people to satisfy their own and society's needs.

Those who are interested in the regeneration of rural economies cannot afford to stereotype the ageing population as a symptom or cause of rural economic decline. The ageing population is not only growing, but it also accounts for a growing proportion of national expenditure and wealth. Older people potentially have an important and increasing contribution to make to rural economies as both residents and visitors to the countryside. Quite apart from the direct expenditure of older consumers, there is also the considerable purchasing undertaken by the public and private sector on behalf of older people. Although the contribution of older people to rural economies is thus not fully understood, it merits much further research and analysis to better inform policy makers and businesses on how best to maximise the potential of older consumers to rural economies and on how to realise the potential value of expenditure on older people's services in rural areas.

Social challenges: the rejuvenation of rural populations

Migration flows within England are creating a gradient of steadily rising average ages running down the settlement hierarchy, from cities to villages, and from densely to sparsely populated areas. However, a totally segregated geography – where the cities were occupied by the young, the single, and ethnic minorities, the suburbs were home to families, and the countryside was the preserve of older people – would be very undesirable. It threatens a polarised politics that would reinforce geographical, social and generational divides. The creation of age-related spatial ghettos would also cut right across the interdependence of the generations, which is still a feature of supportive families, of working communities and of a society that has a sense of where it is coming from and where it is heading.

To avoid such a fate, it is important that rural areas do more to retain or attract younger people. There are clearly issues here to do with affordable housing and suitable employment. However, the largest exit of local young people from rural areas occurs through higher education. With mass higher education, there is the prospect of the majority of young people being stripped away from rural areas. To counter this trend would call for the promotion of more rurally based higher education. The past few years have seen the establishment of university campuses in Lincolnshire, Cumbria and Cornwall, and it would be valuable to learn from the contribution of these ventures to the rejuvenation of rural populations.

Unfortunately, the number of young people is shrinking nationally and there are fewer and fewer of them to go around. What rejuvenates the urban population of England, particularly London, is immigration into the UK. At present there is very little international immigration into the English countryside, although Champion and Shepherd (Chapter 2) do report evidence of the beginnings of an immigrant presence but in much smaller numbers and more transient than in urban areas. Temporary migrants from overseas are already used extensively in the agricultural and horticultural sectors. However, agencies across the country providing services for older people also report considerable difficulties in recruiting and retaining staff. To help overcome such staffing difficulties, immigrants could be encouraged to settle in rural areas. That would need the provision of suitable affordable housing, as well as acceptance by rural communities of families from overseas and ethnic minorities coming to stay (*Diversity Review*, Countryside Agency, 2004a).

A group that rural areas already attract is the pre-retired, but they could make more of them. Pre-retirement is where people from as young as their 40s onwards move to rural localities with a view to eventual retirement, but who at the same time are substantially reshaping their employment, family, leisure and community activities. That reshaping often unlocks a great deal of capital, time and energy. The pre-retired are thus typically a very dynamic element – helping sustain the voluntary sector, in the vanguard of new demands on commercial and public services, and behind the growth in part-time and self-employment and the setting up of new businesses – as they seek to create their version of the good life. Public authorities, service providers and voluntary organisations need to understand this diverse group if they are to draw on the additional resources and energies it brings into rural areas.

Communal challenges: how to ensure the inclusion of older people

It is important that public policy and service providers be responsive to the distinctive re-quirements of people at the different stages of ageing if older people are to live life and con-tribute to the full. If the needs of an ageing rural population are to be met, new formulae will be required for the way funding is distributed by government and regional bodies, and many rural authorities will be obliged to reconsider their priorities.

Inevitably the shifting rural demographic profile in the coming years will see ever more service capacity currently oriented towards younger age groups progressively released. It is critically important that the resources and facilities rendered surplus be systematically redeployed to match the growing bulge in the older age bands. This represents an enormous organisational challenge for public authorities and other service providers.

This has important strategic consequences for future planning and housing allocations, which to date have more or less ignored the needs of older rural residents, the prime focus being on the building of family homes and executive housing. In consequence, much of the rural hous-ing stock is not well suited to an ageing population. Conversion of existing housing as well as new build must meet the changing aspirations and age profile of rural communities. Flexible universal design principles should be adopted to ensure that new houses and conversions are both accessible and adaptable as people age in place.

Much of the Government's current policy of delivery of community services and participation is reliant on a large army of mostly older volunteers who are prepared to give up consider-able time to support their community. The Government, moreover, would like to see a sig-nificant expansion and widening of this involvement, to extend participation in civil society, to overcome social exclusion, to benefit local communities and to improve the responsive-ness of public services (Department for Work and Pensions, 2005). To increase the numbers and maintain the commitment of older volunteers, towards these ends, would call for a more systematic and professional approach to volunteer recruitment and support (Countryside Agency/Age Concern, 2005).

Education has a vital role in helping older people to be active members of their communities, by providing opportunities for learning new skills and for personal development, by providing a forum for discussion of issues common to all older people, and by challenging stereotypical beliefs about ageing. It is unfortunate that, since the 1980s, lifelong learning has been focused too narrowly on those in the workforce. Funding has been concentrated on those aiming for qualifications and there has been little room for older people uninterested in passing examinations. A re-think is required of what we mean by lifelong learning and learning post-work, to encompass specifically the experience and needs of older people and the ways they live their lives (Withnall, 2000). Education has an important role in helping older people to learn about and come to terms with developments in new technology, such as computers (Stephenson, 2002). Involvement in learning has been shown to be beneficial to the health of older people (Aldridge and Lavender, 2000). Education also has a positive impact on the social capital of communities through building self-confidence, skills and sociability (Kennedy, 1997; Moser, 1999).

————

The greying of England's countryside is thus an important social trend which is seeing changes to both older lives and rural living. With proper forethought by individuals and the wider society and by analysing and addressing the economic, social and community challenges, it should have largely beneficial consequences, with older people being enabled to live their lives and to contribute to the full. The greying countryside can also be a laboratory for a wider understanding of the issues that face an ageing society. This needs much more research in areas like consumption, volunteering, service provision and the stimulus for migration. If this work can be done, it will not only enable a comprehensive response to the ageing of our countryside but it could also provide important pointers to how more generally society might deal with demographic ageing.

References and further reading

Abrams, D. (2005) *How Ageist is Britain?* London: Age Concern

Age Concern Research Services (2005) *Analysis of LifeForce 2004/5 Data – Urban/Rural Split* (unpublished)

Aldridge, F. and Lavender, P. (2000) *The Impact of Learning on Health,* Leicester: National Institute for Adult and Community Education

Bennett, K. and Phillipson, J. (2004). 'A plague upon their houses: revelations of the foot and mouth disease epidemic for business households', *Sociologia Ruralis* 44 (3), 261–283

Bennett, K., Carroll, T., Lowe, P. and Phillipson, J. (2002) *Coping with Crisis in Cumbria,* University of Newcastle: Centre for Rural Economy

Boyle, P. and Halfacree, K. (1998) *Migration into Rural Areas,* Chichester: Wiley

Carnegie Trust (1993) *Life, Work and Livelihood in the Third Age,* Dunfermline: Carnegie United Kingdom Trust

Centre for Rural Economy (2000) *Rural Microbusinesses in the North East of England,* University of Newcastle: Centre for Rural Economy

Champion, A. (1996) *Migration Between Metropolitan and Non-Metropolitan Areas in Britain,* End of Award Report for ESRC

Commission for Rural Communities (2005a) *Under the Radar: Tracking and Supporting Rural Home-Based Businesses,* London: CRC

Commission for Rural Communities (2005b) *State of the Countryside 2005,* Cheltenham: Countryside Agency

Continuous Mortality Investigation (2005) quoted in the *Guardian,* 30 September 2005

Countryside Agency (2000) *Not Seen, Not Heard?* Cheltenham: Countryside Agency

Countryside Agency (2003) *Rural Economies: Stepping Stones to Healthier Futures,* Cheltenham: Countryside Agency

Countryside Agency (2004a) *Diversity Review,* Cheltenham: Countryside Agency

Countryside Agency (2004b) *State of the Countryside,* Cheltenham: Countryside Agency

Countryside Agency/Age Concern (2005) *Rural Lifelines,* London: Age Concern

Cressy, R.C. and Storey, D.J. (1995) *Small Business Risk: A Firm and Bank Perspective,* SME Centre Working Paper No. 39

Department for Work and Pensions (2005) *Opportunity Age,* London: DWP

Disney, R., Grundy, E. and Johnson, P. (1997) *The Dynamics of Retirement,* London: Department of Social Security

Ermisch, J.F. (2004) *Parent and Adult–Child Interactions,* Working Papers of the Institute for Social and Economic Research paper 2004–02, Colchester: University of Essex

Findlay, A., Short, D. and Stockdale, A. (1999) *Migration Impacts in Rural England,* Cheltenham: Countryside Agency

Godfrey, M., Townsend, J. and Denby, T. (2004) *Building a Good Life for Older People in Local Communities,* York: Joseph Rowntree Foundation

Jagger, C. (2004) Quality of life for the oldest old, in I. Stewart and R. Vaitilingam (eds) *Seven Ages of Man and Woman,* Swindon: ESRC, 32–35

Jagger, C. et al (2001) 'Patterns of onset of disability in activities of daily living with age', *Journal of the American Geriatrics Society* 49 (4), 404–409

Halfacree, K. (1994) 'The importance of the "rural" in the constitution of counterurbanisation', *Sociologia Ruralis 34,* 164–189

Harrop, A. and Palmer, G. (2002) *Indicators of Poverty and Social Exclusion in Rural England,* Cheltenham: Countryside Agency

Hoggart, K., Buller, H. and Black, R. (1995) *Rural Europe: Identity and Change,* London: Arnold

Huber, J. and Skidmore, P. (2003) *The New Old,* London: Demos

Keeble, D. et al (1992) *Business Success in the Countryside,* London: HMSO

Kennedy, H. (1997) *Learning Works: A Report on the Committee on Widening Participation in Further Education,* Coventry: Further Education Funding Council

Laslett, P. (1989) *A Fresh Map of Life: The Emergence of the Third Age,* London: Weidenfeld and Nicholson

Lowe, P., Murdoch, J. and Norton, A. (2001) *Professionals and Volunteers in the Environmental Process,* Newcastle: Centre for Rural Economy

Marmot, M., Banks, J., Blundell, R., Lessof, C. and Nazroo, J. (eds) (2003) *Health and Wealth in Later Life,* London: Institute of Fiscal Studies

Meadows, P. and Volterra Consulting (2004) *The Economic Contribution of Older People,* A report for Age Concern England

Metz, D. and Underwood, M. (2005) *Older Richer Fitter – Identifying the Customer Needs of Britain's Ageing Population,* London, Age Concern England

Moser, C. (1999) *A Fresh Start: Improving Literacy and Numeracy,* Suffolk: Department for Education and Employment

Mullan, P. (2000) *The Imaginary Time Bomb: Why an Ageing Population is Not a Social Problem,* London: I.B. Tauris

Murdoch, J. (1997) *Why Do People Move to the Countryside?* Report to the Countryside Commission, Department of City and Regional Planning, University of Wales, Cardiff

ODPM/Department of Health (2003) *Preparing Older People's Strategies,* London: Office of the Deputy Prime Minister

Office for National Statistics (1997) *National Survey of Voluntary Activity,* London

Office for National Statistics (2001) *2001 Census,* London

Social Exclusion Unit (2005) *Excluded Older People,* London: SEU

Stephenson, M. (2002) 'Older learners and IT: challenge for inclusion', *Adults Learning* 13 (7), 12–15

Stockdale, A. and Findlay, A. (2001) *The Role of a 'Retirement Transition' in the Repopulation of Rural Areas,* Aberdeen Papers in Land Economy, no. 2001-03. Aberdeen: University of Aberdeen, Department of Land Economy

Warnes, T. and McInerney, B. (2004) *The English Regions and Population Ageing,* London: Age Concern

Wenger, G.C. (1992) *Help in Old Age: Facing up to a Change, a Longitudinal Network Study,* The Institute of Human Ageing, Occasional Papers 5, Liverpool University Press

Wenger, G.C. (1994a) *Understanding Support Networks and Community Care – Network Assessment for Older People,* Avebury Studies of Care in the Community, Aldershot: Ashgate Publishing Ltd

Wenger, G.C. (1994b) *Support Networks of Older People: A Guide for Practitioners,* Centre for Social Policy Research and Development, University of Wales, Bangor

Wenger, G.C. (1995) 'A comparison of urban with rural support networks: Liverpool and North Wales', *Ageing & Society* 15, 89–91

Wenger, G.C. (2001) 'Myths and realities of ageing in rural Britain', *Ageing & Society* 21 (1), 17–130

Withnall, A. (2000) The debate continues: integrating educational gerontology with lifelong learning, in F. Glendenning (ed) *Teaching and Learning in Later Life: Theoretical Implications,* Aldershot: Ashgate

Yates, H. and Jochum, V. (2003) *It's Who You Know that Counts,* London: National Council for Voluntary Organisations

Chapter 2
Demographic change in rural England

Tony Champion and John Shepherd

This chapter analyses the ageing population of rural England. It details changes in the age structure over the past decade, and sets out projections for 25 years hence. These trends are placed in the wider context of demographic change, including migration out of and in to rural areas. The underlying causes of why rural areas have a somewhat older population have changed significantly over the past century. Once it was almost entirely due to a rural exodus – especially of young adults who then raised families in urban areas. In more recent years the effects of this exodus have been compounded by the 'counter-urbanisation' of retirees and middle-aged people.

Demographic ageing is, in fact, a nationwide phenomenon, but it is more pronounced in rural areas because of these age-specific migration flows. In a sense, therefore, rural England – along with the seaside and spa towns that were the traditional destinations of retirement migration – has been acting as the pioneer in the nation's population ageing and is now at the cutting edge of this deepening trend. Hence rural areas provide early experience of the challenges and opportunities that arise when at least half of the population are aged 45 or over, as is likely to be the case nationally by around 2050 – rural England will have passed this particular waymark at least a decade earlier.

The chapter begins with a broad overview of the major patterns of population change affecting rural England, emphasising the extra effect of age-specific migration over and above the general ageing trend. It then goes into more detail about what is meant in this context by 'rural England', taking the opportunity to introduce the new official classification, which was formally adopted in 2005 by the Department for Environment, Food and Rural Affairs (Defra). The latter's six-fold classification of local authority districts (three rural and three urban) is then used to categorise demographic change across rural England in comparison with urban trends, looking first at the recent past and going on to describe the emerging picture provided by the official population projections through to the year 2028. Clear differences are revealed between the three rural types nationally, as well as systematic variations at regional and local scales. This is reflected even more graphically in the patterns of migration evident from the 2001 Census. The chapter concludes by emphasising the sheer scale of the accelerating trend towards rural ageing and some of the policy implications that are a consequence of change in the rural population's age structure.

Population change in rural England: an overview

There are currently five major aspects of population change affecting rural England. The most important is the general progression of the demographic regime, including increasing life expectancy and falling fertility. Some suggest that this amounts to a 'second demographic transition' within the long-term shift from natural increase to natural decrease of the population. Second is the phenomenon of 'counter-urbanisation', whereby a net population exodus from the countryside has been replaced by net in-migration from urban areas. This is a process that is qualitatively different from local suburbanisation and dates back to the 1960s in England, although its scale has fluctuated over time.

Thirdly, in spite of this switch from net migration loss to net gain, rural England continues to be affected by the exodus of young adults. Indeed, as participation in higher education has been growing and as the social structure of the countryside has been shifting towards the middle classes from which university students are still predominantly recruited, this is likely to be an accelerating driver of rural change. Fourthly, in recent years there has been some evidence that rural England is beginning to be affected directly by the surge in net migration from overseas, though the largest cities and other entry points remain the most pressurised areas. Finally, there is the impact of past fluctuations in birth rates, with the main twentieth-century 'baby boom cohorts' now moving into later life. This section provides some background information on each of these five aspects as a prelude to examining their effect on the population size and age structure of rural England.

The new demographic regime

Over the past four decades or so Europe has entered a new phase of demographic development, variously referred to as a 'second demographic transition' (Lesthaeghe and van de Kaa, 1986), 'a new demographic transition' (Faus-Pujol, 1995) and even a 'demographic revolution' (McLoughlin, 1991). In the most basic terms, this appears like a continuation of the (first) demographic transition, primarily because the headline trends remain those of longer life expectancy and lower fertility. However, several aspects are very different. In particular, according to van de Kaa (1987, 2003) and McLoughlin (1991), the move to the second transition also involves a generational switch in attitudes and values from 'altruism' to 'individualism' and a shift in gender power towards the female, both greatly assisted by the 'pill' and altered sexual and partnership behaviour.

Certainly, the emerging demographic regime contrasts greatly with that of 40–50 years ago. Among the main differences are increasing cohabitation, rising levels of couple separation, slower (even negative) natural population increase and surging net immigration from other countries, especially those with weaker economies and those still experiencing the first transition. Alongside these changes and partly linked to them are major changes in population profiles and structures. Population ageing is perhaps the most direct and significant outcome, but other developments include the growth of ethnic diversity, the reduction in average household size, the decrease in traditional family households and the rise of other household types. These developments have been particularly well documented for those countries that started to move towards this new regime in the 1960s, most notably those in Northern and Western Europe, including England (Noin and Woods, 1993; Hall and White, 1995; Coleman, 1996; see also Champion, A.G., 1992, 2001).

Counter-urbanisation

The process of 'counter-urbanisation' involves the shift of population out of urban areas into the countryside, a process described as a 'cascading of population down the settlement hierarchy', with the most rural areas experiencing the strongest rates of net in-migration and the most urban areas seeing the highest rates of net out-migration (Champion, A.G., 1989; Champion, T., 2001). Traditionally, the main element in this shift was the movement of people at or close to retirement age, adding to the numbers of older people living in the countryside (Rees, 1992; Champion et al, 1998).

More recently, the age spread of this urban–rural shift has broadened to include not only greater numbers of early retirees and people 'downsizing' into self-employment and less demanding jobs but also household groups considered as quintessential 'suburbanisers', ie families with school-age children and mainly from middle-class backgrounds (Fielding, 1998; Champion and Atkins, 2000; Champion and Fisher, 2003). While this latter group does help rejuvenate the age structure of rural areas, the effect is short term. This is because in family households that have relocated to a rural area the parents tend to stay put and become 'empty-nesters' who 'age in place' while their grown-up children move away.

The exodus of young people

Children leaving their parental homes in rural England are very largely bound for urban areas, and there is little movement in the opposite direction. Few urban school-leavers move into rural areas, apart from students moving to those universities and colleges with campuses in rural settings and people in very specific lines of work with rural sites such as the armed forces. The types of jobs suitable for school-leavers are much more plentiful in urban areas, appropriate housing is cheaper and more accessible, and there is also the lure of the 'bright city lights' as opposed to the perceived dullness and lack of privacy associated with life in villages and small towns. The movement of young adults thus constitutes a very efficient process of rejuvenation of city populations – one that will be reinforced if they remain in urban areas when they start their families.

The impact of international migration

Until recently the English countryside would not have been thought of as a destination for international immigration. Indeed, the contemporary history of rural areas has almost invariably been one of emigration – as much to the New World as to the growing industrial cities nearer to hand. The notable exceptions were not typical immigrants but would include, for example, the occupants of prisoner-of-war camps and US military bases.

Latterly, however, the English countryside has begun to have an immigrant presence. Just as migrants have pushed across the Rio Grande into the USA and across the Mediterranean into Southern Europe to take up low-paid, casual and often seasonal work in agriculture, forestry and tourism, so a similar process has begun in England. Evidence remains largely anecdotal, especially where this relates to undocumented entries and overstaying visitors. The Worker Registration Scheme and other special arrangements for arrivals from the European Union Accession States in Eastern Europe and elsewhere are, however, indicating that a proportion of these are finding work in rural areas. There have also been a number of well-publicised cases of asylum-seekers being placed in the countryside, sometimes on disused military bases.

However, immigrants settling in rural areas – insofar as they are documented in migration and population statistics – are few compared to those reported in urban areas and are probably a great deal more transient. Instead, the much more important effect of international migration on rural England is an indirect one – the larger the numbers of immigrants accommodated in cities, the larger, it seems, is the volume of 'counter-urbanisation' from those cities, with London being the supreme example of this relationship.

The legacy of past baby booms

A proper understanding of what has been happening to England's age structure recently, and what is destined to occur over the next quarter of a century, must take account of the legacy of past baby booms (and busts). As an example, the effect of the nation's biggest ever baby boom has virtually run its course. The major peak in births in 1900–1914, which became even more pronounced in its subsequent effects due to the high attrition of the previous 'birth cohort' in the First World War, was responsible for the massive increase in people reaching retirement age in the 1960s and 1970s and the doubling of England's older old population since the 1980s.

The baby booms that are now beginning to affect the older population are that of the mid 1940s and the one that began in the later 1950s and peaked in 1965. Numerically, the latter is by far the more important, rightly focusing minds on the potential challenges to the pension system by the 2020s as this group ages into its 60s. The immediate post-war baby boom, however, is also having a substantial impact on the older population, because it is taking the place of the much smaller birth cohorts of the wartime years and of the economically depressed interwar years before that. Currently just reaching pensionable age, the members of this earlier boom will be entering their 80s by the end of the 2020s. The legacy of these birth cycles is now accelerating the population-ageing effects of the longer-term trends described above.

Defining rural England

So far this chapter has presented 'rural England' as a general concept, but it is important that a clear definition is established before demographic statistics are analysed in detail. However, defining 'rural' is not straightforward. Indeed, some academics consider that in cultural, social and economic terms an undifferentiated notion of 'the rural' in a country such as the United Kingdom is outdated (Hoggart, 1990). This view serves to underline the difficulties of definition, but the notion of 'rurality' continues to re-assert itself, not least in the policy domain. This occurs, for example, in considerations of how a dispersed population might be most efficiently provided with health and care services, or where, and how best, to subsidise public transport links, or how to identify the rate at which 'rural' land is being developed. Such concerns require clear geographical definition. The problem is that there is more than one way of doing this, partly because of the contested nature of ideas about 'rurality' but also because different users have different needs. There is no sharp dividing line on the ground between what is rural and what is urban to which all users are prepared to subscribe (for detailed discussion of this point, see Champion and Hugo, 2004). Ideas about rural territory depend greatly on the scale of area at which analysis is taking place, potentially ranging from individual plots of land to a local labour market area or wider region.

It was dissatisfaction with the notion of a definition based upon a simple classification of places as *either* urban or rural that led to a comprehensive review of the use of definitions for official purposes (SERRL, 2002). More significant, however, was the fact that there were a number of different rural definitions in use across government which lacked consistency and clarity in the criteria used. A review was therefore undertaken which recommended that the new definition should be based upon the relatively enduring basis of *settlement structure* rather than the more rapidly changing demographic, social or functional characteristics of places (eg existence of a certain number of shops or, say, primary school).

Classifying rural areas

In 2004 the Office for National Statistics (ONS) published a new definition of rural areas covering England and Wales, launched alongside Defra's Rural Strategy (Defra, 2004).[1] At the most detailed level – that of 2001 Census Output Areas (COAs) – areas are identified, first, as lying within settlements of more than 10,000 population in which case they are termed 'urban' COAs. The rest are called 'rural' COAs and these can be further classified, according to the type of *settlement* in which the majority of the population of a COA lives, as 'rural town and fringe', 'village' or 'hamlet/dispersed'. Rural COAs are also classified by the broader population context in which they are located, which may be 'sparse' or 'less sparse' according to the average number of households at three geographic scales (ie 10, 20 and 30km) around any location. 'Sparse' COAs meet the criterion at all three scales. 'Sparsity' at 10km, which roughly represents a longer than average journey to work, is typical of areas like south Wiltshire, the Cotswolds and the Peak District, while 30km (perhaps a longer range 'call-out' for the emergency services) is typical of north Norfolk, the North York Moors and most of Cumbria. The settlement and context dimensions combined give a six-fold classification of rural COAs as shown in Figure 2.1.

Figure 2.1 The structure of the classification of Census Output Areas

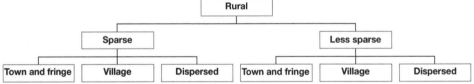

The same principle is used to classify the 'higher-level' census geographies of Super Output Areas and Census Wards, although the size and configuration of these in terms of population distribution does not make it feasible to distinguish between the 'dispersed settlement' and 'villages' categories. At Census Ward level, for example, there is a four-fold classification of 'rurality' that, firstly, separates rural towns from villages and dispersed settlement and, secondly, distinguishes these two categories according to whether they are located in 'sparse' or 'less sparse' areas.

---

1   For a detailed discussion on the methodology see http://statistics.defra.gov.uk/esg/rural_resd/ rural_defn/Rural_Urban_Methodology_Report.pdf.

Rurality and local authorities

Although not part of the formal 'definition' of rural areas, a classification of local authority districts has also been developed for England, prompted primarily by the fact that a large amount of administrative and other data is available only at this level. England's 354 unitary authorities and local authority districts (collectively termed 'LADs') have been allocated to one of six main types. Three types – 176 LADs in all – are overwhelmingly urban in nature, and are called 'Major Urban', 'Large Urban' and 'Other Urban'. The three rural types, with 178 LADs, are called 'Significant Rural', 'Rural-50' and 'Rural-80', according to the proportion of people in rural settlements. Thus 'Rural-80' LADs have between 80 and 100 per cent in rural settlements and 'Rural-50' LADs have more than 50 per cent, while 'Significant Rural' have more than the national average of 26 per cent. Table 2.1 gives the population breakdown as of 2003, the latest year for which official population estimates are available.

Table 2.1 England's population distribution, 2003, by district type

District type	Number of LADs	Residents	% England's total residents
Major Urban (750,000+ pop)	76	17,193,028	35.0
Large Urban (250,000+pop)	45	7,262,314	14.8
Other Urban	55	6,746,403	13.7
Urban total	176	31,201,745	63.5
Significant Rural	53	6,438,371	13.1
Rural-50	52	5,765,408	11.7
Rural-80	73	5,736,608	11.7
Rural total	178	17,940,387	36.5
England total	354	49,142,132	100.0

The relevance for rural policy of this classification lies, in broad terms, in the geographical pattern and location of LADs and the nature of settlement within them. As illustrated in Figure 2.2, the Significant Rural LADs are mainly interspersed with urban England and generally represent the parts of the countryside that are accessible to the larger urban centres or which have a number of smaller urban areas within their boundaries. The Rural-50 LADs are broadly grouped around these, with particular concentrations across southern England and around the edges of the more heavily populated areas of the Midlands and into East Yorkshire. Population in rural settlements – small towns, villages and dispersed dwellings – is in the majority here, and issues of service planning and delivery become increasingly important to more scattered populations. Finally, the Rural-80 LADs mainly occupy those areas generally regarded as being 'deeply rural', including substantial parts of the Southwest, East Anglia, Lincolnshire, Cumbria and Northumberland. These are the rural areas that have particularly attracted older in-migrants and second home buyers.

Figure 2.2 A classification of districts based upon rurality

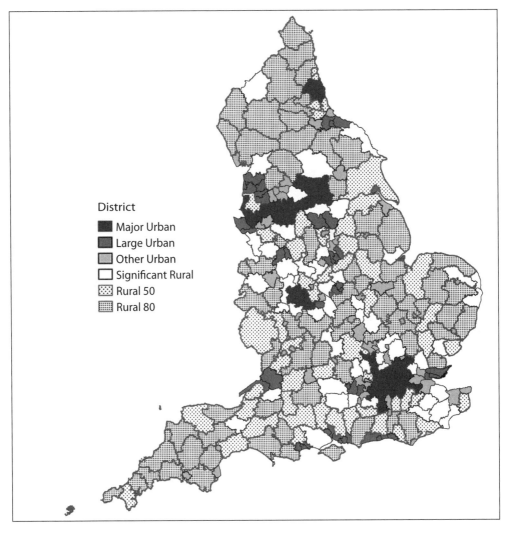

District
- ■ Major Urban
- ■ Large Urban
- ▨ Other Urban
- ☐ Significant Rural
- ▨ Rural 50
- ▨ Rural 80

Figure 2.3 summarises these geographical patterns in terms of the population make-up of four broad regions defined in terms of Government Office Regions (GORs). The graph is dominated by the large number of residents living in the Major Urban LADs in Southeast England (comprising the London, South East and East of England GORs) and Northern England (North East, North West and Yorkshire and the Humber GORs). By contrast, in terms of their rural areas, the four regions are similar in the sense that their Rural-50 districts are quite evenly matched in population numbers to their Rural-80 districts. In three cases, too, the most important type in terms of population size is the Significant Rural, but it is the least important in Southwest England. On this regional basis, it is Southwest England that is the most rural of the four. In fact, over three-fifths of its population (61.3 per cent) lived in the three rural categories in 2003, well above the national figure of 36.5 per cent. Midlands England (comprising the East and West Midlands GORs) was also above the national figure at 43.8 per cent, while Southeast England (34 per cent) was marginally below it and Northern England (26.6 per cent) considerably lower.

Figure 2.3 Population of four broad regions of England, 2003, by district type

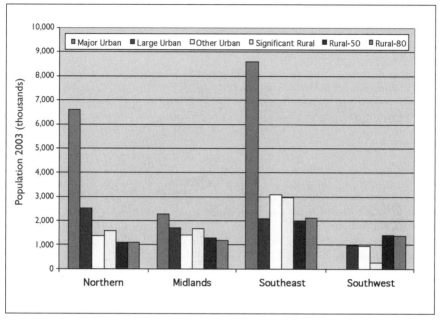

Note: Southwest England contains no Major Urban districts

It is important to note that the picture of England's rural population produced by this LAD-level classification is quite different from that derived from the finest-grained definition. Compared to the 2001 Census figure of 17.9 million people living in the three rural LAD types, the actual population of rural COAs (which is officially taken as the rural population) is just 9.5 million. This differential arises from the fact that, although many of the urban districts contain rural areas and residents, the effect is more than offset by the large numbers of residents in urban enclaves within rural districts, not least because of the decision to include 'market towns' as part of rural England. Given that the LAD classification forms the basis of most of the rest of this chapter, it is important to recognise that this chapter examines the populations of what can be thought of as the broadly rural districts of the country rather than those of non-urban settlements strictly defined.

Population change in the recent past

The two main features of rural England are that its population is growing and that it is ageing at the same time. It is not unique in this, as the same two trends have been happening nationally, but both have been occurring more rapidly in the rural areas, making those areas increasingly distinctive from urban England. Moreover, the pace of these changes is usually greatest in the most rural locations and is fairly general across the regions. These recent trends can be clearly documented by comparing the official population estimates for 2003 with those of 1993. This period has been chosen because it is the most recent span of 10 years for which such data is available; it also neatly dovetails with the 2003-based population projections. The official 2003 population estimates also provide the best indication of the population, because they take into account the undercounting and other deficiencies of the two most recent censuses and, more importantly, they adopt a consistent definition of residents, most notably counting students at their term-time address throughout.

The picture of recent population change is presented in absolute terms in Figure 2.4. Over the decade 1993–2003 the three rural district types (as defined in Table 2.1) together added almost one million to their population, compared to just over three-quarters of a million people gained by England's three urban district types combined. In terms of how the difference was spread across the six broad age groups shown, urban areas substantially outstripped the rural areas in their gain of people aged 30–44 years old, but rural England saw significantly larger increases in 0–14 year olds and 60–74 year olds and a somewhat larger increase in the number of people aged 75 and over. All districts were very closely matched in terms of their gains of 45–59 year olds and their loss of 15–29 year olds.

Figure 2.4 Urban and rural England: population change, 1993–2003, by age group

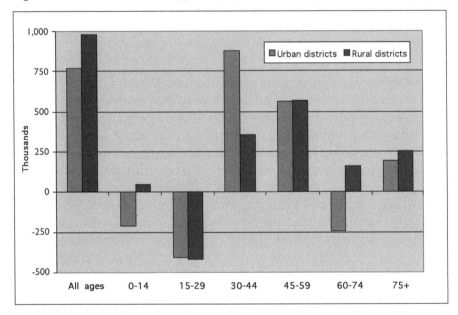

The fact that rural districts contributed well over half of the total population increase over this period is remarkable, given that their share of the overall population of England was not much more than a third. Indeed, the rate of growth in rural districts (5.7 per cent) was more than twice that of urban districts (2.5 per cent) (see Table 2.2). The rural excess in growth rate over the urban districts is especially pronounced for the three older age groups, ranging from a 7 to a 12 percentage point difference. In contrast, the urban districts outstripped the rural districts in the growth rate of 30–44 year olds and experienced a significantly smaller decrease of 15–29 year olds.

Table 2.2 Population change, 1993–2003, for broad age groups, by district type, per cent for decade

District type	All ages	0–14	15–29	30–44	45–59	60–74	75+
England	3.6	-1.8	-8.0	12.2	13.4	-1.1	13.5
Urban	2.5	-3.4	-5.9	13.4	10.9	-5.8	9.4
Rural	5.7	1.4	-12.5	10.0	17.4	6.4	20.0
Major Urban	2.7	-2.6	-4.7	16.1	8.8	-7.5	6.1
Large Urban	1.0	-5.9	-7.4	9.2	11.0	-5.4	10.3
Other Urban	3.7	-2.9	-7.1	10.9	16.3	-1.9	16.7
Significant Rural	4.1	0.0	-12.0	10.2	14.0	3.6	18.5
Rural-50	5.4	1.4	-13.6	9.2	17.4	6.3	20.5
Rural-80	7.8	3.2	-11.9	10.5	21.2	9.5	21.0

Table 2.2 also shows how far these patterns vary across the different types of rural and urban districts. The most striking feature is the extent to which increasing rurality is assoc- iated with the greater pace of growth in the number of the oldest people. For the 75+ group, for instance, it was the Rural-80 districts that saw the fastest growth, with their numbers up by 21 per cent over the 10-year period, followed by the Rural-50 districts and then the Significant Rural districts. Indeed, this relationship extends across all six district types, with the Major Urban type seeing the smallest relative rate of increase in the numbers of much older people. The same pattern is found for the 60–74 year olds, with higher rates of increase with increas- ing rurality and higher rates of decline the more urban the district. The trend is also simi- lar for the 45–59 group, except for the strong growth recorded by the Other Urban districts. Among the three younger age groups, however, only the under-15 group come close to this graduation across the six types, with the main feature for the 15–29 year olds being the broad contrast between urban and rural and with the growth of the 30–44 age group being fairly uniform apart from the faster growth of the Major Urban districts.

Figure 2.4 and Table 2.2 both bear witness to the general ageing of the English population in the 10 years up to 2003, with the overall contraction of the two under-30 age groups and substantial increases recorded by the 30–44, 45–59 and 75+ age groups. Moreover, it is an ageing process that is generally proceeding more rapidly in rural England than for the urban districts, with the former seeing the faster growth in people aged 45 and over and the greater rate of decline in the 15–29 age group. The under-15 age group provides the only sign of a rejuvenation of the rural population but, as we have already noted and will see in more detail later, the effect of this is undermined by the high level of movement of young adults out of the countryside.

Finally, this pattern of population ageing is fairly general across the nation. This is shown in Figure 2.5, using the same four-region breakdown as in Figure 2.3 and highlighting the con- trast in change rates for the under-45 and 45-and-over populations. In Northern England all six district types experienced a clear population ageing between 1993 and 2003, with a rise in numbers aged 45 and over alongside a decline in the number of people aged under 45. But the pace of ageing was greater for the two most rural categories, because while the contraction of the under-45 age group was at a similar rate to that of the more urban districts the rate of increase in the older populations was much higher. Elsewhere in England, the overwhelming picture is one where the older population grew faster than the under-45 population (the only exception being London), with the growth-rate differential between these two broad age groups being greatest for the three rural types and especially the Rural-80 districts. For instance, Southwest England's Rural-80 districts saw their number of people aged 45 and over rise by 17 per cent over the 10-year period compared to an increase of only 1 per cent for people aged under 45.

Figure 2.5 Change in number of people aged under 45 and aged 45 and over, 1993–2003, by district types for four regional divisions of England

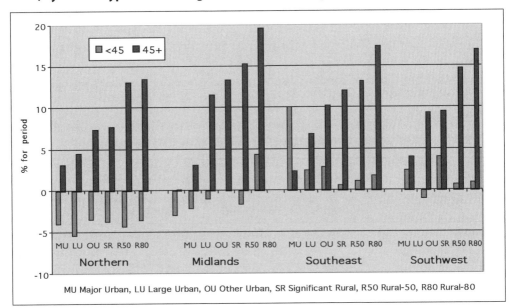

MU Major Urban, LU Large Urban, OU Other Urban, SR Significant Rural, R50 Rural-50, R80 Rural-80

The projected patterns of population change

The latest (2003-based) official population projections are for up to 2028. They indicate the continuation of the trends identified for 1993–2003; in other words, the population of rural England will continue to grow faster and age more quickly than that of urban England. This is perhaps not surprising in that these figures are based on projecting recent trends forward into the future with assumptions being made that the changes that have taken place in fertility and mortality in the last few years will be maintained into the future as will the age-specific patterns of migration. They do not allow for the influence of any policy measures or other developments that have not already been affecting population trends. What additionally the projections provide, however, is, firstly, the specific figures on the extra numbers in each age group and their changing shares of the overall population for each type of area and, secondly, an indication of the effect of the further ageing of the baby booms and busts of the past. Just as the 30–59 age groups swelled between 1993 and 2003 as the baby boomers reached 'middle age', so the projections reveal how these birth cohorts are likely to swell the numbers in their 60s, 70s and 80s by 2028. Perhaps the single most significant figure presented below is that, based on current trends, the Rural-80 districts as a group will find that almost half of their residents will be aged 50 and over by 2028, and the other two rural district types will not be far behind.

Table 2.3 shows the expected level of overall population change for the projection period 2003–2028 for England as a whole and for the separate district types. By 2028 England's total population will be over 55 million people, up by 5.5 million or 11 per cent on the 2003 level. By then, the share of the national total accounted for by the three rural types combined will have risen to 37.8 per cent, up by over one percentage point from its 2003 share of 36.5 per cent. The 5.5 million national increase will be spread almost equally between the urban and rural districts, but the rural districts will experience a considerably faster rate of growth – 15 per cent, as opposed to just under 9 per cent for the urban districts in aggregate. Looking across the six district types, the same pattern of growth rates is found as for 1993–2003. The highest growth rate is expected to be recorded by the most rural type – Rural-80 – with a progressively lower rate of increase as one moves further up the urban hierarchy, with the sole exception of the Major Urban category whose 'out of line' performance is entirely due to the forward projection of London's strong growth of recent years. Moreover, apart from this latter case, it is the most rural type that is expected to see the largest absolute increase in population numbers.

Table 2.3 Projected population change, 2003–2028, by district type, England

District type	Population 2028		2003–2028 change	
	Thousands	% England	Thousands	%
England	55,381.3	100.0	5,535.6	11.1
Urban	34,432.0	62.2	2,787.0	8.8
Rural	20,949.3	37.8	2,748.6	15.1
Major Urban	19,157.6	34.6	1,661.9	9.5
Large Urban	7,804.2	14.1	472.7	6.4
Other Urban	7,470.2	13.5	652.4	9.6
Significant Rural	7,331.2	13.2	813.1	12.5
Rural-50	6,699.4	12.1	859.9	14.7
Rural-80	6,918.7	12.5	1,075.6	18.4

This scale of population growth is primarily due to increases between 2003 and 2028 in the numbers of people aged 60 and over. For England as a whole, these are expected to rise by a total of 5.3 million people, and the 45–59 year olds by a further 0.6 million, while the three younger age groups will contract or grow only marginally (Table 2.4). The rural districts combined account for significantly more than half of the rise in the total number of people aged 60 and over. At the same time, rural areas can expect to see the numbers of 30–44 and under-15 year olds reduce somewhat, thereby accelerating the ageing process, though this will also affect urban England, which in aggregate seems destined to see some shrinkage of its 15–29 age group as well.

Table 2.4 Population change, 2003–2028, for broad age groups, by district type, thousands

District type	0–14	15–29	30–44	45–59	60–74	75+	All ages
England	-119.7	65.3	-350.6	601.4	2,982.0	2,362.0	5,535.6
Urban	-102.1	-39.3	-120.2	499.3	1,511.6	1,036.9	2,787.0
Rural	-17.6	104.6	-230.4	102.1	1,470.4	1,325.1	2,748.6
Major Urban	20.4	-11.3	35.8	429.0	740.5	445.3	1,661.9
Large Urban	-77.9	-30.4	-87.0	16.9	365.6	286.2	472.7
Other Urban	-44.6	2.4	-69.0	53.4	405.5	305.4	652.4
Significant Rural	-11.4	29.8	-75.5	33.1	441.4	400.3	813.1
Rural-50	-13.9	28.6	-81.7	25.0	472.4	429.0	859.9
Rural-80	7.7	46.2	-73.2	44.0	556.6	495.8	1,075.6

Note: totals may not sum exactly because the data for individual districts was rounded.

The increasing size of the older age groups appears even more significant when expressed in terms of their growth rates. Nationally (Figure 2.6, right-hand panel), in 2028 the number of people aged 75 and over is forecast to be more than 60 per cent larger than in 2003, and the number of 60–74 year olds over 40 per cent larger, due to the baby boomers having moved into later life, and on current trends the biggest impacts will be sustained by the rural districts. The rate of increase in the number of people aged 75 and over rises progressively across the urban–rural spectrum, with the Rural-80 districts expected to see almost a doubling in their numbers as opposed to the Major Urban districts' rise of less than 40 per cent. The gradient of growth rates for the 60–74 age group is similarly regular, though the gradient is less steep, rising to an increase of just over 60 per cent for the Rural-80 districts.

Figure 2.6 England: % change in size of broad age groups, 2003–2028

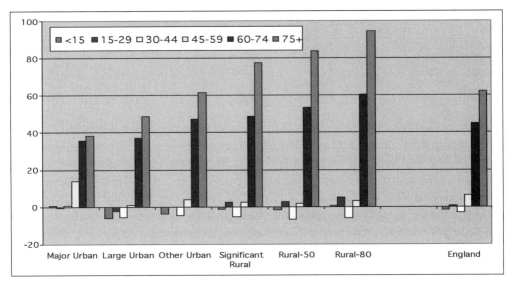

41

Figure 2.7 summarises the projected changes for all rural districts combined, using an age pyramid with 5-year age groups. Superimposing the percentage distribution of 2028 on to that of 2003 shows very clearly the way in which, over this period, the bulge of 30–59 year olds moves up the age ladder to swell all the age groups from 60–64 upwards. It also shows the proportionate increase in the importance of each age group chronologically, being greatest for the 85-and-overs because a large increase in the share of this group is building on a relatively small base. Also striking is the greater proportionate elongation of the bars for older males compared to females. Traditionally there have been far fewer males than females at these higher ages, but this differential is beginning to narrow because of the faster gains in life expectancy for males in recent years. Note that, in absolute terms, the growth in numbers of the very oldest people in rural England is higher than suggested in Figure 2.7, because of the fact that its whole population is growing strongly at the same time. For example, rural England's 85-and-over population is projected to rise by 180 per cent from 310 to 874 thousands, with the male component of this trebling in size from 114 to 345 thousands.

Figure 2.7 All rural: population projection 2003–2028

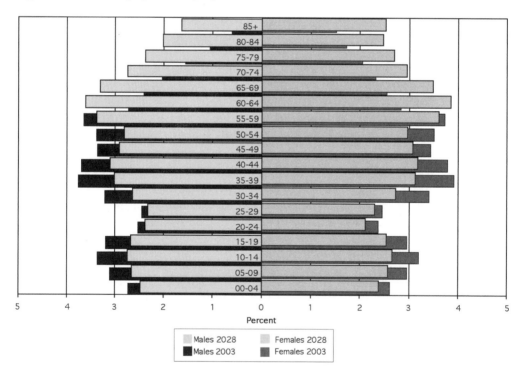

Figure 2.8 shows how the continued ageing of the population is projected to affect the age composition of the different district types. The Rural-80 type already had the highest share of people aged 50 and over in 2003 and this will become even more distinctive by 2028, when little short of half of this type's population are expected to be at least 50 years old. The proportion for the Rural-50 type was a little lower than this in 2003, and consequently its percentage point increase is also just a little lower. Similarly, the Significant Rural type comes just slightly further behind on both accounts. In urban areas less than 30 per cent of the Major Urban type's population was aged 50 and over in 2003, and the projected increase by 2028 is expected to be the lowest of all six types, at barely 5 percentage points.

Figure 2.8 Age composition of England's population aged 50+, 2003 and 2028, for Rural LAD classification, % total population

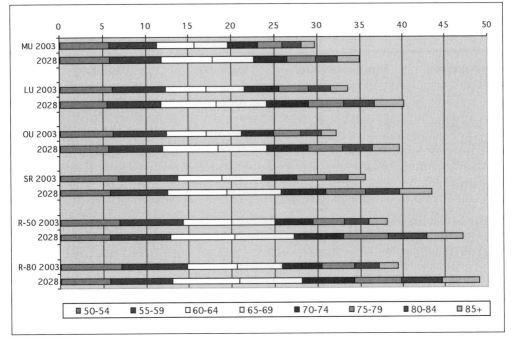

Analysing these trends on a regional basis highlights clear variations in the proportion of older people and in the pace that this is growing. As shown in Table 2.5, in all four regions the rural population is currently older than the urban, and over the 25-year period to 2028 the proportion aged 50 and over is projected to increase faster for the rural districts. Southwest England currently has the largest proportion of its rural population aged 50 and over, while the Southeast has the smallest – a situation that is not expected to change. By 2028, 49 per cent of the rural Southwest's population will be of this age, compared to 44 per cent for the Southeast. The biggest increases in the proportion of older people in rural districts, however, look like occurring in the Midlands and Northern England, tending to close the gap on Southwest England.

Table 2.5 Proportion of population aged 50 and over, 2003–2028, for urban and rural England, by broad regional division

Broad region	2003		2028		% point change	
	Urban	Rural	Urban	Rural	Urban	Rural
Southeast	29.0	36.7	34.7	44.4	5.7	7.7
Southwest	34.0	40.4	39.2	48.9	5.2	8.5
Midlands	31.9	37.4	37.7	47.2	5.8	9.8
Northern	33.0	37.3	39.5	47.3	6.5	10.0

In all the regions it is the most rural district type that already has the highest proportion of older people and will continue to age the most rapidly. Southwest Rural-80 districts are likely to see the proportion of people aged 50 and over reaching 51 per cent by 2028 (Table 2.6). Those of the Midlands and Northern England will not be far behind this.

Table 2.6 Proportion of population aged 50 and over, 2003 and 2028, for the three district types of rural England, by broad regional division

Broad region	Significant Rural		Rural-50		Rural-80	
	2003	2028	2003	2028	2003	2028
Southeast	34.9	41.8	37.8	45.6	38.1	46.8
Southwest	36.7	41.9	39.9	48.1	41.6	51.0
Midlands	35.8	45.1	37.7	47.3	39.4	49.8
Northern	36.2	44.8	37.0	47.9	39.2	50.2

Individual districts vary considerably from these regional aggregates. Altogether, 58 districts – almost 1 in 6 of the England total – are projected to have the majority of their population aged 50 and over by 2028. The ranking is led by Berwick-upon-Tweed, with an expected proportion of 62 per cent in 2028. The next oldest populations will be found in West Somerset, North Norfolk, Rother, East Devon, East Lindsey, West Dorset, South Lakeland, Tendring and Christchurch. All but one of these top ten districts are rural, six of them Rural-80. The exception is Christchurch, which is classified as Large Urban on account of it being part of the urban area of Bournemouth. It is therefore clear that many rural parts of England are now overtaking seaside resorts and spa towns as the places with the oldest populations – although it should be noted that all the top ten are on the coast as well as being rural.

The role of migration in producing rural population ageing

Migration plays an extremely important role in determining demographic structures across England, not least in terms of the number and composition of the older population. As has been demonstrated, the rural ageing process comprises three main types of migration. While traditionally most attention has been given to the arrival of retirees and the exodus of young adults, more recently a third type has become much more important, though its effect on the proportion of older people in a community is not immediate. The main element in the emergence of 'counter-urbanisation' has been the high level of migration into rural England by pre-retirement groups, with the largest rural population gains being of 30 and 40 year olds and their children. While many children leave for urban areas on or soon after leaving school, most of their parents stay for the rest of their lives, 'ageing in place' alongside the locally born and bred. In this section, a variety of analyses is used to illustrate these points, drawing very largely on ward-level data on within-UK migration obtained from the 2001 Census. This provides a more precise definition of settlements than the district-level classification used up till now – one which restricts 'rural England' to settlements of under 10,000 people and accounted for 18 per cent of England's total population in 2001.

Figure 2.9 provides an introduction to the importance of England's rural wards as the net beneficiary of internal migration. In aggregate, they gained almost 30,000 more people than they lost as a result of people changing address within the UK in the 12 months leading up to census day in 2001. This is a greater gain than for any of the other categories shown and indeed is larger than for all the urban areas of under 100,000 residents combined. The graph also shows clearly the classic 'counter-urbanisation' relationship, with the largest conurbations (namely London, West Midlands, Merseyside, Greater Manchester, West Yorkshire and Tyneside) being substantial net losers of migrants and the medium-sized urban areas seeing net gains but not on such a large scale as rural and smaller urban areas. (Note: because the census provides no information about emigration overseas, this graph does not show the effect of net international immigration in helping to offset the within-UK migration losses of the largest six urban areas.)

Figure 2.9 Net within-UK migration balance, 2000–2001, by size of urban area, England, thousands

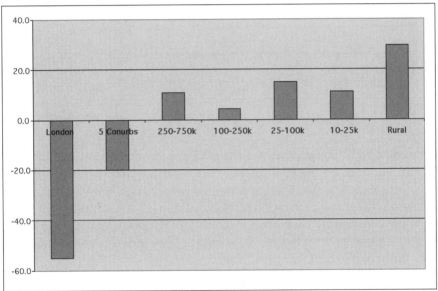

The age breakdown of this population movement reveals very clearly the three ways in which migration is contributing to the ageing of rural England. As shown in the far-right panel of Figure 2.10, the rural wards are net gainers of retirees and the immediate pre-retirement age group, but their main gain is from 30–44 year olds and the under-16 age group. In due course, however, many of the youngest in-migrants – together with local children – move out of rural England, as reflected in the large net losses of the 16–19 and 20–24 age groups, but once the 30–44 year olds have arrived, in net terms they stay and eventually contribute to the swelling of the ranks of older people living in the countryside. The pattern for the six largest urban areas combined (far-left panel of Figure 2.10) is almost the mirror image of this, especially in relation to their net losses of children and the age groups of 30 and over. The two next largest size groups are distinctive only in their net gains of 16–19 year olds, this occurring presumably because of attracting more university students than they send to university elsewhere. Meanwhile, the urban areas of 10,000 to 100,000 people are largely a microcosm of the rural category, but they are bigger net attractors of the 60–74 age groups (and especially the over 75s). It would appear that the countryside and rural towns (of under 10,000 people) do not hold such a strong appeal for older old people when moving.

Figure 2.10 Net within-UK migration balance, 2000–2001, by size of urban area and age group, England

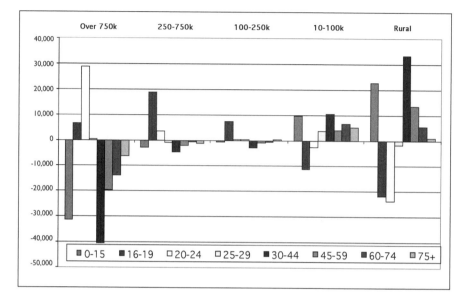

Rural England, as defined at the ward level, is therefore the key migration gainer of older people and the largest cities are the main losers, where 'older' now has to be defined as 30 and over. This is not to imply that the urban areas have experienced no population turnover. In fact, considerable 'cascading' has been taking place. Population is not just moving out of the largest cities directly into rural England; rather, much of the net movement out of the largest cities goes to the next level of the urban hierarchy, but the latter then loses similar numbers to the next level down, and so on (Champion, 2004).

The structure of England's settlements of under 10,000 people, can be analysed combining two two-way classifications. One separates out Rural Towns from the remainder of the countryside which, at the ward level used here, groups the Villages and Dispersed elements of the full rural definition, while the other distinguishes the geographical context of settlements in terms of 'sparse' and 'less sparse'. The resulting four-fold typology indicates considerable variation across rural England in overall migratory growth rates. In the year leading up to the 2001 Census, the strongest performance was recorded by Rural Towns in sparse settings, with a net migration gain relative to their existing population of 0.92 per cent – over three times the overall rate of 0.29 for all of England's rural wards. Next highest, but a long way behind, is the 0.35 per cent migratory gain for the Rural Towns in less sparse areas, with the Villages and Dispersed categories trailing far behind with rates of 0.17 and 0.14 per cent in less sparse and sparse settings respectively.

It is, however, in the behaviour of specific age groups that the differential performance of these four rural types is most marked. Of particular relevance to the older population is the greater appeal of town over village life for older old people. This is evidenced in Figure 2.11 by the net exodus of people aged 75 and over from the Village and Dispersed category, found in both sparse and less sparse contexts but especially the former. As seen previously in Figure 2.10, these are not leaving rural England, but are concentrating in the Towns, producing a 1.5

per cent increase in the 75+ population of those in sparse settings and also some growth in those situated in a less sparse context.

Figure 2.11 Net within-UK migration rate, by age and different rural settlement types, England

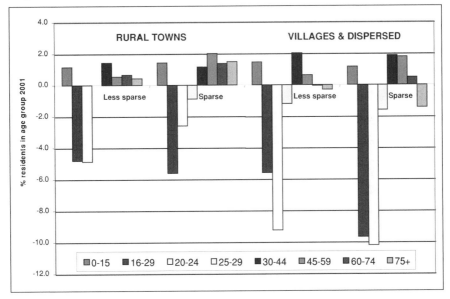

However, perhaps the most striking aspect of Figure 2.11 is the massive haemorrhaging of young adults. This is found for all four types of rural settlement, but is especially severe for the Villages and Dispersed category in sparse areas. The 10 per cent net migration loss of 16–24 year olds recorded in this one-year period from these areas is the equivalent of losing more than three out of every five of this segment of the population if repeated for the 9 years of their passing through this age group (using compound rates). Even for the Villages and Dispersed in less sparse surroundings, on the basis of a 6 per cent annual loss of 16–19 year olds combined with an over 9 per cent loss for 20–24 year olds, the net shrinkage of the school-leaving cohort is over half. If it were not for the substantial net in-migration of older people and their children, the prospects for this type of settlement in rural England would be bleak indeed.

Similar analyses for Government Office Regions (not shown here) suggest that these patterns are prevalent across the whole of rural England. These include the net migration loss of those aged over 75 from the Village and Dispersed type of settlement, the relative attractiveness of Remote Towns for the oldest age groups, the premium conferred by remoteness for the 30–59 age groups, and the high rate of loss of young adults by the sparse Village and Dispersed areas in particular. The pace of these migration changes varies between regions. In Yorkshire and the Humber, for instance, the sparse Villages and Dispersed wards lost almost 14 per cent of their 20–24 year olds in the pre-census year, considerably more than England's overall figure of 10 per cent. In contrast, in the East of England, the rate of loss was under 3 per cent.

It may be that the exodus of young adults will have been accelerating in recent years due to the increasing proportion of school-leavers going on into higher education. It may also be that the exodus of people aged 75+ from the deep countryside has been increasing, as this group will have been particularly disadvantaged by the closure of village shops and post offices and the rationalisation of rural bus services. However, the increased popularity of rural England for middle-aged and middle-class people, already with a 40-year history behind it, shows no sign of abating. Indeed, according to the evidence of the NHS Central Register, overall levels of net out-migration from the larger cities into the more rural counties have in recent years been running at some of the highest levels ever recorded since this data source came on stream in the mid 1970s.

Summary: the ageing of rural England

The purpose of this chapter has been to document the evidence in support of the central theme of this book. It has confirmed that the population of rural England is growing faster than that of the nation as a whole and that it is also growing older more quickly. These observations hold true whether looking back over the developments of recent years or examining the official 2003-based population projections covering the period through to 2028. Moreover, the figures which we have presented for rural England are very significant. Key headline statistics are:

- In the 10 years to 2003, the number of people aged 75 and over living in the 178 local government districts classified as rural rose by 20 per cent, compared to the 9 per cent increase estimated for urban England.

- Between 2003 and 2028 the number of people aged 75 and over in English rural districts is projected to rise by around 80 per cent, and the number aged 60–74 will grow by around 50 per cent.

- At the apex of rural England's age pyramid, the number of males aged 85 and over is expected to treble, while the numbers of people in all the age bands below 60 will be smaller in 2028 than they were in 2003.

Of course, the projections are based on assumptions derived from recent trends in life expectancy, family size and migration, and there can be no absolute certainty about the future. Yet there are sound reasons for accepting this broad picture of the continuing rapid increase in the numbers of older people living in the countryside. In the first place, increasing longevity has been an ever-present factor since the onset of the demographic transition some two centuries ago. Secondly, all those who will be in the older age groups in 2028 have already been born, so the only question is where they will be living. In that regard, there seems to be no diminution in the preference of those aged from their 30s upwards to live in rural areas.

Set against this argument, however, there are scenarios that could potentially challenge this pattern of projected rural population growth and ageing. One concerns choice of retirement area and the increasing tendency of people to seek out coastal and rural areas further south in Europe, which in itself would take some of the pressure off rural England. Alternatively, there is the possibility of a further tightening of housing markets in rural areas resulting from the passage of the post-war baby boomers into pensionable age. In relation to the latter, however, the majority of the people that not only desire a rural lifestyle but are also in a position to achieve it are already living in rural England, having moved there in their 30s, 40s and 50s.

What would be more likely, in a situation of rising housing pressure, would be a slowdown in the rate of urban–rural migration by people at these younger ages, which would not reduce the number of older people living in the countryside for the foreseeable future but would merely serve to accelerate the rise in their proportion. Similarly, though it is not an aspect that this review of demographic change has dwelt on, this sifting of incomers would also have a socio-economic dimension, as less prosperous people (including younger people with less housing equity) would be squeezed out of the market.

The mention of housing pressures goes hand in hand with the recognition that rural England is not a single undifferentiated entity. Within the geographical frameworks used in this chapter, there are two major dimensions of variability. In terms of the three rural district types, it is the most rural – Rural-80 – that currently has the highest median age and is expected to see the largest increase in its proportion of older people over the next couple of decades. These areas tend to be located in the more peripheral and coastal parts of the country and contrast particularly with the Significant Rural category, much of which lies within commuting distance of larger cities. Secondly, there is the distinction between the rural towns and the deeper countryside of villages and dispersed settlements, which featured in our examination of migration patterns. The latter command the higher rates of migration gains for most of the older age groups and, combined with their tighter planning restrictions on new housebuilding, would see the greater impact of any increased trend towards the filtering out of less prosperous incomers. Besides these two dimensions, there is also much regional and local variation that this chapter has not been able to do full justice to. Suffice it here to draw attention to the likelihood of some districts having three out of five people aged over 50 by 2028 and the median age of all Southwest England's Rural-80 districts combined rising to 51 years.

Nevertheless, discussion of geographical variations should not let us lose sight of the advance of the ageing process along a broad front across England, as in so many other countries around the world but especially those that experienced a temporary baby boom in the middle of the last century. It is simply that the rural areas are in the vanguard of this process, with their most rural parts lying at the cutting edge. It is just a matter of timing as to when a particular level of ageing will have been reached in any place, not whether it will actually occur. In due course, unless England goes on receiving large numbers of young immigrants from overseas or fertility rates move sharply upwards, urban areas too will eventually reach the situation described above for rural England. How rural communities cope with the ageing 'wave' over the next few years can be expected to pave the way for the rest of the country.

Acknowledgements

The authors would like to thank Dr Brian Linneker, Research Fellow with the Rural Evidence Research Centre at Birkbeck College, for assembling the Census data within the framework of the new rural classification.

References and further reading

Champion, A.G. (ed) (1989) *Counterurbanisation: The Changing Pace and Nature of Population Deconcentration,* London: Edward Arnold

Champion, A.G. (1992) 'Urban and regional demographic trends in the Developed World', *Urban Studies* 29 (3/4), 461–482

Champion, A.G. (2001) 'A changing demographic regime and evolving polycentric urban regimes: consequences for the size, composition and distribution of city populations', *Urban Studies* 38 (4), 657–677

Champion, A.G. and Atkins, D.J. (2000) Migration between metropolitan and non-metropolitan areas in England and Wales, in R. Creeser and S. Gleave (eds) *Migration within England and Wales using the ONS Longitudinal Study*. ONS Series LS no. 9, London: The Stationery Office, 1–15

Champion, T. (2001) 'The continuing urban–rural population movement in Britain: trends, patterns, significance', *Espace, Populations, Societes* 2001-1-2, 37–51

Champion, T. (2004) 'The counterurbanisation cascade in England and Wales since 1991: the evidence of a new migration dataset', *Belgeo* 1–2, 85–102

Champion, T. and Fisher, T. (2003) 'The social selectivity of migration flows affecting Britain's larger conurbations: an analysis of the 1991 Census Regional Migration Tables', *Scottish Geographical Journal* 119, 229–246

Champion, T. and Hugo, G. (eds) (2004) *New Forms of Urbanization: Beyond the Urban/Rural Dichotomy,* Aldershot: Ashgate

Champion, T., Atkins, D., Coombes, M. and Fotheringham, S. (1998) *Urban Exodus,* London: Council for the Protection of Rural England

Coleman, D. (ed) (1996) *Europe's Population in the 1990s,* Oxford: Oxford University Press

Defra (2004) *Rural Strategy 2004,* London: Department for Environment, Food and Rural Affairs

Faus-Pujol, M.C. (1995) Changes in the fertility rate and age structure of the population of Europe, in R. Hall and P. White (eds) *Europe's Population: Towards the Next Century,* London: University College London Press, 17–33

Fielding, T. (1998) Counterurbanisation and social class, in P. Boyle and K. Halfacree (eds) *Migration into Rural Areas: Theories and Issues,* Chichester: John Wiley, 41–60

Hall, R. and White, P. (eds) (1995) *Europe's Population: Towards the Next Century,* London: University College London Press

Hoggart, K. (1990) 'Let's do away with rural', *Journal of Rural Studies* 6 (3), 245–257

Lesthaeghe, R. and van de Kaa, D.J. (1986) Twee demograpfische transities?, in D.J. van de Kaa and R. Lesthaeghe (eds) *Bevolking: Groei en Krimp,* Deventer: van Loghem Slaterus

McLoughlin, J. (1991) *The Demographic Revolution,* London: Faber and Faber

Noin, D. and Woods, R. (eds) (1993) *The Changing Population of Europe,* Oxford: Blackwell

Rees, P.H. (1992) Elderly migration and population redistribution in the United Kingdom, in A. Rogers (ed) *Elderly Migration and Population Redistribution,* London: Belhaven

SERRL (2002) *A Review of Urban and Rural Area Definitions,* a report to the Office of the Deputy Prime Minister, Occasional Monographs No. 2, Birkbeck College

Tarling, R. et al (1993) *The Economy of Rural England,* London: Rural Development Commission

van de Kaa, D.J. (1987) 'Europe's second demographic transition', *Population Bulletin* 42 (1), 1–57

van de Kaa, D.J. (2003) Second demographic transition, in P. Demeny and G. McNicholl (eds) *Encyclopaedia of Population,* New York: Macmillan Reference USA, 872–875

Chapter 3

'A place in the countryside' – migration and the construction of rural living

Irene Hardill

Introduction

A place in the country is an aspiration for many, and particularly so for a large number of middle-aged and older people. This chapter focuses on the individuals behind the statistics, concentrating on the motivation and social trends driving a move to the country. The perceived quality of the rural environment is one of the most important factors in the appeal of rural areas as places to live. Surveys reveal that rural dwellers are more content than urban dwellers (Cabinet Office, 1999). Some 89 per cent of people living in rural areas said they were content with where they live, compared with 20 per cent in cities. In one national survey, 71 per cent of people expressed the view that the quality of life is better in the countryside than elsewhere, and 66 per cent said that they would move there if they could do so (ibid). In consequence, rural areas are among the fastest growing parts of England – in terms of both population and employment. In Chapter 2 Tony Champion and John Shepherd describe counter-urbanisation as migration 'cascading down' the urban hierarchy to rural settlements such as market towns and villages. Two broad groups stand out in this migration to the countryside: middle-aged and older people and younger households with dependent children.

Given the significant contribution of in-migrants to the shifting rural demographic profile, it is important to identify the drivers behind the decisions of individuals, if the broader economic and social implications are to be understood. This chapter provides a more in-depth study of such drivers, by analysing the experiences of a group of late middle-aged migrants who have moved to the rural Midlands; individuals who in later life had the opportunity and wherewithal to realise that aspiration of finding 'a place in the country'. The chapter explores what propelled them and what attracted them to a rural area. Their motives and experiences prove to be many and varied. What they have in common is a geographical relocation to a house in a rural area. This residential relocation is typically part of a complex set of domestic and employment changes that households undertake in what might be considered a mid-life transition. The adults in these households have made far-reaching and interlinked mid-life decisions about rearranging their family and work relations. The change of house and scene is also a change of direction chosen to fit the household to what is seen as the next stage in their lives. In this way rural residential locations are imbued with certain functions for living, wherein the stages and stations of later life are fitted together.

Hagerstrand (1969) conceptualised migration in terms of movements through an individual's life course, regulated by 'stations' (homes and workplaces) at which a person stays for varying lengths of time. People's 'life-paths' take them through a network of stations, the aggregate of many life-paths forming an intricate but far from ordered fabric. As Salt (1988, page 397) recognises, 'consideration of the movement of an individual in life (career)-path terms can throw fresh light on … channels of mobility among particular groups'. Another way of conceptualising migration is to focus on the home, in terms of a 'housing ladder' or a 'property ladder'. This was a device used by building societies and estate agents in particular to emphasise the investment potential of house purchase (Munro and Madigan, 1998). The ladder began with a 'starter home' for the first-time buyer, with the implicit expectation of subsequent advancement up successive rungs of the hierarchical property market. As such the image was seen to provide a 'life plan' which appealed to notions of self-improvement and future security and which commanded widespread popular support (Saunders, 1989). The idea of a housing ladder embraces financial accumulation: each successive step is buoyed by accumulated equity and capital gain acquired in the previous property.

The property hierarchy is closely associated with an archetypal family life cycle, in which young adults (whether single or as couples) are expected to make their first house purchase in the city close to work, where flats, small houses and starter homes are available.[1] As the household expands and its income rises and/or the value of its property increases, there may be a move to a more definitely suburban, out of town or small town location. It is at this stage that children's schooling may play a key role in choosing a location. Finally, once the family grows up, there may well be a move to a smaller house or a bungalow near the sea, or a flat near to adult children. This represents a simplified but powerful image of a socially sanctioned life cycle of self-improvement which meshes easily with many of the perceived advantages of home ownership, including:

- the ability to reduce housing costs in later life;

- a form of savings which is seen as credit worthy;

- the accumulation of an asset which will ultimately be 'something to leave to the children'.

Residential decisions and housing search are intrinsically tied to the household, how it functions as a decision-making unit, and the weighting of power relations within it. Residential migration is a highly disruptive process for all those involved, particularly in moves involving considerable distances – it disrupts and fragments a household's social space (Seavers, 1999, page 151).

The choice of a home in a rural area involves the choice of not only a particular residential property but also the neighbourhood/locality as part of this 'living space', a space which extends beyond the dwelling itself out into the surrounding physical, socio-economic and socio-cultural environment. Moreover, the choice of a rural home often involves moving from an urban housing market to a rural one. Some moves from housing markets in London and the South to rural areas may be influenced by house price differentials (Countryside Agency, 2004). Moving home in mid to later life may result in the release of equity tied up in property, thereby enabling the household members to undertake a lifestyle change (eg 'downsizing' by

---

1   While this may have been the case, today with escalating property prices it is hard for young adults to get on the first rung of the property ladder.

moving to a retirement bungalow, or the search for a less pressured job in a rural as opposed to an urban labour market, or becoming one's own boss by becoming self-employed).

Migration to the countryside: a lifestyle and life course decision

Enormous changes have occurred to the pattern of the life course for men and women in England, which has traditionally[2] been divided into three rigidly defined stages: 'school age', 'working age' and 'retirement' (for a fuller account see Meadows, 2004, page 15; Warnes and McInerney, 2004, page 8). The transitions between each stage in the life course have become much more complex, characterised by greater fluidity. Working life is now characterised by risks of unemployment related to redundancy, the termination of contracts, outsourcing and career stagnation, and these risks have altered the duration and concept of 'working life' (Hardill and Van Loon, in press) such that half of men and a third of women now retire before they reach the state pension age (Disney et al, 1997). This binary is already blurred as men and women retire before state pension age and some work beyond it. A recent study found that overall employment rates for women at age 60 and men at aged 65 stand at 8 per cent and 9 per cent respectively (Smeaton and McKay, 2003). There are a number of reasons for continuing to work beyond the state pension age. These include financial reasons, because of inadequate pension provision, but there are also skill-related reasons. Those with highly valued skills and qualifications have a range of choices to continue working, including on a part-time basis or through self-employment. Huber and Skidmore (2003, page 59) call for a redefinition of 'retirement' to recognise the blurring of the work/retirement binary.

The population aged over 50 years forms a heterogeneous component of the population, with hybrid identities. Older people's lives have been shaped by increasing individualisation, mobility and 'mosaic' lifestyles, which are generating more single-person households. As a result of changing family forms as well as broader patterns of economic and social restructuring, what was a largely homogeneous 50+ age group has become fragmented (Stacey, 1998, page 17; Beck and Beck-Gernsheim, 2002). Chronological age is already a less useful predictor of patterns of living with older people being increasingly diverse in their characteristics. Indeed, as they approach state pension age there is an expectation of a further three decades of life, because of an increase in life expectancy, but this life is likely to be radically different to that of their parent's generation (Scales and Scase, 2000).

Champion and Shepherd's (Chapter 2) analysis of the 2001 Census has shown that migration is helping to alter the distribution of older people around the country. Migration rates vary greatly by age (the age group 25–44 are the most likely to move), with older people moving around the least, but the migration of older adults is significant over longer distances associated with moves around retirement age (ibid). Among older age groups outward flows are strong from London (especially those aged 45–59 years, somewhat smaller for those aged 60–74 years and least for 75+) (ibid). The regions that stand out as beneficiaries of migration flows of older adults are the Southwest, followed by the East Midlands and the East of England. Moving to the countryside occurs at mid-life, and involves households. The dominance

---

2   Through custom, as envisioned in the Beveridge Plan of 1942 and with the advent of the Welfare State (see Warnes and McInerney, 2004, page 8).

and relative influence of household members can change at different stages in the migration process, and it is necessary to distinguish between:

- the impetus to move and the actual decision to move;

- the general destination area and the specific housing search space (Seavers, 1999).

The move to the countryside can therefore be thought of as a mid-life transition as family and work relations are rearranged. The decision to move to a rural area could be:

- Work-related: relocation because of a new job as part of the pursuit of a career largely by male partners in households. Such moves may impact adversely on the career/job aspirations of female partners (Hanson and Pratt, 1995; Hardill, 1998). The choice of residence is often related to the male partner's pattern of commuting.

- A pre-retirement strategy: relocation for lifestyle reasons. The decision to move house is inextricably linked to a radical change in labour market position, which results in a less stressful job, bringing about a major lifestyle change, such as the move from full-time to part-time work, or the move from employee to self-employed status ('elderpreneurs') (Baines et al, 2002; Huber and Skidmore, 2003; Oughton et al, 2003).

- A retirement strategy: moving house occurs with withdrawal from the labour market, with early retirement (sometimes called 'freedom 50') or with retirement at state pension age.

Migration in the East Midlands

Currently the East Midlands comprises the counties of Derbyshire, Leicestershire, Nottinghamshire, Northamptonshire and Lincolnshire, and the unitary authorities of Derby, Leicester, Nottingham and Rutland (Figure 3.1). The draft revision of the East Midlands Regional Planning Guidance (East Midlands Local Government Association, 2003) identifies five sub-areas which have some internal coherence, two of which, the *Peak sub-area* (National Park and surrounding areas) and the *Eastern sub-area*[3] (Lincolnshire, Rutland and the eastern parts of Northamptonshire and Leicestershire), are predominately rural in character. The Eastern sub-area has a traditional settlement structure of dispersed towns and rural hinterlands, and parts of the area suffer from peripherality, especially eastern Lincolnshire along the coastal strip (ibid).

The region is composed of a mosaic of physical and socio-economic landscapes; it extends from the intensively farmed Fens in the east across to the central scarplands and the cluster of free-standing urban centres, such as Nottingham, and then westwards to the hills of the High Peak. Vast areas of the region were untouched by industrialisation (and deindustrialisation); indeed, the principal activity through much of Northamptonshire and southern Leicestershire remained agriculture. However, farming is no longer the foundation of the rural economy today, nor is it the lynchpin of rural society.

The East Midlands has a significant rural population with over 40 per cent of the population classified as living within a rural district, compared with 28.5 per cent of the population for

3 The Eastern sub-area falls into a number of sub-regional housing markets including Corby-Kettering and Wellingborough, Nottingham, Leicester, central Lincolnshire, coastal Lincolnshire, and Peterborough/Welland (DTZ Pieda, 2005).

England (Champion, 2005). The region is therefore an interesting case study in examining in more depth rural immigration through the eyes of the individuals who have chosen to relocate there.

Figure 3.1 Map showing the counties/unitary authorities and districts in the East Midlands

Map reproduced courtesy of Stephen Hincks, University of Liverpool

Figure 3.2 Population change, 1993–2003, for the rural classification of local authorities in the East Midlands (%)

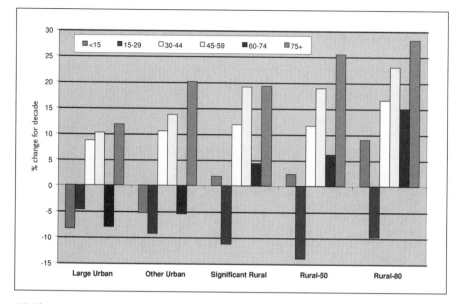

NB *There are no Major Urban areas in the East Midlands, classed as settlements with 750,000 or more population*

Source: 2001 Census, Office for National Statistics

The regional population statistics demonstrate that the East Midlands shows similar trends to the other English regions (see Chapter 2). Figure 3.2 illustrates population change, 1993–2003, for the East Midlands; it shows clear differences between the urban and rural districts within the region. Urban parts of the region recorded a decline in young and older people: that is people aged less than 29 years and those between 60 and 74 years. The rural population in the region grew largely because of the growth in the numbers of middle-aged and older adults, mirrored by a decrease in the number of young people (between 15 and 29 years) in these communities. These trends are likely to continue. Figure 3.3 presents population projections for 2003–2028, and while it is predicted that all areas, urban and rural, will see their population aged over 60 years increase, it will be particularly pronounced for rural areas. It is forecast that many urban areas will also see a reduction in their population of people under 44 years of age.

In the East Midlands population growth due to in-migration to rural areas has been particularly concentrated (see Figure 3.4). The NHS Central Register provides an estimate of the net migration in to the East Midlands over the period of March 2001 to December 2003. Most of the rise in population in the East Midlands over the past few years has come from Eastern England and the Southeast. Almost 40,000 more people are estimated to have moved to the East Midlands from these regions than have gone in the opposite direction. Further to this, over 13,000 more people have moved from London to the East Midlands than vice versa. The only areas to which the East Midlands has lost population are Scotland, Wales, Northern Ireland and the Southwest (and the net out-migration to these regions was less than 5,000 in total). Overall, the net migration to the East Midlands between March 2001 and December 2003 is estimated to be over 61,000.

Figure 3.3 East Midlands: change in size of broad age groups, 2003–2028

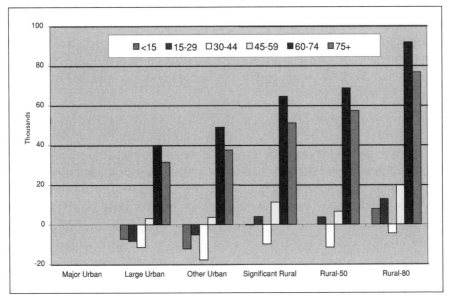

NB *There are no Major Urban areas in the East Midlands, classed as settlements with 750,000 or more population*

Source: 2001 Census, Office for National Statistics

Figure 3.4 East Midlands: percentage change in size of age groups due to net within-UK migration, 2000–2001, for rural and urban wards

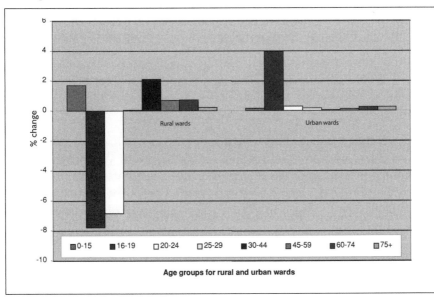

Source: 2001 Census, Office for National Statistics

In-migrants tend to be aged 30–44 years, in couple households. Crucially this group remain in the region, they semi-retire or retire in situ (Figure 3.3). The migration statistics from the 2001 Census record all people in an area who have moved there in the past year. For the East Midlands while 2,089 individuals of pensionable age moved into the region 1,416 left (a net gain of 673), compared to 37,721 couples who also moved to the region and the 27,932 who left (a net gain of 9,789 individuals[4]). A large proportion of these in-migrants were those relocating to the rural East Midlands.

At county level, Northamptonshire and parts of Leicestershire have witnessed population growth because of their proximity to the prosperous markets of the Greater South East. Growth in the southern part of the region is set to continue under the Sustainable Communities Plan. Northamptonshire has been earmarked for major new growth clustered around Northampton, Corby, Kettering and Wellingborough. Some communities in Lincolnshire are expanding because of retirement and pre-retirement migration (see Table T33 Theme Table on Migration, 2001, Census and Champion, 2005).

Migration to the countryside: a case study of the East Midlands

The empirical evidence used to tell the story of the individuals behind the region's demographic statistics presented in this chapter is drawn from material collected in a study of in-migrant households to the Eastern sub-area of the East Midlands. This uses a qualitative approach to providing material to create a picture of the lived reality of growing older in rural England and is based on two main sources:

● Structured self-completion questionnaires covering 113 in-migrant households: 43 (38 per cent) had an adult aged between 40 and 50 years and 44 (38 per cent) an adult aged over 50 years. Of these 44 households 18 had an adult aged over 60 years and 26 one between 50 and 59 years. Within the 44 households there were a total of 75 adults aged over 50 years.

● Semi-structured face-to-face interviews with a representative sub-set of 43 of the 113 in-migrant households: a third of the subset (14 of the 43) had an adult aged over 50 years present.

The household (rather than the individual) is frequently the key unit involved in migration decisions and many moves are prompted by non-job-related decisions. Most moves are over short distances, but the main focus of this chapter is on those households who have made longer-distance moves. Households who moved into the study area between 1980 and 1996 were interviewed. This has the advantage of spanning a period of quite varied economic conditions rather than being limited to the situation prevailing in a single year. Secondly, it permits the examination of people's circumstances before as well as after their move, including retirement, redundancy, bereavement, dependent children leaving home and marital breakdown. In this chapter, both the self-completion questionnaires and the face-to-face interviews are analysed. A total of 75 individuals (mean age of 48 years at the time of the move, and a mean age of 53 years at the time of the interview) from the 44 households provided life history information, of which 27 were aged over 60 years.

4   Of individuals who are part of couple households.

The in-depth interviews are used to explore how the in-migrants construct their own meanings and identities for themselves resulting from their decision to move to the country (Moustakas, 1994). The reasons for relocating to a rural area are not only diverse but constantly changing because 'the interplay of gender, class, age and location is not static' (Chapman and Lloyd,1996, page 2). An analysis of the motivations for moving to rural parts of the East Midlands as expressed by the interviewees are therefore a result of a complex interplay of a range of factors and these need to be analysed at the level of both the individual and the household. The 44 in-migrant households with an adult aged over 50 years at the time of the move can be grouped in four types:

- 12 households (3 of whom participated in in-depth interviews) indicated that the relocation was principally **work-related**. Household relocation was triggered by one household member getting a new job, which was beyond commuting range from the previous family residence and a home in a rural area was chosen. Such moves adversely affect the labour market position of female partners (see James and Sarah).

- For three households with dependent children the move was undertaken solely for **lifestyle choices**, the search for more suitable housing combined with a search for the social side of village life, including good schools (see Mike and Suzy). The lifestyle choice may include the step into self-employment.

- 14 households (7 of whom participated in in-depth interviews) moved in their 50s **planning for retirement**. For some this was a conscious decision as part of a pre-retirement strategy, which entailed the search for a more suitable home, such as a bungalow, especially in an area where property prices were such that they gained equity release. Moreover, relocation and changing housing market was accompanied by a change in labour market position, such as a less stressful job, either part-time or full-time. For some this less stressful situation was achieved by the step into self-employment (see Maureen and Rob). One key lived reality of these moves was the necessity of having access to a motor vehicle.

- For 15 households (of which 4 participated in in-depth interviews) the house move was combined with **labour market withdrawal** (for 12 of the households it was early retirement; for 3 households it was at state pension age) (see Jenny and Glynn). Whether or not this was their final move was dependent upon transport and access to services.

TYPE ONE: WORK-RELATED

James (a full-time self-employed consultant) and Sarah (a retired former part-time university researcher) are both in their late 50s, have two grown-up children, and have lived together for over 35 years. His job has always 'led', and as a result they have moved from London to Lancashire to Essex and to rural Leicestershire. They moved in the late 1980s from rural Essex (he had a job in the East End of London) to a small village two miles from a market town in Leicestershire because of his job. James commented that 'his job was "king"… everything else secondary'. That said they chose a location almost 20 miles away from his employer, in an urban area where he was Production Director, as he didn't want to see employees on a weekend. Moreover the family preferred village life, but one with access to the facilities of a town, especially good schools for the children. Within 6 years of living in the East Midlands he had been made redundant twice; this was not new to James as he had experienced redundancy before he moved to the East Midlands. He 'sort of "fell" into self-employment' as he was offered a consultancy by a business contact, and has subsequently built up a client base in part due to old business contacts as well as contacts gained through work undertaken for a Business Link. The decision to remain in rural Leicestershire and take self-employment was made to enable Sarah and him to stay put as they did not want to move yet again; Sarah was particularly keen not to move as she had found an absorbing job as well as being embedded in village life. She has recently retired from that job and is enjoying a very active retirement.

In most households one partner tended to be instrumental in making the initial decision to move. In the case of those households for whom the move was job-related, the decision to move tended to be made by the person, largely a male partner, with the 'lead' career (James in the case of James and Sarah, above). The initial decision was then followed by a period of negotiation between the partners, of compromise, and 'trade-offs' between 'him' and 'her', between domestic and work priorities. Job-related reasons also dominated the decisions for moving into the area for couples with partners aged between 40 and 50 years. Take for example one former bank manager with an organisational career (47 years; partner 46 year old homemaker) who said, 'we came to … [Lincolnshire because] I was a Bank Manager and took a promotion to come and manage the local branch … it was just a way of life … you know that you go with the job'. He went on to note that, 'at the time it was bank policy that you live in the town where you work because the Bank Manager is supposed to be part of the community, but that has now changed'.

The labour market impact of a rural residential choice more adversely affected female members of in-migrant households than male members (Hardill, 1998). An earlier analysis of all in-migrant households (ie those aged above 50 years as well as those aged under 50 years) found that while two-thirds of the in-migrant women who held jobs before the move managed to find jobs (but often with downward occupational mobility) after the move, one-third withdrew from the labour market (including taking early retirement or were unwaged) (ibid). For some of the women aged over 50 withdrawal from the labour market was part of the lifestyle choice, but this was less so for women under 50; there is evidence that household asymmetry was reinforced by the move to a rural area (see also Little, 1997).

TYPE TWO: LIFESTYLE CHOICE

After a spell working abroad, Mike, a 55 year old (currently unemployed journalist) said, 'I returned to a job in the City. I was prepared to travel 60 minutes, Grantham is 65 and had a grammar school'. Suzy, his wife (also 55 years and also now unemployed) went on to say, 'we didn't like the Canadian education system ... we took the map of England, and drew a circle round 60 minutes from London ... we had a look at Lincolnshire ... there was a grammar school ... we still wanted to be in a village ... it was within our price range'. Their daughter (26 years, office worker) said, 'my father had a job in the City ... he didn't want to live in London ... he needed greenery, we all did. We'd grown up in the Prairies ... we needed space and air ... my father drew a circle round central London ... he didn't want to travel more than an hour and a half a day ... we found this part of the world'. The east coast main line was one of the key reasons why this household, and indeed others, opted for the study area. They chose an accessible rural residential location, with good communications, in their case to London, and their initial search was not specifically confined to the study area. Since moving to the area Mike has been made redundant and Suzy has encountered problems in finding a job. They love the area but admit that they face the dilemma of either taking a job with lower status available locally or travelling some distance within the East Midlands or further afield for higher status and better paid jobs, but both feel that they are encountering ageism in their job searches. Their children have benefited from the local education system and have both been to university.

Those households who moved for lifestyle reasons placed emphasis on the quality of village life, especially social and economic amenities. In our 'village – we are well served. We have a post office and a general store, a butcher and licensed grocer, newsagent, three pubs'. Others focused on activities, 'there's an awful lot that goes on'. Suzy (see above), who is unemployed, emphasised the positive aspects of village life, especially social activities in the village hall. 'We have a village hall ... a very good facility. Gerald's wife said that, 'everything centres around the village hall ... we get heavily involved ... it's just a strong community spirit ... that came to the fore when we had heavy snow and power cuts here for three days ... neighbours popping round to make sure everything was OK'. However, a couple in their 70s said that, 'there are a lot of social clubs. But what you find is that it is all the incomers who take them over, or set them up. In my club, for example, there is one member from [local town]; the other six are incomers (from Kent, Essex, London and Manchester)'.

While it is fair to say that mixed feelings were expressed about the nature of their lived experience of rural life, the interviewees were asked if the area had lived up to expectations, and on the whole the answers were positive. Suzy has positive views, 'Oh yes ... you feel more relaxed ... it's a slower pace ... I suppose it's being in a village [there is a] pleasant ambience in which to reside, people are very helpful to one another'. Anne also said, 'we like it and we are happy living here'. An even more positive response was given by Mandy, 'better than yes. We were a bit dubious about moving here ... but it grows on you'.

The interviewees expressed feelings about being 'insiders' and 'outsiders' in village life, and some felt locals were unfriendly. Mandy said, 'apart from making friends, we are happy with everything. My husband is better because he's got a little job'. But she went on to say that it has been 'a bit disappointing. I was hoping there was going to be a Women's Institute or something like that, that I could join and get to know people. At the moment I tend to be in the house'. A woman in her 50s also said that it's quite difficult to get involved in this village, well I've tried to'. But then others spoke in a more positive way emphasising friendliness, and that they had moved to a welcoming inclusive rural community. Jenny has been made to feel 'very welcome, I have found that with everyone', as has another woman in her 50s, 'I like the area I like the people … we have had ten super years and enjoyed it (live in village of 500 near [town in Lincolnshire]'). One man in his 60s says that he has, 'enjoyed the peace and quiet and the people are friendlier, people speak to each other. You speak to somebody in the South they look back at you as though you are about to attack them or something like that'.

Geoff and Anne get on with, 'the neighbours, we get on well with all of them. The community spirit is improving … it's quiet and pleasant'. Lynn said that, 'I just like the community life. To walk down the street and stop and pass the time of day with someone because you know them; I like it here' and this positive view was shared by her partner Steve. Jenny also feels that there is, 'plenty to do, we went line dancing last night in the village hall … we like to mix because we have been in the hotel business'.

There has been a considerable growth in the number of people, especially older rural in-migrants, both men and women – whose legal and contractual status is one of self-employment. Indeed becoming self-employed alongside choosing rural living is a second key lifestyle theme for the surveyed in-migrant households. The actual work situation of the older self-employed is far from that of the traditional small business owner (Corden and Eardley, 1999, page 209). Increased insecurity in job contracts and dissatisfaction with their terms and conditions of employment are resulting in some adults adopting an entrepreneurial strategy (Sennett, 1998). They move from employee to self-employed status, often drawing on their social networks and business contacts using their accumulated skills and expertise. Few employ others and they tend to work from home as 'consulting seems the road to independence' (Sennett, 1998, page 19).

The decision to become self-employed may be made to enable the in-migrant household to remain in a rural area, as is illustrated by James and Sarah, and Gerry (self-employed editor) and Jenny (self-employed information broker). Gerry and Jenny are both under 50 years of age but have become self-employed since moving to the study area. They have been together since university and have two daughters (aged 8 and 12 years), and live in a semi-detached house in a small village in Northamptonshire. They moved here from London a decade ago, specifically for a rural lifestyle, and Gerry looked for jobs within commuting range of their chosen village. Although the decision to move was essentially Gerry's, Jenny is very happy with the decision and wouldn't move back to a town, 'I think I'd find it quite difficult [to move back to a town] … I think I would find it overpowering to live in a street situation again. Jenny trained as a librarian, but withdrew from the labour market when she had children. She spent the past 10 years 'looking after the children', before the move and after. Prior to Jenny returning to the labour market she did an IT course that has enabled her to retrain and return to part-time work, as a self-employed home-based teleworker. She is an information broker, and has 'started up a nice little sideline in book indexes for various publishers, which is very lucrative'. While Jenny is now working, their lifestyle is still based on the premise of a home-based wife, with her job secondary to her role as prime carer.

Gerry has also become self-employed because his employer,

> '… relocated the operation back to London. I wasn't going to start commuting again, so I took the voluntary redundancy option and decided to go freelance. I'd been doing a certain amount of freelance anyway. So it was just a question of moving over to full freelance'.

He works in a profession with a long tradition of freelance work (Oughton et al, 2003). Technology and social networks have enabled some managers and professionals to become self-employed and take control of their lives. He noted: 'book publishing is in turmoil at the moment, so nobody is investing in staff. The trend is away from in-house staff, more towards outworkers who are engaged just for the period that they are required, … because of the technology we no longer produce proofs in the old fashioned way … it's all done on screen now'.

TYPE THREE: PLANNING FOR RETIREMENT

Maureen (61) and Rob (late 50s) moved 3 years ago from Derbyshire to Lincolnshire, and this move was linked to a semi-retirement strategy. They live in a converted chapel in the Fenlands. Maureen is a retired former secretary, who said that their move coincided with and was, 'because of [my] early retirement from work, and then thinking I'd like to get away somewhere quiet, live in peace and quiet ready for retirement'. Rob is not retired; he works about 20 hours per week, and he articulated the decision as a search to relocate home (and the business) to where property prices were less. His business is not tied to one specific geographic location, he is self-employed, with no employees, but his business has assumed less importance. As he said, 'I wanted semi-retirement … I wanted space [for the business] my workshop is a double garage … my overheads are much reduced, with the land we've got about half an acre, we could afford to pay cash and still have a bit of change in my pocket'. He went on to say, 'I did some work in [Lincolnshire] while I was still living in Derbyshire. Maureen came with me and she looked in some of the estate agents, we'd talked of moving, and she'd said no to Lincolnshire. She discounted it as uninteresting, but she looked in the estate agents and couldn't believe the prices, for what you get'. They have found peace and quiet for retirement, and admit that living out 'in the sticks' has many negatives; however, as Maureen went on to say, 'it is usually one's own choice and negatives become positives'. Maureen also added, 'Rob's business is drying up a bit', but they are not totally dependent on the business as an income stream for their lifestyle, and his work has become more of a hobby.

The transition into retirement is undergoing substantial change (for a fuller discussion see Chapter 5). People are experiencing extended retirement because of moving out of paid work during their 50s; for some it is a choice but for others it is the result of economic restructuring, and 'employability' issues relating to their lack of transferable skills, as well as ageism in the workplace. For Maureen and Rob relocation was made possible because Maureen retired from paid work and Rob was self-employed in a business that was not tied to one area. David Brooks (2000, pages 108–109) has suggested that for some people, including older adults, business values are different, 'business is not about making money; it's about doing something you love. Life should be an extended hobby … in this way business nourishes the whole person'. Brooks suggests that a counter-cultural mental framework has come to the business world (ibid, page 111). In a similar vein Beck (2000, pages 54–55) suggests there is more of a 'cross-over between employer and day labourer, self-exploiter and boss on their own account … with the objective of moulding their own lives rather than conquering world markets'. For some, therefore, making money and maximising profits are not the key motive, and high-pressure careers and large incomes may be traded in for a less frantic and more creative life by becoming self-employed in a different area of activity mid or later on in one's career (Knowsley, 1999). Self-employment as part of a strategy for personal nourishment is therefore often accompanied by migration to a rural area (see also Baines et al, 2002; Oughton et al, 2003). The businesses run by in-migrants can add to the asset base of rural communities, and these 'life-style' businesses include post offices, village shops, and bed and breakfast. Many such businesses are created to generate an income, rather than to expand and grow (ibid).

Geoff and Anne moved planning for retirement. Geoff (56 years, full-time job) said, 'well I retired, or at least I was made redundant from the army in 1992 and we had lost our roots by then. We decided we wanted to live somewhere near the centre of the country because of the way our children have spread themselves around. We came to have a look around in the middle of 1991, when we thought this was going to happen. We happened to choose Northamptonshire as a central point. Within a week of coming up we'd seen this place and thought we want to live here. We made an offer on this house the same week in fact'. His partner Anne (55 years, homemaker) commented that they wanted to live, 'north of the M25, we came further out for a cheaper house. It didn't matter where in the country we lived. We found a house and fell in love with it'. Of the 75 adults aged over 50 years who participated in the research one-third have retired from paid work since moving to the study area, half remain in paid work (but of these one-third are now either part-time or self-employed); 11 per cent are homemakers and 7 per cent are unwaged.

Some of those households whose move was part of a retirement plan indicated that their move into the study area was to capitalise on house price differentials. These moves have been from London and the South East to the East Midlands. Some were in a position to withdraw from the labour market (see Steve) while others need an income stream (as with Geoff and Paul below). Steve (54 years, retired) said, 'I had been made redundant a couple of times in recent years (in the South East) and it sort of sped up our thoughts of moving and we looked around and got details from various builders across the country and that's why we came in this direction (Lincolnshire). We came to [small town] and we liked it … we liked the price of the bungalow … moved a year ago'. His partner Jenny (60 years, retired) noted, 'Steve had been out of work for over a year … we had already decided to come here. We came up here in the July to look around and the next month I was made redundant as well'. So with both of them made redundant, they decided to capitalise on their assets, move north, and retire early. For Paul (63 years, full-time job) and Mandy (59 years, homemaker) the move was purely because it was a cheaper area to buy a house. Mandy said, 'that was the only reason … my husband had a small business and it folded up. It wasn't paying, so we just had to get out, sell the house and pay off debts. We'd seen in the newspapers that this was a cheaper area to buy so we used to come out and have a look around'. Paul also said, 'We were self-employed and going bankrupt. We had to sell the house to clear debts, basically. Then move down market. This was a cheaper area, so basically we were compelled to'. Mandy, 'would have loved to go to Scotland. I was dreading coming here, it's so flat'. Paul needed to secure a job, since the household needed the additional income, and was able to do so. Mandy is a homemaker, and they have their daughter and family living nearby. Paul enjoys his work and he anticipates working beyond state pension age, 'basically working on into retirement hopefully. I can't sit and read. It bores me silly; I've got to be doing something'.

TYPE FOUR: HOUSE MOVE AND LABOUR MARKET WITHDRAWAL, RETIREMENT AND 'WINDING DOWN'

Jenny (61) and Glynn (65) have been self-employed for a decade and a half and bought their bungalow in a small village with few amenities in Lincolnshire for their retirement. Since they have been married they have had 23 house moves. They bought the bungalow 12 months ago while they were still in business running a hotel in South Wales. They used to spend one week in every month at the bungalow during a transitionary period while they were trying to sell their business in South Wales. Until this move their moves had always been dictated by business. 'On this occasion we have retired ... it is fairly rural out of the rat race for want of a better expression because we are looking to wind down. We have had a very hectic working life [in the hotel trade], we can buy anywhere in Britain because we have no ties or whatever'. Although they said they had no ties they have two sons but they did not want to move near to either of them. Jenny noted, 'we actually had an offer on a house in Lancashire, just outside Southport, and I saw this advertisement [for Lincolnshire in the national press] and got the details of the bungalow, and was very impressed with the sizes of the rooms and you know money wise'. They had no preconceived ideas as to where they wanted to retire other than somewhere in rural England, and this decision was swayed by attractive property prices. They have positive views of the village and according to Jenny they have been made to feel, 'very welcome, I have found that with everyone'.

Some interviewees talked about their move in terms of a housing ladder. For Jenny and Steve, 'the idea of the bungalow was to be a final move and to get ahead a bit ... a bungalow is easier when you get older and the years roll on'. Mandy explained that 'my husband is 63 and I am 59 ...well we shall be retired. So we are quite happy just pottering around quite honestly... we shall stay here, touch wood, it's our last move'. She went on to say that, 'it's not easy at our age to make friends quickly', and so was not anticipating a further move and having to settle into another area.

One important aspect of rural life is the quality of public transport. Some in-migrants moved to what they described as quite isolated areas, where access to a car was essential. The loss of a car can alter feelings as has happened to one 78 year old woman. Her son said, 'my mother she hates it. I don't think she actually hates it, but she has some bad feelings'. She explained that they 'were a two car family, now we're back to one. I didn't have to rely on [son] then. We could do our own thing we don't do our own thing so much now'. So her negative feelings were related to the loss of their car and associated mobility and being dependent upon her son for a trip to the supermarket, etc. But she did also say, 'but I'm happy enough here I wouldn't personally want to go back to the South East'. Another couple said of their village, 'you need transport, if you rely on public transport forget it, it doesn't exist'. Suzy reinforced this by saying, 'public transport – tends to operate at times that suit the bus company rather than the village generally'. Mike her husband talked about when, 'we went for a period without a car. It was murderous [shopping]. It's impossible for the elderly who are alone'. Anne also noted that in her rural area there is 'patchy public transport'. She went on to say that their village is all right, 'as long as you are not too old because you are cut off'.

Geoff and Anne have, 'no plans to move. We like it here and certainly we are looking at 20 years until we can't manage it any more. We've got quite a big garden to look after and that will be the limiting factor at some point. While we can still climb stairs and do the garden we've no intentions of moving'. Anne did wonder, 'perhaps when we get too old to drive. Because we are stuck if we can't drive'. So Anne did see problems ahead for them when they loose mobility. A couple in their 60s said that, 'there could be extraneous things or if I suddenly got arthritis, so that I'm less ambient, I think we would look for something more in suburbia than we are currently. I think things like public transport and access to other facilities would have a much higher priority, after having lived here for nine years and realising how restricting it can be'. Suzy said they would move, if we had to, 'to be honest I've got to the stage where I do hate packing up. We like it. There are a lot of worse places that we could live'. One 59 year old woman, Sheila, was thinking ahead, 'as you get older you realise you need some facilities nearby or very good neighbours because when the day comes and you couldn't drive you are absolutely stuck. It does pose a problem as you get older that you have such a lot of travelling to facilities. I think all the time you are fit to be able to live in this sort of environment is great but as you get older it could pose problems. I think if you got to the stage when you couldn't drive or you had lost your partner and you had never been able to drive then I think you would have to look to move somewhere that had a bus or a train service'. At the moment she is working part-time and her husband, who is 64, has a full-time job; they have a car and good health, but the realities of living in a small village when they are less mobile is on her mind.

Conclusions

As has been noted in this chapter increasing numbers of people are choosing to live in rural parts of England, including the East Midlands. This process has accelerated in recent decades within a context of increasing affluence, a rising rate of private car ownership, and of the blurring of the working life and retirement binary because of changes in the duration and concept of working life. Rural in-migration has radically altered the region's rural landscape, economically and socially: it is a place to live and work, and a place to retire to, or 'opt out' in. As has been illustrated through the use of case studies above the reasons for moving to the rural parts of the East Midlands are diverse. In most households one partner tended to be instrumental in making the initial decision, but there followed a period of negotiation between partners, with an element of compromise, 'trade-offs' between 'him' and 'her', such as between domestic and work priorities, as well as trade-offs between dependent children and parents, as access to schools is prioritised.

The popular myth that most people who move to rural areas are retirees needs to be dispelled. In-migrant households span the working life and retirement binary. Migrating to the countryside is the result of far-reaching and interlinked mid-life decisions about rearranging household, family and work relations. The change of house and scene is also a change of direction chosen to fit the household to what is seen as the next stage in their lives. While some in-migrants anticipated that this move would be their last, others felt that they may have to move again when their resources, supports and skills for independent living decline, especially if they are unable to drive a car, tend the garden or manage the stairs.

Acknowledgements

This research was funded by the ESRC (grant R000236072), and was undertaken by Irene Hardill, Anne Green, David Owen, Anna Dudleston and Stephen Munn. The views expressed here are those of the author alone.

References and further reading

Baines, S., Wheelock, J. and Oughton, E. (2002) A household based approach to the small business family, in D. Fletcher (ed) *Understanding the Small Family Business,* London: Routledge

Beck, U. (2000) *Brave New World of Work,* Cambridge: Polity

Beck, U. and Beck-Gernsheim, E. (2002) *Individualization: Institutionalised Individualism and Its Social and Political Consequences,* London: Sage

Brooks, D. (2000) *Bobos in Paradise: The New Upper Class and How They Got There,* New York: Simon and Schuster

Brown, R. and Danson, M. (2003) '"Going grey": demographic change and the changing labour market in Scotland', *Local Economy* 18 (4), 291–305

Cabinet Office (1999) *Rural Economies: A Performance and Innovation Unit Report,* London: Cabinet Office

Champion, A. (1996) *Migration Between Metropolitan and Non-Metropolitan Areas in Britain,* End of Award Report for ESRC

Champion, A. (2005) Ageing and migration trends, in *Regions for All Ages: The English Regions and Demographic Ageing: Key Trends and Issues,* Sheffield: Regions for All Ages

Champion A. and Townsend A. (1990) *Contemporary Britain,* London: Edward Arnold

Chapman, P. and Lloyd, S. (1996) *Women and Access in Rural Areas,* Aldershot: Avebury

Corden, A. and Eardley, T. (1999) 'Sexing the enterprise: gender, work and resource allocation in self-employed households', in L. McKie, S. Bowlby and S. Gregory (eds) *Gender, Power and the Household,* Basingstoke: Macmillan, 207–225

Countryside Agency (2004) *State of the Countryside Annual Report,* Wetherby: Countryside Agency

Disney, R., Grundy, E. and Johnson, P. (1997) *The Dynamics of Retirement: Analyses of the Retirement Survey,* DSS RR42, London: Department of Social Security

DTZ Pieda (2005) *Identifying the Sub-Regional Housing Markets of the East Midlands* (ref 04054719), available via http://www.goem.gov.uk

East Midlands Local Government Association (2003) *Regional Guidance for the Spatial Development of the East Midlands,* Leicester: Leicestershire County Council

Hagerstrand, T. (1969) 'On the definition of migration', *Scandinavian Population Studies* 11, 63–67

Hanson, S. and Pratt, G. (1995) *Gender, Work and Space,* London: Routledge

Hardill, I. (1998) 'Trading places: case studies of the labour market experience of women in rural in-migrant households', *Local Economy* 13 (2), 102–113

Hardill, I. and van Loon, J. (in press) Individualization and 'identity-risks' in dual career households, in D. Perrons et al (eds) *Gender Divisions and Working Time in the New Economy,* Cheltenham: Edward Elgar, Chapter 10

Hardill, I., Bentley, C. and Cuthbert, M. (in press) The East Midlands Region, in I. Hardill, P. Benneworth, M. Baker and L. Budd (eds) *The Rise of the English Regions?* Routledge: London

Huber, J. and Skidmore, P. (2003) *The New Old. Why Baby Boomers Won't be Pensioned Off,* London: Demos

Knowsley, J. (1999) 'High-fliers quit the City rat race for a stress-free career in garden design', *Sunday Telegraph* 4 July 1999, 19

Little, J. (1997) 'Constructions of rural women's voluntary work', *Gender, Place and Culture* 4 (2), 197–209

Meadows, P. (2004) *The Economic Contribution of Older People,* London: Age Concern England

Moustakas, C. (1994) *Phenomenological Research Methods,* Thousand Oaks, CA: Sage

Munro, M. and Madigan, R. (1998) 'Housing strategies in an uncertain market', *The Sociological Review* 46 (4), 714–734

Office for National Statistics (2003) *Regional Trends,* page 38

Oughton, E., Wheelock, J. and Baines, S. (2003) 'Micro-businesses and social inclusion in rural households: a comparative analysis', *Sociologica Ruralis* 43 (4), 331–348

Salt, J. (1988) 'Highly skilled migrants, careers and international labour markets', *Geoforum* 19, 387–399

Saunders, P. (1989) 'The meaning of "home" in contemporary English culture', *Housing Studies* 4 (3), 177–192

Scales, J. and Scase, R. (2000) *Fit and Fifty?* Economic and Social Research Council, available at http://www.esrc.ac.uk/esrccontent/PublicationsList/fifty/down.html

Seavers, J. (1999) Residential relocation of couples: the joint decision-making process considered, in P. Boyle and K. Halfacree (eds) *Migration and Gender in the Developed World,* London: Routledge, 151–171

Sennett, R. (1998) *The Corrosion of Character,* New York: Norton

Smeaton, D. and McKay, S. (2003) *Working After State Pension Age: Quantitative Analysis, Department of Work and Pensions,* Research paper no. 182, London: DWP

Stacey, J. (1998) *Brave New Families: Stories of Domestic Upheaval in Late Twentieth Century America,* New York: Basic Books

Warnes, T. and McInerney, B. (2004) *The English Regions and Population Ageing,* London: Age Concern England

Chapter 4

Rich and poor in the countryside

Alana Gilbert, Lorna Philip and Mark Shucksmith

Introduction

Income is an important determinant of overall quality of life: a divide between rich and poor is as much a feature of older, as of younger, age groups. Indeed, with state pensions having declined in real terms over the past 25 years, the gap between rich and poor pensioners has increased (Bardasi et al, 2002). On the one hand, poverty rates among older people are high. On the other hand, more older people than ever before are financially comfortable and in a position to enjoy their later life – a period in the life course when work and family constraints are lifted, giving time to pursue activities that contribute to a good quality of life.

Most existing research about income in later life has been conducted from a nationwide per-spective: a rural dimension is difficult to find. As this book has established, the rural population is older than the urban population and ageing at a faster rate. But how many of these rural older people are poor and how many are comfortably off, or even rich? We often read about wealthy people retiring to attractive rural areas. Indeed, a new acronym – 'woopies', well-off older persons – has appeared in recent years. Equally, we know that many older people in rural areas survive on low incomes and experience difficulties in mobility and access to services. It is now well known that poverty and affluence occur in close proximity in rural Britain, making rural poverty less easy to identify and to address (Shucksmith, 2003; Commission for Rural Communities, 2005). This chapter explores the evidence about inequality of in-come among older people in rural areas, drawing upon data from the British Household Panel Survey (BHPS). It also considers some of the causes and consequences of income differences among the older rural population.

Later life and rural poverty

A survey of rural deprivation in Essex, Suffolk, Shropshire, the Yorkshire Dales and Northum-berland in the early 1980s was the first to establish the strong association between later life ('old age') and poverty in rural England.

> 'Single elderly households accounted for one-third of the poor on average … Households composed of elderly people were far and away the most vulnerable to poverty.'
>
> (Bradley, 1987, page 164)

There were affluent older people too, but there were considerable variations in the mix of income between the study areas:

*'Elderly households in the lowland localities were mainly from local families, with the ma-
jority living almost entirely on their state pensions and other welfare benefits. The reduced
vulnerabilities of elderly households in the Dales, Shropshire and Northumberland coast
areas reflects the recent retirement to these areas of more affluent couples. Even so, most
of those who had retired to those areas in the 1960s and early 70s – many of whom had
subsequently suffered the bereavement of a spouse – were found to be living on quite inadequate incomes, with few assets.'*

(ibid, page 165)

Research a decade later in rural areas in Scotland (Shucksmith et al, 1996) and in England and
Wales (Cloke et al, 1994, 1997) found very similar patterns, with variations between areas likewise shaped by their experiences of in- and out-migration and labour market effects. These
studies showed that many older people survived on extremely low incomes, relying primarily
on the state pension and often unaware of such entitlements as Housing Benefit, Invalidity
Benefit [replaced by Incapacity Benefit and at the time of writing about to be reformed], Income Support, Disability Living Allowance or Attendance Allowance.

Recent research for the Countryside Agency (2003) shows that, in England, a quarter of pensioners in private households in rural districts are living on a low income, defined as less than
60 per cent of the median household income. The proportion in urban districts is similar. In
total, 630,000 pensioners in private households have a low income and a third of them live in
rural England. In remoter rural areas, 29 per cent of low income households contain someone
aged over 60. This research also examined the extent to which older people in rural areas are
reliant on state transfers. Around 1 in 10 pensioners in private households in rural areas rely
on the state pension and state benefits alone. Two-thirds of these older person households
consist of only a single person. When residents in care homes are included as well, half of the
people aged over 60 in rural England are found to be dependent solely on the state pension.
Most, though, do not claim the range of welfare benefits to which they are entitled (Countryside Agency, 2003) and there is evidence that benefit take-up rates are systematically lower
in rural areas (Gordon et al, 2000; Harrop and Palmer, 2002). There is accumulating evidence,
then, that poverty in later life is widespread in rural areas of England. Single-person households, many of whom rely heavily upon the state pension and yet who fail to claim their other
benefit entitlements, are particularly likely to experience poverty.

Beside this poverty there is also affluence within the older rural population. The particular mix
in any locality reflects differential patterns of migration and structural differences in labour
markets, which affect income levels locally both before and, after retirement. While this mix
itself may vary over time (Age Concern, 1996; Help the Aged, 1996; Wenger, 2001), individuals
and their households face varying fortunes through their life course (Glasgow et al, 1993).

This chapter examines the variations in the financial situation of rural older households. It
begins by reviewing alternative explanations, and considers the various sources of income in
later life and then presents the results of new analysis of the British Household Panel Survey.
This provides important longitudinal evidence by tracking a sample of households throughout the 1990s and enables the actual dynamics of poverty and affluence among older households in rural areas to be explored. Finally, relationships between income and quality of life are
examined, to establish some of the consequences of income status in later life.

Theoretical perspectives on income in later life

Vincent (1996) argues that the causes of poverty and affluence in 'old age' are the same – only magnified – as those during the earlier years of people's lives:

> *'The inequalities in the rest of society are reproduced in old age, and appear to be ampli-*
> *fied. After retirement, the inequalities resulting from low pay, unemployment, disability, ill*
> *health, sex discrimination and racial discrimination are carried through into old age. The*
> *decline in the value of savings and pensions … means the worst off are the very old.'*
>
> (Vincent, 1996, pages 23–24)

For the poor, the older one gets, the poorer one becomes, and thus inequality between rich and poor increases with age.

To understand the causes of poverty and affluence in people's later life, then, we must go beyond cross-sectional studies of poverty among older people and look back to their earlier lives to investigate the sources of inequalities in their life histories. At the same time, to understand how these inequalities are amplified in older age the ways in which older people obtain, or fail to obtain, income from various sources must be analysed.

Glasgow et al (1993) reviewed theoretical perspectives used to explain poverty among people in younger age groups. They suggested extending these theories to provide a life course perspective on older people's income status in rural areas. For rural areas of the USA, they came to the conclusion that:

> *'to fully understand the ability of individuals to accumulate wealth and access to pen-*
> *sions and higher Social Security levels in old age, we must be able to identify not only their*
> *human capital, but the industrial and occupational sectors of their employment, and the*
> *types of job mobility they have experienced throughout their lives. Gender and race further*
> *influence their access to particular types of jobs and the returns they make for their educ-*
> *ation and human capital attributes.'*
>
> (ibid, page 268)

The localities in which they have lived are a further factor. For example, individuals will fare worse in localities where the economic base is dominated by low skilled, low wage jobs, whereas those who live in areas where skilled, well-paid jobs are available will fare better. They go on to argue that individuals in rural areas are particularly disadvantaged in most or all of these respects because skilled, well-paid jobs are less commonly found in rural areas, particularly remote rural areas. A cost of living dimension should, however, be considered alongside this American perspective. If one is on a low income is it better to live in a low wage, low cost areas? If one is retired is it an advantage to live in an area where wages are low? This analysis emphasises sources of private and market-derived (employment) income. In other national contexts, among developed countries, the welfare state plays a greater role than in the USA, where publicly provided pensions and other state benefits play a minor part in supporting older people.

Sources of income in later life

Income in later life is determined by a range of factors including an individual's employment and income history, the age they cease to participate in the labour market and the nature of pension provision, benefit entitlement and uptake, savings and investments. This section will review employment and income patterns to demonstrate how the type of area in which someone spends their working life influences their income and thus their ability to make private provision for later life. It will then briefly consider the transition from work to retirement and how that affects income. Finally, the various sources of income in later life – from the market (employment), but also from the state, the voluntary sector and friends and family (Philip and Shucksmith, 2003) – will be reviewed.

Employment and income histories

Income levels in later life will reflect an individual's employment and income history during the course of their working life. The broad employment structure of urban, remote rural and accessible rural areas in England is similar, but income levels are variable. Defra (2004, page 22) reported that 'average household incomes are higher in accessible rural areas (median £28,150 per annum) than in either urban (median £26,000) or remote rural (£23,000)'. Overall, 'remote rural areas have the lowest average household incomes'. Pay levels display a similar pattern, with remote rural areas having considerably lower average gross weekly earnings than accessible and urban areas.

This income pattern is not a recent phenomenon. Most older people who have always worked in remote rural areas will have received wages below the national average during their working life. A low income while in employment limits an individual's ability to make private provision for their retirement. As this book has established, over the past four decades counter-urbanisation has become an important phenomenon across rural areas, bringing in usually more affluent newcomers. Many in-migrants, as they reach later life, are wealthier than the 'local' older population in their new community. The differential in income status between locals and incomers can be a source of tension within the community.

As Anne Green demonstrates in Chapter 5, we no longer live in a society where everyone retires at a conventional retirement age (normally 60 for women and 65 for men). There are an increasingly large group of people (11 per cent of those aged 65–69) who are choosing for a variety of reasons to stay in employment, either on a full- or part-time basis. Employment income therefore continues to be an important source of income for some older people, alongside pensions and savings.

The transition from work to retirement

The transition from work to retirement occurs in many different ways and at different ages, with a variety of implications for income in later life. For some the transition from work to retirement involves a switch from full-time to part-time or more casual forms of employment in the years leading up to retirement. This is associated with a reduction in income in the immediate pre-retirement years, which may hinder the ability to make last-minute financial provision for later life. For others working life continues into the late 60s and early 70s, either from financial necessity or a desire to remain active in the workplace.

Pay and labour market participation peak for many in the early 50s. It is then that financial measures designed to maximise income in retirement are often made. However, if one is made redundant at this age it can be difficult to re-enter the labour market with knock-on effects for income in later life. Bardasi et al (2002, page 156) have noted that the incidence of low income in retirement among those who are unemployed or disabled immediately before retirement is higher than among part-time and especially full-time workers. On the other hand, early retirement packages from private or company schemes mean that it has not been unusual to retire below the state pension age with full pension benefits intact; however, this is likely to decrease rapidly because of the impact of the European Union's Age Directive. The work-to-retirement transition and employment and income histories are thus important determinants of income in later life.

Income in retirement: state provision

The UK basic pension is insufficient on its own to provide an income above the poverty threshold. The link between wages and the state pension was severed in 1980. Pensions have decreased in real terms since then: in 2003 the basic state pension for couples was only 17 per cent of the average wage. Many therefore rely on additional benefit entitlements. Looking back, Kempson and White (2001) found that, for those aged over 65 in rural England, 'year-on-year changes in benefit payments appeared to be associated with many of the moves into poverty'. Since 1997, this trend has been reversed, and pensioner poverty has been reduced through increased benefit entitlements and the introduction of means-tested, income guarantee schemes (Howarth and Kenway, 2004). The Minimum Income Guarantee was introduced in 1999/2000 and was replaced in 2003 by the Pension Credit scheme. The latter guarantees a minimum income of £109.45 a week for single pensioners and £167.05 for couples (compared with the average income in 2000/2001 of £24,100, or £463 a week, reported in Regional Trends 38, Office for National Statistics 2004). Specific income-related problems for older people have been addressed by, for example, extending winter fuel allowances to all those aged 65+ and the provision of free television licences to those aged over 75.

This illustrates the significance of the state's role in providing an income for older people. However, it is unclear to what extent older people in rural areas have shared in these improvements. The proportion of pensioners in long-term receipt of the Minimum Income Guarantee was much lower in rural districts than in urban districts, despite similar proportions experiencing low income (Harrop and Palmer, 2002).

The Government's increasing emphasis on means-tested benefits rests upon the basic assumption that the benefits will be claimed. However, special effort is required to reach older people unaware or unconvinced of their welfare entitlements (see, for example, DSS, 1999; Shucksmith, 2000). Three years after the launch of the Minimum Income Guarantee, 83 per cent of pensioners on low incomes knew nothing about the scheme (Help the Aged and MORI, 2002, see http://news.bbc.co.uk/hi/english/business/newsid_2051000/2051567.stm). Likewise, the National Audit Office (2004) found that only 47 per cent of people on low incomes were aware of the Social Fund[1] and take-up was particularly low among ethnic minority groups and older people.

Income in retirement: private provision

Apart from the state, the most common sources of income in retirement are private provision (a personal, occupational or stakeholder pension, income from an annuity or other investment income), equity release and inheritance. Occupational pensions and investment income account for most of the difference between the poor and the better off in retirement. The amount of investment income received by all pensioners almost doubled between 1979 and 1996/97. Average pensioners' incomes are growing faster than average earnings, and the gap for women is narrowing (DSS, 2000). Private occupational pensions are, however, much more available to men. This reinforces the vulnerability of older women to a low income.

The recent UK crisis in money-purchase pension funds and the Government's plans to end final salary pension schemes in some public sector occupations suggest that continuing improvements to pensioner income from private provision cannot be taken for granted. Providing for a decent income in retirement is costly for employers and employees. Since 1988 it has not been compulsory for employers to oblige their employees to join company pension schemes. As a result, many people who work in the private sector, or who work part-time, have not made provision for their retirement and there has been a steep decline in the percentage of firms with an occupational pension scheme.

Another potential source of retirement income is from releasing equity bound up in property. The UK has become a nation of homeowners, and house prices have risen apace (the Halifax House Price Index records a 500 per cent increase in UK house prices between 1984 and 2004). In many parts of the country even a modest home can be a substantial financial asset and downsizing or moving to a cheaper housing market area can release substantial amounts of equity. However, releasing equity in this way is not a choice that all older people are willing or able to make and, even if funds are released from the sale of property, the money may be required to pay for care and support services.

Increasing longevity may also have a significant impact upon intergenerational wealth transfers. A typical age to inherit a house from parents may be just as one's own retirement approaches. Notwithstanding the impact of the 'ski-ing' generation – those who are 'spending the kid's inheritance' in their retirement – this type of financial inheritance is likely to become an important source of further wealth polarisation among the older community.

An analysis of rural older people's income

The British Household Panel Survey (BHPS) began in 1991 and is an annual survey of over 5,000 households, covering around 10,000 individuals. If any individual leaves the household, the new household in which they reside is added to the survey. Income data from nine waves

---

1   The following awards under the Social Fund are available to older people who meet qualifying criteria for the respective award at the time: Budgeting Loans, Crisis Loans, Community Care Grants, Funeral Payments, Cold Weather Payments, and Winter Fuel Payments.

of the BHPS has been used (1991 to 1999 inclusive). The 1999 wave is currently the most recent for which rural identifiers are available to fit the needs of this study.

The rural sample from the BHPS reported here is for Great Britain as a whole. This keeps the sample as large as possible, providing robustness where the rural sub-samples are small.[2] In this classification remote rural areas of England include, for example, the South West, the North East and North West, north Yorkshire, Lincolnshire, East Anglia and The Marches. Accessible rural areas include, for example, the South East, the Cotswolds, Warwickshire and Cheshire (see Figure 4.1).

The BHPS sample

To allow a comparison of older age groups with the population as a whole, data for people under 55 is reported alongside three sub-groups of the older population: those 55–64, 65–75 and over 75. Details of the sample by geographical and age sub-groups are show in Table 4.1.

Table 4.1 Sample size by geographical and age sub-groups (Great Britain)

| | Age group | | | |
	Under 55	55–64	65–74	75+
Remote rural				
Male	2,504	470	394	330
Female	2,444	482	597	584
Accessible rural				
Male	6,553	1,021	847	450
Female	6,753	1,106	1,063	866
Non-rural				
Male	17,399	2,626	2,379	1,424
Female	18,868	2,837	3,031	2,429

n = 77,457 (this is all BHPS respondents for whom an income value was recorded)

2   The rural sub-samples follow those used by Gilbert et al (2003). They were identified using the Local Authority District information available in the BHPS. The rural definition for England is that used by Tarling et al (1993), which classifies Local Authority Districts into remote rural, accessible rural, coalfield areas, urban and metropolitan areas. As no similar classification was available for Scotland and Wales, the Local Authority Districts were defined consistent with the Randall definition. Rural districts were defined as those where population density is less than one person per hectare. These rural districts were then classified as remote or accessible rural depending on their proximity to urban centres.

Figure 4.1 Tarling classification of remote rural, accessible rural and urban for local authorities in England

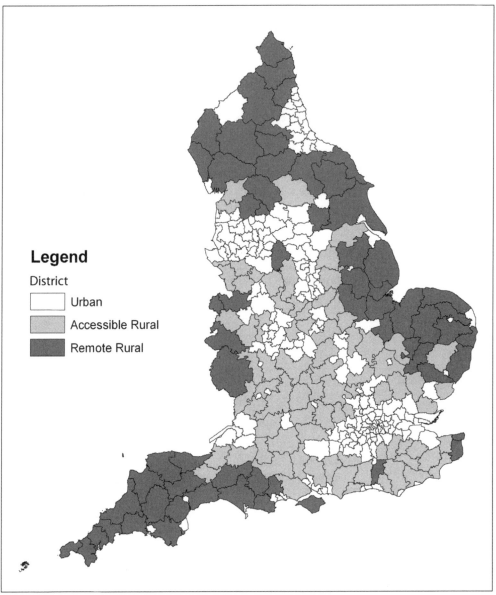

Map reproduced courtesy of Birkbeck College, London

Overview of individuals' income

The income variable provided by the BHPS is gross household income. As this chapter is focusing on individuals rather than households, the values for household income are inflated to 1999 values and then attributed to individuals (see McClements, 1978, for details of this procedure). Table 4.2 presents mean annual incomes by geographical sub-areas and by age group.

Table 4.2 Mean annual income (attributed to individuals)

	Age group			
	Under 55	55–64	65–74	75+
Remote rural				
Male	£13,678	£12,822	£8,981	£10,026[3]
Female	£13,034	£10,670	£8,370	£7,519
Accessible rural				
Male	£16,321	£15,624	£10,754	£9,031
Female	£15,269	£13,519	£9,030	£7,536
Non-rural				
Male	£14,765	£13,058	£9,518	£8,158
Female	£13,792	£11,707	£8,181	£7,022

n = 77,457

Note that the mean annual income is pooled for the years 1991–1999, covers the whole of Great Britain and reports 1999 values, equivalised

From Table 4.2 it can be seen that, generally, income falls with increasing age. Other analysis of the same waves of the BHPS (Bardasi et al, 2002) found that the oldest age cohorts were always poorer than younger cohorts of retired people. The notable exception is males aged 75+ in remote rural areas: further examination shows this deviation from the trend to be mainly due to a small number of individuals with very large incomes skewing the average income figure.

Geographical variations in income are evident in Table 4.2. Those living in remote rural areas have the lowest incomes (the exception being those aged 75+), followed by those in non-rural areas, while the highest incomes are for those who live in accessible rural areas. This pattern is not just a 'post-retirement' one – it is also established in the under-55 groups. The marked income differential between remote and accessible rural areas highlights the importance of differentiating between types of rural area.

A consistent feature is that women have lower levels of income than men for all age groups and geographical locations. The gap is smallest (6–7 per cent) for the under-55 age group, and it worsens with older age. It is particularly marked in the 75+ age groups in rural areas (reaching 17 per cent in accessible rural areas and 25 per cent in remote areas). Irregular female working patterns in earlier life are reflected in considerable income disadvantages upon retirement (Ginn and Arber, 1996). This effect would seem to be exacerbated by the casual and part-time nature of much female participation in rural labour markets (see, for example, Little and Austin, 1996).

3   The male 75+ rural figure is so high because a handful of individuals had very high incomes, skewing the data and inflating the mean value.

Source of income

Table 4.3 reports the various sources of income recorded from the BHPS sample as a percentage of an individual's income. Note that state pensions – the basic pension and SERPS – are included within 'benefit income'. This is because, firstly, the state pension is a means-tested benefit and, secondly, some people's state pension is in practice combined with other benefit payments.

Table 4.3 Source of income as a percentage of total annual income (attributed to individuals)

		Source of household income			
	Age band	Private pension income	Benefit income (incl state pension)	Labour income	Investment income
Remote rural	Under 55	1.6%	6.9%	87.7%	3.0%
	55–64	17.0%	11.9%	62.8%	7.7%
	65–74	32.2%	43.8%	10.3%	13.0%
	75+	24.8%	50.0%	9.6%	15.2%
Accessible rural	Under 55	1.1%	4.3%	90.3%	3.4%
	55–64	16.1%	9.7%	64.8%	9.1%
	65–74	31.2%	39.6%	16.7%	12.2%
	75+	28.9%	53.2%	5.5%	12.0%
Non-rural	Under 55	1.2%	7.0%	87.7%	2.6%
	55–64	13.8%	17.2%	61.8%	6.8%
	65–74	25.4%	47.9%	16.8%	9.4%
	75+	22.4%	60.0%	9.1%	8.1%

n = 77,457. Due to rounding and the omission of transfer income, rows will not sum to 100. Note that the data is pooled for the years 1991–1999, covers the whole of Great Britain and reports 1999 values, equivalised

Unsurprisingly, private pension income is insignificant for the those aged under 55. In all three types of area the proportion of total income from private pensions is highest for the 65–74 age group but is still below a third of total income. Of note is the decreasing importance of private pension income between the 65–74 and 75+ age groups. This could reflect the fact that those currently over 75 were less likely than younger age groups to make private provision for their retirement. It may also reflect a gender dimension: fewer women than men have private pension provision and women comprise a higher proportion of the those aged over 75 than men. In general, private pensions account for a higher proportion of total income in remote and accessible rural areas than is the case in non-rural areas.

Perhaps the most striking feature of Table 4.3 is the importance of benefit income to the overall income of older people. This category includes state pensions and other benefits, such as Income Support, Housing Benefit, Council Tax Benefits and Winter Fuel Payments. The proportion of income derived from benefits increases with age, and comprises the most important source of income, accounting for at least a half of total income for those aged 75+. For all age groups benefit income is most important for the non-rural individuals in the sample, and it compensates for their lower incomes obtained from private pensions. Higher benefit take-up rates in urban areas compared to rural areas are a contributory factor. Although not reported in our analysis presented in Table 4.3, it is worthwhile noting that a higher proportion of older women's income comes from benefits whereas a higher proportion of men's income comes from private pensions (Bardasi et al, 2002).

The proportion of household income made up of labour income decreases as individuals reach their mid 60s, and the transition from paid employment to retirement takes place. Of note, though, is the fact that reaching state pension age does not result in all individuals ceasing to be economically active (further analysis of income by household composition indicated that this labour income was not due to another member of the household bringing home a wage). Table 4.3 shows that labour income accounts for 16.7 per cent of household income of those aged 65–74 years living in accessible rural areas, compared to 10.3 per cent in remote rural areas. Factors such as the range and accessibility of employment opportunities may explain the difference between these figures and those of urban areas.

The proportion of investment income increases by age band until 75+, at which point (except for the remote rural group) it tails off a little. Although for most people investment income is small or insignificant, the older they are the more it figures in their overall income. In the 75+ category income investment falls, perhaps because the relative value of investments has decreased with inflation or because the capital has been drawn down. Further research is required to provide a more detailed explanation of why the proportion of investment income for each age band is consistently somewhat higher in rural than in non-rural areas.

Do sources of income for 'poor' and 'rich' older people, here defined as less than 50 per cent and more than 150 per cent of mean household income respectively, differ? Table 4.4 identifies the relative sources of income for the low income group, and Table 4.5 identifies the sources for the high income group.

Table 4.4 Low income group's source of income as a percentage of total household annual income (attributed to individuals)

| | Age band | Source of household income | | | |
		Private pension income	Benefit income	Labour income	Investment income
Remote rural	Under 55	1.1%	52.9%	40.8%	2.2%
	55–64	15.7%	50.9%	22.1%	9.0%
	65–74	8.3%	84.1%	3.0%	4.6%
	75+	8.9%	86.1%	0.3%	4.8%
Accessible rural	Under 55	1.5%	45.9%	44.6%	2.6%
	55–64	15.0%	53.3%	20.9%	10.5%
	65–74	6.8%	84.4%	2.3%	6.0%
	75+	5.2%	89.8%	0.2%	4.7%
Non-rural	Under 55	0.6%	60.9%	29.8%	1.9%
	55–64	10.3%	65.4%	17.2%	6.8%
	65–74	8.0%	86.6%	1.8%	3.3%
	75+	7.4%	88.7%	0.3%	3.6%

n = 12,642. Due to rounding and the omission of transfer income, rows will not sum to 100. Note that the data is pooled for the years 1991–1999, covers the whole of Great Britain and reports 1999 values, equivalised

Table 4.5 High income group's source of income as a percentage of total household annual income (attributed to individuals)

| | Age band | Source of household income | | | |
		Private pension income	Benefit income	Labour income	Investment income
Remote rural	Under 55	1.7%	2.2%	91.9%	3.7%
	55–64	13.7%	2.5%	76.8%	6.6%
	65–74	44.8%	14.4%	17.4%	21.9%
	75+	29.0%	20.4%	17.7%	32.7%
Accessible rural	Under 55	0.7%	1.2%	93.9%	3.8%
	55–64	13.8%	2.8%	73.3%	10.1%
	65–74	40.3%	15.9%	26.4%	16.9%
	75+	44.3%	26.2%	10.7%	18.7%
Non-rural	Under 55	1.1%	1.7%	93.1%	3.1%
	55–64	10.5%	4.4%	77.1%	7.7%
	65–74	30.0%	16.6%	38.2%	14.7%
	75+	33.1%	18.8%	29.9%	17.0%

n = 21,059. Due to rounding and the omission of transfer income, rows will not sum to 100. Note that the data is pooled for the years 1991–1999, covers the whole of Great Britain and reports 1999 values, equivalised

It is clear from Tables 4.4 and 4.5 that the proportion of income obtained from different sources does differ for the low and high income groups and within these groups there are additional variations by geographical location and by age group.

The low income profiles are broadly similar between geographical areas, with benefit income exceeding labour income even for those aged under 55. After then, with labour income declining sharply across all areas, the profiles converge onto a heavy dependence on benefit income for those aged 65 and over. Private pension and investment income do show minor peaks in the 55–64 age group, especially in the rural areas, where they reach averages of 9–11 per cent and 15–16 per cent respectively, suggesting an early retirement effect. But after 64 benefits account for 78 per cent or more of the income of low income groups whatever the areas. This clearly illustrates the importance of the benefit system, including the state pension, designed as it is to ensure that, regardless of where one lives, a minimum income is sustained.

For the high income group, in comparison, there is greater divergence between geographic areas with age. However, the starting point is high levels of labour market income for those under 55 in all areas. Although there is then some decline, for many labour market income remains a sizeable proportion of their income into their late 60s and beyond. This group in rural areas may include farmers and other landowners, self-employed people and part-time professionals and business executives.

The income status of high income groups in their working life puts them in a better position to make financial provision for their later life. Private pensions thus figure prominently in the income profiles of those aged over 65, especially in the rural areas. Investment income additionally is an important source, especially in remote areas. This illustrates the long-term financial benefits of being able to enact saving and investment plans for retirement.

For the high income group place of residence does appear to have an effect. In remote rural areas there is a marked decrease in the proportion of income from private pensions between the 65–74 and the 75+ age groups, a pattern which is not evident in accessible or non-rural areas. This could be a reflection of the financial status of wealthy retired migrants who move into remote rural areas in their 50s and 60s but whose capital is reduced by the time they reach 75. The proportion of labour market income after the age of 65 is most significant for the non-rural group, being twice as important as an income source as it is for the remote rural group. This could reflect more labour market opportunities in non-rural areas.

The dynamics of older people's income

One of the great advantages of the BHPS is that it tracks individuals, to enable the annual household income of selected individuals to be studied as it changes over time. It is therefore possible to distinguish income mobility over time from transient fluctuations in income, allowing what Jarvis and Jenkins (1998) call 'permanent' income differentials to be observed within a sample. Examining income mobility among the older population is, they argue, particularly 'relevant to policy issues such as the design of retirement pensions and income insurance schemes, public and private' (ibid, page 428).

The unit of analysis is each recorded year-on-year transition. [4] The small number of individuals who move between the non-rural, remote rural and accessible rural areas between successive waves are excluded from the analysis. The sample was divided into two age groups, under 65 and 65+, in order to keep the numbers in the three geographical area categories large enough for meaningful statistical analysis. Income data is presented in such a manner as to facilitate the identification of 'poor' and 'rich' individuals, defined, as above, as less than 50 per cent and more than 150 per cent of mean household income respectively. Table 4.6 summarises income transitions between 1991 and 1999.

Table 4.6 Transition matrix – summarised income transitions between 1991 and 1999

	Remote rural		Accessible rural		Non-rural	
	Under 65	65+	Under 65	65+	Under 65	65+
a. From under 50% median income in one time period to:						
Under 50%	60.5%	75.5%	56.1%	75.5%	63.9%	70.4%
Between 50 and 150%	38.4%	23.9%	40.9%	23.8%	33.4%	29.2%
Over 150%	1.1%	0.5%	3.0%	0.7%	2.7%	0.5%
b. From over 150% median income in one time period to:						
Under 50%	1.3%	2.7%	1.6%	2.0%	1.0%	1.7%
Between 50 and 150%	25.1%	35.2%	18.0%	30.3%	20.1%	34.7%
Over 150%	73.7%	62.2%	80.4%	67.7%	78.9%	63.6%

Sample size = 77,457

Table 4.6 is read as follows: of those aged under 65 in remote rural areas who have under 50 per cent median income in one year, 60.5 per cent will still have under 50 per cent median income in the next year, 38.4 per cent will have moved up to the 50 per cent to 150 per cent of median income band, and 1.1 per cent will have moved up to the over 150 per cent of median income band.

Of those in the under 50 per cent median income band, individuals aged 65 and over are more likely to remain in that income band the next year than those aged under 65. Conversely, those aged under 65 are more likely than those aged 65 and over to move up one or two income bands. This illustrates that it is easier for people of working age to improve their income over time than it is for those who have reached retirement age. It appears that the people over 65 in non-rural areas find it easier to move out of the lowest income band over time. The transition matrix shows that of those aged 65 and over who start off in the under 50 per cent band, those in remote rural and accessible rural areas are more likely than their non-rural counterparts to still be in this band in the next year. This could reflect less contact with the benefit system, whether because an individual is not aware of benefits they are entitled to or because of a reluctance to claim a benefit.

For individuals in the over 150 per cent median income band, those aged 65 and over are more likely than those aged under 65 to be in a lower band in the next year. High income individuals living in accessible rural areas are the most likely to still be in that income band the next year. Older people living in remote rural areas are the most likely to drop one or even

4   Each recorded transition may be defined as each move from year 1 to year 2, from year 2 to year 3, etc. Everyone in the original sample who was present in two successive waves is included.

two income bands. This demonstrates that even the highest income groups are vulnerable to a steadily decreasing income as they age.

The transition matrix illustrates a number of things. It demonstrates the changeability of an individuals' income over time. This is in line with Jarvis and Jenkins' (1998) analysis of the first four waves of the BHPS, where it was also observed that most income mobility is short range. Older people, even the most wealthy, are more likely than younger people to experience a decline in their income over time. Location affects income change for those who start off in the highest income band, with older people living in remote rural areas being more likely than those living in accessible rural areas to move out of the 150 per cent of median income band.

The persistence of low and high income

An alternative way of examining the longitudinal income data is to consider the persistence of low and high income. The sample from which the data in Table 4.7 is derived consists of 31,635 individuals. It is smaller than the sample used to compile earlier tables because it only includes those who have been in the BHPS panel for all nine waves under examination (1991–1999) and who have not changed their rural/non-rural category or under/over 65 age category. High income persistence was also quantified but is not reported in this chapter. The tiny sub-samples for the over 65 age groups led to the results being statistically invalid and any summary table of those results would be misleading.

Table 4.7 Low income persistence

	Remote rural		Accessible rural		Non-rural	
Spell length (years)	Under 65	65+	Under 65	65+	Under 65	65+
1	63.6%	56.9%	47.7%	57.9%	52.3%	58.9%
2	44.8%	48.3%	25.3%	48.1%	35.2%	43.8%
3	34.6%	45.0%	19.6%	36.5%	26.0%	33.5%
4	20.9%	39.9%	16.7%	30.7%	20.3%	26.4%
5	19.0%	39.9%	12.7%	25.1%	16.4%	23.8%
6	17.3%	35.8%	10.7%	21.7%	10.4%	18.8%
7	9.6%	31.6%	10.7%	17.9%	5.6%	18.8%
8	9.6%	31.6%	10.7%	17.9%	5.6%	18.8%

Sample size = 31,635

Table 4.7 uses 1991 as the base year and, for those individuals who had a low income in 1991 (50 per cent or less of median income), records how many have yet to escape a low income by 1992, then 1993, etc. Low income persistence is much greater among those over 65 than those under 65, and is most pronounced in remote rural areas. We can see this by looking at how long it takes at least three-quarters of a particular group to get out of the low income category. The accessible rural under-65 group achieve this after 3 years, and the remote rural and non-rural ones after 4 years. Among people aged over 65, however, those living in non-rural areas take 5 years, those in accessible rural areas 6 years, and still after 8 years almost one-third of those living in remote rural areas have not yet escaped the low income catego-ry. Such persistent low income suggests that benefits – the most likely mechanism of lifting a low income older person out of poverty – are not reaching this demographic sub-group. There could be structural failures within the benefit system and/or cultural resistance to ben-efits within the older population underpinning this trend.

Persistent low income also points to structural poverty rather than a temporary dip in income due to some passing misfortune. For example, if you have 1 year in low income but are in high income for the other 7 years, then you may have had savings to tide you over a low income period. Alternatively, if you borrowed money to help make ends meet, you can repay the loan when your financial situation improves. If you are frequently in the low income category these options are unlikely to be available. For the working-age population changing job, or securing employment after a period of unemployment, are common ways to improve one's financial status. This option is not available for those over 65. A boost of income in retirement is nor-mally associated with claiming a state benefit for the first time, becoming eligible for a new benefit or receiving a rise in pension income, but such increases are unlikely to be high in real terms.

The effects of income upon quality of life for older people

Income and overall financial status are important determinants of quality of life and life satis-faction. Gabriel and Bowling (2004) investigated older people's quality of life and noted that many respondents in their study associated a good quality of life with financial security. Financial security means, for example, not having to worry about paying utility bills or an unexpected household repair. An adequate income, particularly having money left over once necessities are paid for, makes it easier for people of all ages to get out and about, to enjoy life, to be independent and to retain control and autonomy.

More older people than ever before are reaping the benefits of private pensions and in-vestment income. Many live their retirement in financial security and this is known to be an important determinant of life satisfaction. However, as demonstrated in the tables above, a sizeable minority of older people live on very low incomes and have a negligible chance of moving out of low income in the future. Although quality of life is determined by a multitude of factors, the remainder of this chapter considers how income status may affect quality of life, by considering selected aspects, or domains, of life for older people (health, car use and self-reported well-being) by means of illustrating the association between income status and other aspects of life.

Self-assessed health status

Between 1991 and 1998 the BHPS asked the following question: 'Please think back over the last 12 months about how your health has been. Compared to people of your own age, would you say that your health has on the whole been …' The possible responses were excellent, good, fair, poor and very poor. Table 4.8 records the percentage of respondents recording good or excellent health status by income group, age group and geographical location. Note that the score represents a subjective measure of health status (as opposed to an objective measure such as that provided by a medical practitioner) and may reflect differences in expectations and attitudes of people in different age groups and living in different areas.

Table 4.8 Percentage reporting good or excellent health by income group, age group and geographical location

	Age group			
	Under 55	55–64	65–74	75+
Remote rural				
Under 50% median income	70.9%	56.1%	56.5%	50.2%
Over 150% median income	81.6%	82.7%	88.8%	76.3%
Accessible rural				
Under 50% median income	72.4%	57.7%	57.8%	54.1%
Over 150% median income	81.2%	82.5%	77.3%	73.4%
Non-rural				
Under 50% median income	61.7%	47.8%	49.0%	47.7%
Over 150% median income	81.6%	75.4%	77.2%	75.3%

Sample size = 11,319 (low income) and 18,731 (high income)

For each age and geographical area grouping, those with an income over 150 per cent of the median enjoy better self-reported health status than their low income counterparts. This is in line with the findings of other research, such as that reported by Blaxter (1987) where a positive correlation between self-reported low health status and low income was recorded and Gnich and Gilhooly's (2000) observation that higher socio-economic status (associated with higher incomes) delays mortality, morbidity and disability until comparatively later in life. Although high income does not preclude an individual suffering ill health per se, it does make some forms of preventative health care easier to achieve. For example, eating a healthy diet or heating one's home adequately is easier for those with a high income, and high income groups are likely to belong to the social classes associated with low rates of smoking.

Among the under 50 per cent median income group, for each of the three geographical locations, a greater proportion of those under 55 report good or excellent health than the 55–64 and 65–74 age groups. Unsurprisingly, the 75+ group have the lowest proportion reporting good health. Among the over 150 per cent median income group there is no readily identifiable pattern of good health, although, as would be expected, a lesser proportion of the 'rich' 75+ age group enjoys good health than the younger 'rich' age groups.

In the under 50 per cent median income category, a higher percentage of those in accessible rural areas enjoy good or excellent health than those in the same age groups in remote rural areas who, in turn, enjoy better health than those in non-rural areas. Again, with the over 150 per cent median income category there is no such clear pattern. Among those aged under 55 there is practically no difference, among those aged 55–64 remote and accessible rural dwellers enjoy better self-reported health than those in non-rural areas, among people aged 65–74 those in remote rural areas enjoy better health than those in the other areas, and among the 75+ age group the differences are very small.

With the exception of those under 55 with over 150 per cent median income, those in remote rural areas seem to enjoy comparatively better health than those in non-rural areas. However, the differences are too small to allow us to draw meaningful conclusions.

Car usage

Accessibility is an important cross-cutting issue for all those who live in rural areas. Problems associated with personal mobility are particularly acute for the older population.

> '... being mobile means being able to get around and lead an active life. Mobility is especially important for older people, many of whom have a fear of becoming dependent on other people for transport, or – worse still – of becoming housebound'
>
> (Fell and Foster, 1994, page 20)

> '...having a car gave their lives quality as it meant they did not have to rely on public transport or on lifts from other people, and they could be independent'
>
> (Gabriel and Bowling, 2004, page 688)

Dependency upon private cars characterises rural Britain. It has been demonstrated that older people throughout the Western world are more likely than ever before to have a driving licence, to take more trips by car and to do so more often as a car driver (Rosenbloom, 2001). Analysis of the Scottish Household Survey showed that pensioner households are less likely than other households in rural Scotland to run a car (Philip et al, 2003). It was also shown that a considerable drop off in car availability occurs between the age band 65–74 and 75+ regardless of where an individual lives, although older people in rural areas in the oldest age group are more likely than older people in non-rural areas to have a car available.

The BHPS asked, in 1991, 'Have you got a car or van, or is there one you have use of?' and in subsequent waves 'Do you normally have access to a car or van that you can use whenever you want to'. While car ownership cannot be inferred from this data, it does provide an indication of personal mobility, most important in rural areas where public transport services are more limited than in urban areas.

Table 4.9 Percentage reporting 'have use of car' by income group, age group and geographical location

	Age group			
	Under 55	55–64	65–74	75+
Remote rural				
Under 50% median income	80%	84%	66%	31%
Over 150% median income	96%	95%	98%	81%
Accessible rural				
Under 50% median income	65%	66%	49%	31%
Over 150% median income	95%	98%	98%	85%
Non-rural				
Under 50% median income	51%	53%	37%	18%
Over 150% median income	90%	92%	78%	72%

Sample size = 8,814 (low income) and 19,305 (high income). Note that individuals who responded that they did not drive have been excluded from Table 4.9.

Table 4.9 shows, for each area type and for both income bands, the proportion of those who can drive and who have access to a car is similar for the under-65 age bands but decreases with each successive band. This is more marked for those who have an income under 50 per cent of the median income than for those with the highest income. The proportion of those who can drive who have access to a car is always less for the under 50 per cent median group than the over 150 per cent median group. The most marked drop in car use is between the 65–74 and 75+ age groups with below 50 per cent median income in remote rural areas.

A number of factors are likely to explain these findings. The need to reapply for a driving licence at the age of 70 is likely to lead to some drivers giving up their licence voluntarily and some being required to relinquish their licence on health grounds. Older women are less likely to drive than older men (although the differential is much less for younger women). Many have never held a licence, and others suffer when their spouse dies or gives up driving: the latter will be captured in Table 4.9. A physical impairment preventing the ability to drive is likely to explain why car use for the 75+ age group in remote and accessible rural areas is similar in both income bands.

Sitting above these factors is the role played by income. Running a car can be expensive and lower income older person households may decide that the cost of running a car when it ceases to be required to travel to and from work outweighs the benefits of personal mobility. This will be more likely for those who live within easy access of shops and services or have access to a reasonable public transport service and may explain why car use among those aged 65–74 in accessible rural areas is lower than that noted for the same age group who live in remote rural areas. The proportion of those who can drive who have access to a car is also, for both income bands in each age group, always greater for the remote rural group than the non-rural group. The difference is most marked though in the under 50 per cent median income groups – a reflection perhaps of the greater need to have use of a car in remote rural areas than in non-rural areas where the less well off have access to 'better' public transport.

Income status in later life does not necessarily protect older people from the accessibility constraints that result from not having a car but, if personal health permits, wealth makes it easier for an older person to maintain their personal independence by running a car.

Self-reported well-being

The BHPS includes a suite of 12 self-assessed questions about well-being including, for example, 'Have you recently … lost much sleep over worry', 'Have you recently … felt constantly under strain?', 'Have you recently … been able to enjoy your normal day-to-day activities?' and 'Have you recently … been feeling reasonably happy, all things considered?' The BHPS included a self-reported well-being measure based on these 12 questions, employing a scale running from 0 to 36 (see Cox et al, 1987, for further details). The well-being figures presented in Table 4.10 represent the average value of scores on that 36 point scale: the lower the number, the higher the self-reported well-being of an individual.

Table 4.10 Self-reported well-being

	Age group			
	Under 55	55–64	65–74	75+
Remote rural				
Under 50% median income	11.68	11.61	10.94	11.48
Over 150% median income	10.60	9.81	8.53	10.47
Accessible rural				
Under 50% median income	11.79	12.86	11.69	11.90
Over 150% median income	10.60	9.83	10.17	10.61
Non-rural				
Under 50% median income	12.28	12.09	11.61	11.87
Over 150% median income	10.59	10.30	9.45	10.74

Sample size = 12,153 (low income) and 20,792 (high income)

For each age/rural grouping, those with incomes greater than 150 per cent of the median have a greater level of self-reported well-being than those who have incomes less than 50 per cent of the median. More detailed analysis of the data indicates a gradual increase in well-being with increasing income. It would appear, then, that wealth or financial security is an important determinant of subjective well-being, perhaps simply because financial security prevents older people worrying about many aspects of day-to-day life. For remote rural and non-rural dwellers, self-reported well-being increases with age band up to the 65–74 band. It is unclear whether this reflects the transition into retirement and a concurrent improvement in well-being post-retirement followed by a drop off in well-being in the oldest age cohorts often associated with deteriorating health status, or whether other factors are at play.

Self-reported well-being decreases with advancing age: for the 75+ age group well-being is lower than in the 'young-old' years. This could be associated with the decline in income associated with advancing age, reported earlier, which can create ongoing worry for much older people. It could also be associated with aspects of ageing such as failing health, feelings of isolation, reduced personal autonomy, limited contact with friends and families and a loss of mobility and independence, which are largely independent of financial circumstances.

Life satisfaction

The BHPS also included a life satisfaction question 'How dissatisfied or satisfied are you with … your life overall'. This question was only asked from 1996. This question was answered using a seven-point scale, with seven being most satisfied. There appear to be relationships between income status and geographical locations and the self-reported life satisfaction scores (Table 4.11).

Table 4.11 Life satisfaction scores

	Age group			
	Under 55	55–64	65–74	75+
Remote rural				
Under 50% median income	4.99	5.18	5.82	5.59
Over 150% median income	5.42	5.55	5.87	5.58
Accessible rural				
Under 50% median income	4.92	5.07	5.52	5.55
Over 150% median income	5.29	5.66	5.76	6.04
Non-rural				
Under 50% median income	4.74	4.94	5.57	5.39
Over 150% median income	5.26	5.51	5.89	5.52

Sample size = 5,733 (low income) and 9,454 (high income)

Irrespective of income group, for remote rural and non-rural areas, life satisfaction increases up to age group 65–74 and then drops. For the accessible rural group, life satisfaction increases for each successive age band. Life satisfaction for the low income groups is less than for the high income groups, but for the 75+ age group in remote rural areas there is a negligible difference between the scores for the low and high income groups. This could be an illustration of the suggestion that perceived financial adequacy is a substantially stronger predictor of life satisfaction than objective indicators of socio-economic status, reported by Gnich and Gilhooly (2000). In effect, the oldest members of the remote rural population are the most content with their financial status and other aspects of their lives. There does appear to be a geographical dimension to life satisfaction for the low income group. With the exception of the 65–74 age group, those in remote rural areas report higher life satisfaction than those in accessible rural areas, who in turn report higher life satisfaction than those in non-rural areas – but the differences are small. For the high income group there is no geographical pattern. It may therefore be inferred that living in a rural area makes a low income status more bearable.

Considering health status, car use, self-reported well-being and life satisfaction from an income perspective has suggested that, for the older population, there are some distinctively rural aspects to financial status and other aspects of life.

Conclusions

While a large proportion of older people are financially secure in later life, a significant minority of older people spend their retirement in poverty. The analysis of BHPS data reported in this chapter indicates a clear geographical dimension to income status in later life. Older people in accessible rural areas are the most affluent, while those in remote rural areas are the worst off. Non-rural areas lie in-between the two broad rural categories, but their characteristics are often closer to remote rural than accessible rural areas. Women are more likely to have a low income in later life than men, are more reliant upon the state pension and other benefits for their income and are less likely to have private pension provision than men.

Low incomes during retirement are likely to reflect earlier employment and income patterns. Pre-retirement income is a very accurate predictor of retirement income. In addition to gendered labour market participation rates and salary differences, the impact of the employment sector will be reflected in income during retirement. Remote rural areas are typically low wage economies. Regardless of the effect of financially secure older migrants moving into remote rural communities, unless the structural pattern of employment changes the geographical pattern of income in later life presented in this chapter is unlikely to change.

The longitudinal analysis demonstrated that income decreases with advancing age and that if an older person starts retirement in a low income they are very unlikely to improve their financial circumstances. The analysis also highlighted the importance of benefit income to the overall income of older people. Improvements to the financial status of older people may still be achieved with well-targeted benefits information and advice and measures to persuade older people to claim what they are entitled to. The persistence of low income in remote rural areas in particular was highlighted. This could be alleviated at least in part by measures to improve the lower than average uptakes of various state benefits, particularly in remote rural areas. More broadly, this highlights a societal problem, and one that can only become a more pressing concern as the population ages. To improve the financial status of future generations of pensioners will require input from the state, and, perhaps most importantly, better planning for retirement by people while they are still in the labour force as financial planning needs to start well before planned retirement age to be effective.

The analysis presented in the final section of the paper indicates that there is a relationship between rurality and aspects of quality of life for older people. While a high income is generally associated with the highest self-reported well-being and health status and life satisfaction it appears that living in a remote rural area boosts these scores for the low income group, particularly among the oldest age group.

There has been a focus upon the most financially disadvantaged older people in this chapter and in other research exploring income status and dynamics in later life. If the circumstances of the rural older poor are not improved through the Government's social inclusion agenda, it will have failed a sub-group of rural society whose numbers are steadily increasing. However, there is increasing affluence among the older population across the country. Examining the characteristics of the financially secure proved difficult with the BHPS data because of small sample sizes in the high income group. Investigating this end of the income distribution within rural society and the growing polarisation between rich and poor older people would be a useful and interesting focus of future research.

This chapter has highlighted the fact that the financial circumstances of older people vary with advancing age and that there is a clear geographical variation in income status, with remote rural areas faring worse than accessible rural areas. These trends are worthy of more detailed investigation, especially the longitudinal analysis which allows income transitions to be examined. In particular, if the new urban–rural classification was applied to income data, the impact of 'rurality' on an individual's financial status could be explored in even greater depth.

Acknowledgements

The British Household Panel Survey data used in this article was made available through the UK Data Archive. The data was originally collected by the ESRC Research Centre on Micro-Social Change at the University of Essex, now incorporated within the Institute for Social and Economic Research. Neither the original collectors of the data nor the Archive bear any responsibility for the analyses or interpretations presented here.

The authors wish to thank Nick Buck for adding the rural identifiers which enable the analysis in this chapter to be reported.

References and further reading

Age Concern (1996) *Older People in Rural Areas,* London: Age Concern

Association of Consulting Actuaries (2001) *Placard* Issue 19, May/June 2001

Association of Consulting Actuaries (2002) *Placard* Issue 20, Dec 2002/Jan 2003

Bardasi, E., Jenkins, S. and Rigg, J. (2002) 'Retirement and the income of older people: a British perspective', *Ageing & Society* 22, 131–159

Barry, B. (2002) Social exclusion, social isolation and the distribution of income, in J. Hills, J. Le Grand and D. Piachaud (eds) *Understanding Social Exclusion,* Oxford University Press

Beatty, C. and Fothergill, S. (1999) *Labour Market Detachment in Rural England,* Rural Research Report 40, Rural Development Commission

Blaxter, M. (1987) 'Evidence of inequality in health from a national survey', *The Lancet* 4 July 1987, 30–33

Bradley, A. (1987) Poverty and dependency in village England, in P. Lowe, A. Bradley and S. Wright (eds) *Disadvantage and Welfare in Rural areas,* Norwich: Geobooks, 151–174

Cartmel, F. and Furlong, A. (2000) *Youth Unemployment in Rural Areas,* York: York Publishing Services

Chapman, P., Phimister, E., Shucksmith, M., Upward, R. and Vera-Toscano, E. (1998) *Poverty and Exclusion in Rural Britain: The Dynamics of Low Income and Employment,* York: York Publishing Services

Cloke, P., Milbourne, P. and Thomas, C. (1994) *Lifestyles in Rural England,* A research report to the Department of the Environment, the Economic and Social Research Council and the Rural Development Commission, London: HMSO

Cloke, P., Goodwin, M. and Thomas, C. (1997) *Rural Wales: Community and Marginalisation,* Cardiff: University of Wales Press

Commission for Rural Communities (2005) *State of the Countryside 2005,* London: The Countryside Agency

Countryside Agency (2003) *Older People in Rural England:* research note

Cox, B.D. et al (1987) *The Health and Lifestyle Survey,* London: Health Promotion Research Trust

Defra (2004) *Social and Economic Change and Diversity in Rural England,* London: Department for Environment, Food and Rural Affairs

DSS (Department of Social Security) (1999) *Income Related Benefits – Estimates of Take-Up in 1996/7 (Revised) and 1997/8,* London: Government Statistical Service

DSS (Department of Social Security) (2000) *Retirement Pension Information,* available at http://www.dss.gov.uk/lifeevent/benefits/retirement_pension.htm

Evason, E., Dowds, L. and Devine, P. (2002) 'Pensioners and the Minimum Income Guarantee: observations from recent research', *Social Policy and Administration* 36 (1), 36–45

Fell, S. and Foster, A. (1994) *Ages of Experience. A Survey of Attitudes and Concerns Among Older People Living in Scotland,* Age Concern Scotland, Scottish Consumer Council and the Senior Studies Institute, University of Strathclyde

Gabriel, Z. and Bowling, A. (2004) 'Quality of life from the perspective of older people', *Ageing & Society* 24, 675–691

Gilbert, A., Phimister, E. and Theodossiou, I. (2003) 'Low pay and income in urban and rural areas – evidence from the British Household Panel Survey', *Urban Studies* 40 (7), 1207–1222

Ginn, J. and Arber, S. (1996) 'Patterns of employment, gender and pensions: the effect of work history on older women's non-state pensions', *Work, Employment and Society* 10 (3), 469–490

Glasgow, N. (2003) Older rural families, in D. Brown and L. Swanson (eds) *Challenges for Rural America in the Twenty-First Century,* Pennsylvania: Penn State Press, Chapter 6

Glasgow, N., Holden, K., McLaughlin, D. and Rowles, G. (1993) The rural elderly and poverty, in *Rural Sociological Society Task Force on Persistent Rural Poverty, Persistent Poverty in Rural America,* Boulder, Colorado: Westview Press, Chapter 9

Gnich, W. and Gilhooly, M. (2000) Health, wealth and happiness: studies in financial gerontology, in G. Corley (ed) *Older People and Their Needs. a Multi-Disciplinary Perspective,* London: Whurr Publishers, 17–34

Gordon, D., Adelman, L., Ashworth, K., Bradshaw, J., Levitas, R., Middleton, S., Pantazis, C., Patsios, D., Payne, S., Townsend, P. and Williams, J. (2000) *Poverty and Social Exclusion in Britain,* York: Joseph Rowntree Foundation

Harrop, A. and Palmer, G. (2002) *Indicators of Poverty and Social Exclusion in Rural England 2002,* The Countryside Agency, CAX117

Help the Aged (1996) *Growing Old in the Countryside,* London: Rural Development Commission

Howarth, C. and Kenway, P. (2004) *Why Worry Any More About the Low Paid?* London: New Policy Institute

Jarvis, S. and Jenkins, S. (1998) 'How much income mobility is there in Britian?', *The Economic Journal* 108, 428–443

Johnson, P. and Stears, G. (1995) 'Pensioner income inequality', *Fiscal Studies* 16 (4), 69–93

Kempson, E. and White, M. (2001) 'Ways in and out of low income in rural England', unpublished report to the Countryside Agency

Little, J. and Austin, P. (1996) 'Women and the rural idyll', *Journal of Rural Studies* 12, 101–111

McClements, L.D. (1978) *The Economics of Social Security,* London: Heinemann

Monk, S., Dunn, J., Fitzgerald, M. and Hodge, I. (1999) *Finding Work in Rural Areas: Bridges and Barriers,* York: York Publishing Services

National Audit Office (2004) *Helping Those in Financial Hardship: The Running of the Social Fund,* London: The Stationery Office

Philip, L. and Shucksmith, M. (2003) 'Conceptualising social exclusion', *European Planning Studies* 11 (4), 461–480

Philip, L., Gilbert, A., Mauthner, N. and Phimister, E. (2003) *Scoping Study of Older People in Rural Scotland,* Edinburgh: Scottish Executive Social Research

Office for National Statistics (2004) *Regional Trends,* available at http://www.statistics.gov.uk/statbase/Product.asp?vlnk=836

Rosenbloom, S. (2001) 'Sustainability and automobility among the elderly: an international assessment', *Transportation* 28 (4), 375–408

Shucksmith, M. (2000) *Exclusive Countryside? Social Inclusion and Regeneration in Rural Britain.* York: Joseph Rowntree Foundation

Shucksmith, M. (2003) *Social Exclusion and Poverty in Rural England: A Review of Recent Research,* Report to the Countryside Agency, Defra and ESRC, available at http://www.defra.gov.uk/rural/pdfs/research/esrc_rural_seminars.pdf

Shucksmith, M., Chapman, P. and Clark, G. (1996) *Rural Scotland Today: The Best of Both Worlds?* Ashgate

Social Security Committee (2000) *Seventh Report (Pensioner Poverty),* HC606, London: The Stationery Office

Tarling, R. et al (1993) *The Economy of Rural England,* London: Rural Development Commission

Vincent, J.A. (1996) *Inequality and Old Age,* London: UCL Press

Wenger, C. (2001) 'Myths and realities of ageing in rural Britain', *Ageing & Society* 21, 117–130

Wiggins, R.D., Higgs, P.F.D., Hyde, M. and Blane, D.B. (2004) 'Quality of life in the third age: key predictors of the CASP-19 measure', *Ageing & Society* 24, 693–708

Chapter 5

Employment and the older person in the countryside

Anne E. Green

Introduction

While some older people withdraw from employment before state pension age, others work on beyond this point. Older people represent a significant source of expertise and experience, both as employees and employers, and can enhance the welfare of the local community through their contribution to a diverse economy. For example, older people are more successful in starting a business than their younger counterparts. However, not all older people want to continue in work or have the opportunity to do so, while others have little alternative but to work or seek work. Against a background of labour market trends which include an increasing concentration of the population in older age groups as birth rates decline and the post-war baby boom cohorts age, there is an increasing concern to ensure high levels of employment among older people. As part of a wider strategy of culture change, from October 2006 the Government will introduce regulations prohibiting age discrimination in employment, occupation and training to remove age-based barriers to recruitment and retention of older people.[1] This chapter describes older people's involvement in the rural economy, including the diverse patterns of later working life and the different timings and transitions people take between employment and retirement.

Countering perceptions

At the outset it is important to counter conventional perceptions – first, about employment in rural areas, and, secondly, about the nature of older people's involvement in the economy. Misperceptions on both of these fronts constrain the opportunities facing older people in rural areas, and can skew policy interventions.

First, with regard to employment, traditionally rural areas have been viewed as being dominated by agriculture, fishing, forestry and extractive industry, with a population largely employed locally. However, although still significant in some local areas, employment in these sectors has contracted inexorably over time, and the employment structure of rural areas has become increasingly similar to that of urban areas (Countryside Agency, 2003a). Indeed, four key sectors employ over 80 per cent of employees in rural workplaces: public administration, education and health; distribution; manufacturing; and banking and financial services. While it remains the case that most residents of rural areas work close to home, others seek employment opportunities in urban areas, so underlining the importance of links between urban and rural areas.

---

1   This chapter uses data drawn from the 2001 Census, which has been aggregated to show urban–rural categorisation of local authority districts. For more explanation on the urban and rural definitions used, see the detailed discussion in Chapter 2.

Secondly, retirement is often perceived as an 'event' occurring when individuals reach state pension age. Yet it may be more useful to think in terms of 'gradual trends' rather than 'sudden changes' at a particular age (CROW, 2004a). As noted by Vickerstaff (2004), 'many people would like to exercise more choice about passing through a "retirement zone", rather than "jumping off the cliff" into the unknown territory of permanent and all-encompassing retirement'.

Key themes

Five key themes run through this chapter:

- *Ageing* has important and pervasive implications for the labour market. In turn, the labour market profoundly structures the experience of ageing for individuals. Withdrawal from the labour market in particular is a crucial stage in the ageing process for many. Ageing takes on particular significance for rural areas given not only that the local population is growing older but also that there is a characteristic loss of younger people through selective out-migration and a gain of older people through in-migration.

- *Broader labour market trends and the national and international policy* **context** *are important.* Despite greater devolution in strategy formulation, policy implementation and delivery to regional and local levels, legislation and policy relating to employment and pensions emanate from national and European levels. Rural areas feel the impact of changes in the global economy and of structural changes in the labour market, albeit filtered through distinct sectoral and occupational structures at regional and local levels. A case in point is that recent discussion and policy pronouncements on the role of older people in employment have occurred against the backcloth of a 'tight' labour market. It cannot be assumed that current policy and attitudes would prevail in different economic circumstances.

- *There is* **diversity** *in experience* – both between individuals and between areas. Older people in rural areas are a varied group. Moreover, there is evidence that polarisation increases with age, as past experience shapes future attitudes and options, such that 'every older worker is different'. Likewise, rural areas are diverse and are diverging in their employment restructuring (Performance and Innovation Unit, 1999). Despite facing the same overarching trends, there is no single storyline that captures the full complexity of economic trends (and their outcomes) in rural areas. Of course, diversity in experience is not unique to rural areas or to older people. A pertinent question therefore is whether and how a rural context generates specific opportunities and constraints for older workers.

- *A focus on* **transitions** *is helpful* in illuminating the choices and constraints facing older people in rural areas. However, there is limited statistical evidence available on transitions of older people in rural areas. Ideally such a focus requires a longitudinal approach, in which individual experiences are traced through time. For an example of this sort of approach see Chapter 4 (Gilbert, Philip and Shucksmith), where the trajectories of older people into relative poverty or relative affluence are systematically examined. Most longitudinal studies though are based on national samples, with any spatial disaggregation limited to a regional level. Information sources enabling identification of 'rural' (or 'urban') areas are generally cross-sectional (ie they relate to a particular point in time). So, in this chapter, inferences about older people in rural areas have had to be drawn from a mix of longitudinal analyses undertaken at national level and cross-sectional analyses relating to rural areas, as well as material from case studies.

- *The role of **self-employment** merits more attention* given its greater prevalence among older people than younger people, and in rural areas than in urban areas. Indeed, self-employment has been identified as a crucial driver of rural economies, both in terms of entrepreneurial activity and as a source of income and employment for a significant part of the rural workforce (Countryside Agency, 2003a). It has also been identified favourably as a possible component in flexible retirement strategies and in household income portfolios. However, given the 'diversity' of experience outlined above, it is important to consider when and where self-employment can and does play a positive role, and in what circumstances it is indicative instead of other opportunities being constrained.

Participation in employment

National trends and policies

Labour market analysts make a distinction between the 'economically active' (defined as those participating in the labour market, by being in employment – either as employees or self-employed – or by being unemployed) and the 'inactive' (defined as those who are retired, looking after the home or family, the permanently sick and full-time students). Many of those who are 'inactive' lead busy lives, making important contributions not only to household well-being but also to the local economy and social life through unpaid work, informal caring, volunteering and other activities. However, Government rhetoric and policy gives prominence to participation in employment as a means of generating national wealth, combating poverty and fostering inclusion of individuals within society.

Until a hundred years ago most people continued in employment until death. Gradually, throughout the twentieth century, pensions were introduced as a means of supporting people living after they had left employment. Eventually a system of contributory state pensions was established, with state pension ages of 65 for men and 60 for women[2] (Smeaton and McKay, 2003). Accordingly, labour market analysts conventionally define males aged 16–64 years and females aged 16–59 years as being of 'working age'. Given the focus in this chapter on 'older people', the analyses presented here encompass the 50–74 years age group.[3]

The proportion of men who are economically active is higher than that for women in all age groups. However, the gap has been narrowing over recent decades and, for older people in particular, very different trends are evident.

Looking at men first, in the 1950s and 1960s in the UK, at least 95 per cent of those aged 55–59 years and at least 87 per cent aged 60–64 years were economically active. In the period between 1975 and 1995 the proportion of men aged 55–59 years who were economically active declined from 93 per cent to less than 74 per cent. For men aged 60–64 years the decline was more dramatic, from 82 per cent to 50 per cent. This decline in economic activity among

---

2   These are subject to further change in the future.

3   74 years is the upper 'cut-off' for collection of statistics on employment from the 2001 Census.

older men has been the subject of considerable analysis and discussion (Campbell, 1999) and has been identified as one of the most remarkable labour market trends of modern times (Duncan, 2003).

Another important but contrasting socio-economic trend over the latter part of the twentieth century was the increase in the number of women seeking employment in the formal economy (Hakim, 2000). Between 1951 and 1971 the proportion of women aged 55–59 years who were economically active increased from 29 per cent to 51 per cent. In the period from 1975 to 1995 when increasing numbers of older men became inactive, the proportion of women aged 55–59 years who were economically active remained constant at around 52–56 per cent.

In the 1980s, when the trend towards early exit from the labour market for men was most dramatic, relatively little concern was expressed about it. At a time of mass unemployment, coinciding with a large cohort of young people seeking to enter the labour market, older workers tended to be viewed as 'less deserving' than younger ones who had their working lives ahead of them. Labour market policy at this time focused on young people. It illustrates how attitudes towards the role of older people in the labour market can change over the economic cycle. Traditionally, older workers fulfil a 'buffer' role: being foremost candidates for shedding in a 'slack' labour market (ie when unemployment is high) and one among a number of candidate groups to be encouraged to return to employment in a 'tight' labour market. In the current context of continuing economic growth, a 'tightening' of the labour market and the ageing of the population, policies to increase the labour market participation of older people have stressed the business case for engaging older workers, the promotion of equal opportunities and diversity policies, and anti-age discrimination legislation (Duncan, 2003). Despite evidence of a gradual change in employers' policies (Taylor, 2003), age discrimination remains a pervasive barrier to older workers.

Another challenge for policy is that, if displaced from the labour market, older people tend to be less likely to re-enter than younger people (Barham, 2002). In recent years there has also been greater emphasis on an active labour market policy, including for older people (as exemplified by the extension of the New Deal to those aged 50+). However, the targeting of the 'inactive' (as opposed to the unemployed claiming Jobseekers' Allowance) has complex implications for older people – for whom 'age' may be only one aspect of the disadvantage they face in gaining employment and who may have no wish or expectation of work.

Trends in economic activity have not impacted evenly on older people. Older men with no qualifications (often with lower earnings) have experienced the largest increases in inactivity. Many of this group, especially those from manufacturing and extractive industries, have become 'long-term sick'. A third of males with no formal qualification aged 55–64 were inactive because of sickness and disability in 2000, compared with fewer than 5 per cent of those with higher education. This exit route from the labour market is more apparent in 'slack' than in 'tight' local labour markets (Beatty and Fothergill, 1999) and often reflects constrained choices or involuntary decisions. As with men, older women are less likely to have certified qualifications than younger women, and those with no qualifications are less likely to be economically active than women with high level qualifications (Collis et al, 2000). Many of these older women see themselves, or are seen by others, as 'housewives' rather than retired even though they may have had extended periods of full or part-time employment.

After those with no qualifications, the next largest declines in economic activity for older men have been among those with higher vocational qualifications. This is the group most likely to have an occupational pension, and many of them have exited the labour market voluntarily, with increasing take-up of early retirement opportunities (Disney et al, 1998) – which some now regard as a norm.

Employment rates

The employment rate (ie the percentage of people within a defined sub-group who are in employment) is dependent on the state of labour demand, and is also influenced by a complex interplay of economic and social factors interacting at various levels: from the individual and the family, to the community and the local labour market, up to the national and global levels. A range of factors including economic growth, and a change in attitudes and pension policy has seen the trend for a decline in the employment rate for people aged over 50 halted and reversed (Scales and Scase, 2000). Labour Force Survey data for Great Britain indicates that in autumn 2004 older people's employment rate was 70.7 per cent overall, compared to 66.6 per cent in 1999 and 62.4 per cent in 1992. However, the levels remain well below those of the late 1970s and early 1980s.

Figure 5.1 shows employment rates by 5-year age groups for older men and women in England in 2001. Rates for women are consistently lower than for men, but show the same general pattern of decline by age. Slightly less than three-quarters of those who are in their early 50s are in employment, but thereafter proportions decline rapidly: to just over three-fifths for those in their late 50s and down to just over a third for those in their early 60s. This is indicative of older workers (particularly males) having taken advantage of early retirement schemes or having been made redundant and becoming inactive. Others though have continued in work, and in the 65–69 and 70–74 years age groups 11 per cent and 5 per cent of persons respectively are in employment.

Figure 5.1 Employment rates by gender for persons in England aged 50–74 years, 2001

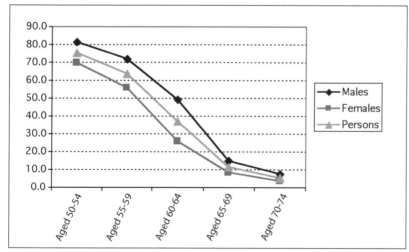

Note: Calculated as the numbers in employment as a percentage of the people in the age group

Source: 2001 Census of Population, Standard Table 28

Figure 5.2a shows the percentage point difference in the employment rate for older men for each of the six urban and rural categories of districts relative to the England average. Figure 5.2b portrays similar information for women. These charts show employment rates are higher than average in all categories of rural area, for both older men and women in each 5-year age group (but also in aggregate for all those aged 16–74 years[4]). Figures 5.3a and 5.3b concentrate on the three 'Rural' categories and show the proportional differences (in percentage terms) between the local and the England employment rates for each age group. The charts show how the higher rural employment rates are relatively greater among those aged over 65 and in the more 'rural' districts.

Figure 5.2a Percentage point difference in employment rates for older men by urban–rural category relative to the England average, 2001

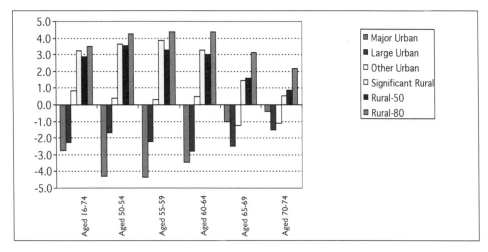

Figure 5.2b Percentage point difference in employment rates for older women by urban–rural category relative to the England average, 2001

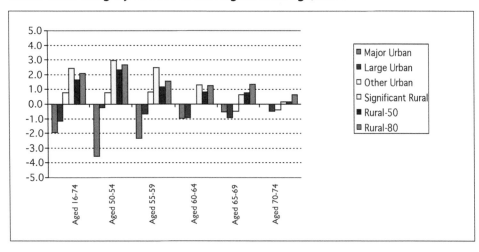

Source: Census of Population, 2001; aggregated to urban–rural categorisation of districts

4   The age range for which 2001 Census data on employment is available.

Figure 5.3a Percentage difference in employment rates for older men in 'Rural' categories relative to the England average, 2001

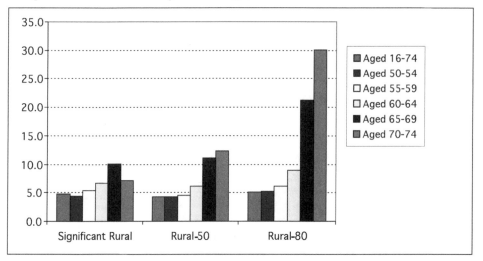

Figure 5.3b Percentage difference in employment rates for older women in 'Rural' categories relative to the England average, 2001

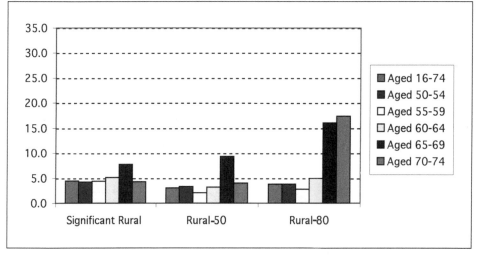

Source: Census of Population, 2001; aggregated to urban–rural categorisation of districts

Indeed, the most 'rural' districts (those categorised as 'Rural-80') consistently display the highest employment rates for men in all age groups shown, and this is especially pronounced in the older age groups (see Figure 5.2a). In the age groups from 50 to 64 years, male employment rates in the 'Rural-80' category are consistently 4 percentage points greater than the England average. In contrast, in the 'Major Urban' category employment rates for men in their 50s are consistently 4 percentage points lower than the England average. Relative differences in local and national employment rates for men are most pronounced in the oldest age groups and in the most 'rural' (ie the 'Rural-80' category) districts (see Figure 5.3a).

Differences in employment rates relative to the England average are less pronounced for women, indicating less urban–rural variation in their experience. However, as for men, female employment rates are consistently higher in 'rural' than in 'urban' areas, but the precise geographical patterning does differ. For women, the 'Significant Rural' areas display the highest employment rates up to state pension age. This might indicate a greater range and variety of employment opportunities for women in those rural areas with stronger ties to urban areas. For women over 65, however, the 'Rural-80' category displays the highest employment rates, as for men. To understand why, it is necessary to examine economic position by age group and gender in more detail, to gain an insight into the labour market transitions of older people.

Changes in economic position by age

Figure 5.4a profiles the economic position of older men in rural areas in England (ie the 'Significant Rural', 'Rural-50' and 'Rural-80' combined). Figure 5.4b presents similar information for women. Four categories of the economically active are distinguished: part-time employees, full-time employees, the self-employed and the unemployed. 'Inactivity' is also disaggregated into four categories: retired, looking after the home, permanently sick and other inactive.[5]

The proportion of people in employment declines in each successive age group. For both men and women in rural areas between the ages of 50 and 64 the decline in employment is sharpest among full-time employees. For women the decline in part-time employment occurs more gradually, such that, from the age of 55, part-time employees outnumber full-time employees. For older men, the share of the age group working as part-timers actually increases between the ages of 50 and 64 such that there are proportionally more men in their late 60s than in their early 50s employed part-time.

Likewise, the decline in the proportion in self-employment occurs later and more gradually than for full-time employees. After age 64, the numbers of older men in self-employment outnumber both part-time and full-time employees. The role of self-employment and part-time employment in transitions out of economic activity in rural areas is explored further below.

Only a small proportion of older men and women are unemployed. Regarding the economically inactive in rural areas, more older men are recorded as permanently sick than older women, while more older women are recorded as looking after the home than older men. From age 65 for men and 60 for women, the retired comprise the largest proportion of economically inactive people – a category which further expands and eclipses the others.

Again it is interesting to pose the question whether rural areas are distinct in any way. Figures 5.5a and 5.5b compare the economic position of older men and women respectively, in rural areas relative to the England average. Some key features are common to both older men and older women in rural areas. First, the greater than average share of self-employed in rural areas is apparent in all five age groups for both men and women. Disaggregation by the three 'Rural' categories (not presented here) indicates a clear gradation, with self-employment more important the more rural the area. Secondly, similar or greater than average shares of older people (and especially older women) are part-time employees in rural areas than in England as a whole.

---

5   Students are not included in the classification as only a very small proportion of older people describe themselves as students.

Figure 5.4a Economic position of older men in rural areas by 5-year age groups, 2001

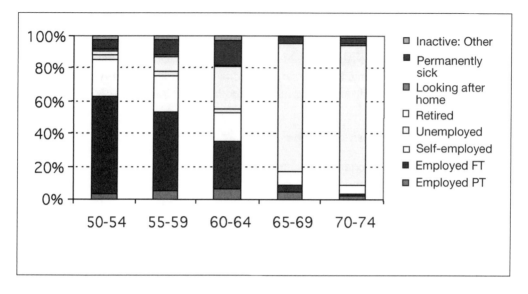

Figure 5.4b Economic position of older women in rural areas by 5-year age groups, 2001

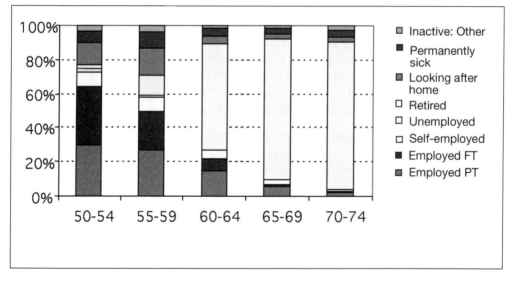

Source: Census of Population, 2001; using urban–rural categorisation of districts

This suggests that part-time employment plays a more important role in transitions out of employment for older people, and especially older women, in rural areas than in urban areas. A third key feature is that permanent sickness accounts for a smaller proportion of older men and women in rural areas than for England as a whole. This suggests that 'sickness' is a less significant route to inactivity in rural than in urban areas. Unemployment and other inactivity also account for smaller shares of older people in rural areas than nationally.

Figure 5.5a Percentage point difference in economic position of older men in rural areas by age group relative to the England average, 2001

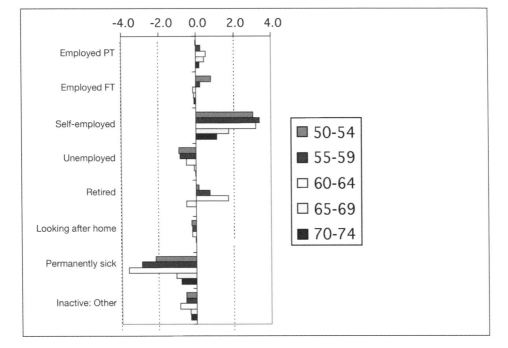

Figure 5.5b Percentage point difference in economic position of older women in rural areas by age group relative to the England average, 2001

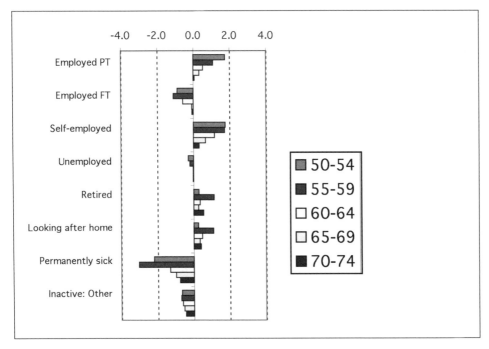

Source: Census of Population, 2001; using urban–rural categorisation of districts

There are also important differences and geographical variations in the experience of ageing and economic activity, between older men and older women. First, across rural areas, a smaller than average share of older women in all age groups are full-time employees, with the exception of age groups 50–64 in 'Significant Rural' areas where the share of older women who are full-time employees is actually higher than average. For men too, in 'Significant Rural' areas the share of full-time employees is greater than average in all age groups. This is also the case for men in the 'Rural-50' districts but only up to age 64. In contrast, in the 'Rural-80' category the share of full-time male employees is lower than average in all age groups.

A second important gender difference is that greater than national average shares of older women in rural areas describe themselves as 'looking after home'. More detailed disaggregation reveals that this proportion is higher in the 'Rural-80' category than elsewhere. This would concur with a line of feminist analysis that identifies rural areas (and particularly more sparsely populated rural areas) as places where traditional 'home-centred' roles of women are reproduced (Little and Austin, 1996; Little, 1997). Older women in rural areas are also more likely to describe themselves as 'retired' than across England as a whole, especially in their late 50s.

Inactive men between the ages of 50 and 64 in rural areas are more likely to be retired than in urban areas. Disaggregation by rural areas suggests that in these age categories it is only in the 'Rural-80' and 'Rural-50' categories that the proportion who are retired is greater than average.

Overall, the profiles outlined give the appearance that exit from the labour market and into retirement is a more gradual process in rural areas than in urban areas. However, this impression cannot be confirmed by cross-sectional data of the type used here. On close inspection, indeed, the picture may be one of greater diversity in experience of the timing of exits from employment in rural areas, and, more particularly, in the most remote rural areas, than elsewhere – with some retiring well before state pension age and others continuing in employment, especially self-employment, long afterwards.

The role of self-employment

Self-employment is particularly important for older people. The Labour Force Survey for Great Britain indicates that, in autumn 2004, 17.7 per cent of people aged between 50 years and state pension age were self-employed, compared with 12.2 per cent aged 25–49 years and less than 4 per cent of people aged 16–24 years. The information on economic position outlined above highlights the even greater significance of self-employment in rural areas (see also Countryside Agency, 2004).

Indeed, self-employment and entrepreneurship have been identified as key features of the flexibility of rural labour markets. They have also been highlighted as a significant element, along with part-time work and temporary work, in some strategies of transition from formal employment to retirement for older people in rural areas. Lissenburgh and Smeaton (2003) argue that, on the whole, self-employment provides better quality flexible employment than part-time or temporary employment. Yet self-employment is not always feasible or desirable (Yeandle, 2005). In a qualitative study of those working after state pension age, Barnes et al (2004) indicate that, while those who had been self-employed and continued in the same job tend to be satisfied and often continue in work as long as possible, others who took up self-employment around state pension age as a crisis move for financial considerations tend to be less satisfied.

One characteristic that the self-employed share is a tendency to continue working after the state pension age (McNair et al, 2004). It is probably that characteristic, rather than any substantial shift from employee status to self-employed, that accounts for the high proportion of the self-employed among individuals working after state pension age (Smeaton and McKay, 2003). The apparent picture of a more gradual transition from employment to retirement in rural areas, with self-employment as a possible intermediate stage, may simply obscure the greater mix of distinct 'routes' from employment to retirement, including a higher proportion of self-employment, in rural areas. Of course, that is not to deny the possibility that for some individuals self-employment may play an important role in a transition from formal work to retirement, perhaps by allowing a gradual reduction of the time and effort devoted to employment-related activities.

The self-employed are a diverse group, encompassing the spectrum from the most vulnerable to the most successful within the rural workforce. McNair et al (2004) identify three distinct clusters of self-employed: first, about 30 per cent who have high incomes and high level formal qualifications; secondly, about 40 per cent who are skilled craftspeople; and, thirdly, about 30 per cent who are unqualified and on low incomes. As noted above, some enter self-employment reluctantly, out of necessity when they find that other options are limited or unavailable (Bryson and White, 1997). People in this category are unlikely to be seeking to take big risks and expand their business. Others actively pursue self-employment, for positive reasons, and typically work full-time. It is this group who are likely to be most open to support for expanding their businesses. Yet others enter self-employment for 'lifestyle' reasons, perhaps associated with 'self-fulfilment' or 'wanting to be their own boss'. Another group comprises those for whom self-employment supplements other sources of household income – including employment, pensions, state benefits and savings (DTZ Pieda, 2004). Indeed, individuals in this group might be both self-employed and employees. It is among this group that older people – often working part-time, or partially retired – are particularly prevalent. Sources of older workers' household income might thus be very diverse including contributions from employment, pensions, savings and self-employment.

Industrially, the incidence of self-employment is especially marked in agriculture and construction (each with around 42 per cent of workers self-employed), other services (21 per cent self-employed), real estate/renting/business services (18 per cent), and hotels/restaurants/catering (14.5 per cent). Yet self-employment in rural areas is not only about these traditional sectors: while half of the rural self-employed work in construction, wholesale and retail and real estate/renting/business services, only a tenth are in agriculture or manufacturing.

Over and above the sectoral composition of the rural economy, therefore, there do seem to be geographic factors at work that foster or impel greater self-employment in rural areas.

The nature of employment

In this section the focus shifts to consider the nature and quality of employment in rural areas, since this has important implications for older people's opportunities and experience of the economy and work.

Sectoral composition and trends

In the medium-term, a continuing decline of employment in primary and manufacturing industries, and a growth of employment in services are expected (see Figure 5.6; Wilson et al, 2004). By 2012 it is projected that agriculture, hunting, forestry and fishing will account for just over 1 per cent of total employment (280,000 jobs) in England as a whole, and manufacturing for just under 11 per cent (2.75 million jobs). Business and miscellaneous services are projected to have the largest employment gains, rising to nearly 30 per cent of total employment by 2012 (7.7 million jobs). Distribution, transport, hotel and catering will account for a similar proportion of jobs.

Figure 5.6 Changing industrial profile of employment in England, 1982–2012

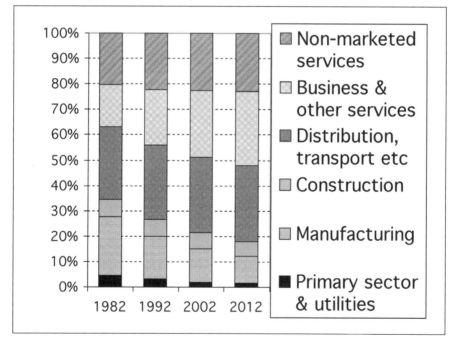

Source: Working Futures (Wilson et al, 2004)

Changes in industrial structure have implications for the gender balance of employment and for the status of the jobs being generated (whether full or part-time employment or self-employment, etc). Recent trends have tended to provide opportunities for part-time rather than full-time employment. Women have been the main beneficiaries of these trends, while men have suffered the brunt of job losses in primary and manufacturing sectors.

Table 5.1 shows the industrial profile of employed residents aged 50–74 years compared with all employed residents (note that the pattern of workplace-based employment would be slightly different from the residence-based picture shown here). At national level, these older residents are disproportionately concentrated in five key sectors: agriculture, hunting and forestry; manufacturing; construction; education; and health and social work. These might be characterised as 'ageing sectors'. All except health and social work are disproportionately present in rural areas and thus contribute proportionately more than other sectors to the older age profile of employed residents there. This, of course, is particularly so with the agricultural sector.

In the three 'rural' categories, there is a greater than average representation of older workers in agriculture; for example, nearly 6 per cent of older employed residents in the 'Rural-80' category are engaged in this sector. More detailed disaggregation highlights the ageing in this sector more starkly. For example, a quarter of the agricultural workforce in Yorkshire and the Humber is aged 65 and over and just 4 per cent is under 35. This has major implications even in a sector which is in decline (as highlighted in more detail in the sub-section on replacement demands below).

Table 5.1 Industrial profile (percentage) of residents in employment in England by urban–rural categories – all ages and for those aged 50–74 years, 2001

	Major Urban	Large Urban	Other Urban	Significant Rural	Rural-50	Rural-80	ENGLAND
All ages							
Agriculture, hunting and forestry	0.5	0.8	0.8	1.8	2.7	4.2	1.5
Fishing	0.0	0.0	0.0	0.0	0.0	0.1	0.0
Mining and quarrying	0.2	0.2	0.2	0.3	0.3	0.4	0.2
Manufacturing	12.6	15.8	16.8	15.9	16.1	15.1	14.8
Electricity, gas and water supply	0.6	0.8	0.8	0.8	0.7	0.7	0.7
Construction	6.1	7.0	6.8	7.1	7.2	7.4	6.8
Wholesale and retail trade; repairs	16.3	17.2	18.0	17.2	16.8	16.5	16.9
Hotels and restaurants	4.6	4.8	4.7	4.5	4.5	5.5	4.7
Transport, storage and communications	7.6	6.9	8.1	6.6	6.4	5.9	7.1
Financial intermediation	6.1	4.9	4.3	4.4	3.9	3.1	4.8
Real estate, renting and business activities	15.5	11.9	11.8	13.0	11.9	11.4	13.2
Public administration, defence, social security	5.4	5.9	5.4	5.4	6.3	6.3	5.7
Education	7.7	7.8	7.5	7.8	7.9	7.8	7.7
Health and social work	10.8	11.3	10.3	10.4	10.6	10.5	10.7
Others	6.1	4.7	4.5	4.7	4.7	5.1	5.2
Aged 50–74 years							
Agriculture, hunting and forestry	0.6	1.0	1.0	2.5	3.6	5.6	2.1
Fishing	0.0	0.0	0.0	0.0	0.0	0.1	0.0
Mining and quarrying	0.2	0.3	0.2	0.3	0.4	0.5	0.3
Manufacturing	14.8	17.4	18.0	16.7	15.9	14.7	16.0
Electricity, gas and water supply	0.5	0.6	0.7	0.6	0.6	0.6	0.6
Construction	7.2	7.8	7.4	7.6	7.8	7.8	7.5
Wholesale and retail trade; repairs	15.1	15.7	16.3	15.9	15.7	15.8	15.6
Hotels and restaurants	3.6	3.8	3.7	3.5	3.6	4.6	3.8
Transport, storage and communications	7.5	7.0	7.9	6.4	6.4	6.0	6.9
Financial intermediation	3.3	2.7	2.6	2.8	2.5	2.1	2.8
Real estate, renting and business activities	13.6	11.6	11.5	13.0	12.3	11.9	12.5
Public administration, defence, social security	5.1	5.4	5.0	4.9	5.3	5.0	5.1
Education	9.9	9.4	9.2	9.5	9.5	9.0	9.5
Health and social work	12.9	12.7	11.9	11.6	11.7	11.4	12.2
Others	5.8	4.6	4.5	4.7	4.7	5.0	5.0

Note: The shaded figures indicate a greater share of employed residents in a category than for England

Source: Census of Population, 2001 – Standard Table 36; aggregated to urban–rural categorisation of districts

A disproportionate number of older rural workers can also be found in construction, manufacturing and education. In the case of manufacturing, the effect is somewhat offset by the fact that employed residents in manufacturing in rural areas are somewhat younger than the average for the sector (in urban areas sharp declines in manufacturing employment have meant that the age profile of those employed is disproportionately weighted towards older workers).

The age profile of employment in the health and social work sector is no older in the rural categories than in the urban ones. However, this does not mean that ageing in specific sub-sectors or occupations does not pose key issues for the future, with many workers in the health sector coming up to retirement age. For example, it can prove difficult to recruit GPs to some remote rural areas, partly because of some of the distinctive features of such labour markets, including limited employment options for dual career households and lack of established communities for a practice to draw on for support (Rural Health Forum, 2005).

Occupational composition and trends

Growth of employment in services has favoured professional and associate professional occupations, caring and personal service occupations (including hairdressers, nursery nurses, nursing auxiliaries and sports and leisure assistants) and sales and customer care occupations. These trends are projected to continue over the medium term. The decline in employment in manufacturing has led to disproportionate losses of manual jobs – notably in elementary (ie unskilled), operative (ie semi-skilled) and skilled trades occupations.

Table 5.2 shows the occupational profile of employed residents aged 50–74 by gender and the urban–rural categorisation of districts. In all three 'rural' categories there is a greater than average proportion of employed residents who are managers and senior officials or in professional occupations or in skilled trades occupations, all of which have an older than average age profile. However, administrative, clerical and secretarial occupations, which also display an older than average age profile, are under-represented in rural areas.

There are marked differences in occupational profiles by gender. Across England, two-fifths of employed men aged over 50 years are in managerial or skilled trades occupations, with somewhat higher proportions (42–45 per cent) in rural areas. In contrast, the largest single proportion – 1 in 4 – of women aged over 50 years in employment are in administrative, secretarial and clerical occupations, followed by elementary occupations (nearly 15 per cent of all female employed residents aged 50–74 years). The next largest occupational groups for older female rural residents in employment are personal service occupations, managers and senior officials; associate professional and technical occupations; and sales and customer service occupations (which has a disproportionate share of younger workers).

Table 5.2 Occupational profile (percentage) of residents aged 50–74 years in employment in England by urban–rural categories, 2001

	Major Urban	Large Urban	Other Urban	Significant Rural	Rural-50	Rural-80	ENGLAND
Males 50–74							
Managers and senior officials	19.2	17.9	18.1	22.2	22.0	21.7	20.1
Professionals	12.7	11.7	11.1	13.0	12.9	12.6	12.4
Associate professionals and technical occupations	11.0	10.5	10.2	10.9	10.9	10.5	10.7
Administrative, clerical and secretarial	5.8	5.2	5.2	4.6	4.6	4.1	5.0
Skilled trades	18.1	20.7	19.8	19.9	21.0	22.9	20.0
Personal service	2.7	2.5	2.4	2.1	2.0	2.0	2.4
Sales and customer service	2.6	2.6	2.5	2.2	2.2	2.1	2.4
Operatives	15.8	16.5	17.4	14.4	14.2	13.7	15.4
Elementary occupations	12.1	12.4	13.3	10.5	10.3	10.4	11.6
Females 50–74							
Managers and senior officials	9.9	9.7	9.7	11.0	11.6	12.9	10.7
Professionals	10.6	8.8	8.4	10.2	10.2	10.3	9.9
Associate professionals and technical occupations	11.5	9.9	9.9	10.7	10.7	10.6	10.7
Administrative, clerical and secretarial	26.7	25.0	25.0	25.4	24.2	22.3	25.1
Skilled trades	2.5	3.0	2.7	3.2	3.7	4.6	3.2
Personal service	11.6	12.4	11.9	11.7	12.1	12.2	11.9
Sales and customer service	9.5	11.6	11.9	10.4	10.3	10.2	10.5
Operatives	3.4	4.1	4.2	3.6	3.4	3.2	3.6
Elementary occupations	14.3	15.6	16.3	13.8	13.7	13.7	14.5

Note: Percentages greater than the England average are shaded

Source: Census of Population, 2001 – Census Area Statistics Table 33, district aggregation

Replacement demands

In discussions of labour market trends and the changing structure of employment, the emphasis tends to be on net increases in numbers of jobs in particular sectors and occupations (referred to by labour market analysts as 'structural' or 'expansion demand'). Yet even more important than this in terms of job opportunities for older people, and for rural areas with their older than average workforce, are requirements resulting from 'replacement demand'. Even in sectors and occupations where employment has declined, or is projected to do so, there is likely to be a demand for new recruits to offset effects of retirement (particularly in sectors and occupations characterised by relatively large shares of older workers), and labour mobility.

In sectors which have an older than average age profile, or which have suffered recent sharp economic downturns (so contributing to a poor image which may be off-putting to potential recruits), replacement demand is a particularly important issue. In rural areas, agriculture and construction are sectors exhibiting these characteristics. Hence, despite the downturn in employment in agriculture, there are relatively few new recruits to take over from those retiring. So, in rural areas 'traditional' sectors and some 'traditional occupations' (including some of the skilled trades occupations) are as likely as the expanding sectors, if not more so, to face labour shortages. Young people tend to regard expanding sectors and occupations as more attractive than 'traditional' ones. In such instances, older people may have the opportunity to continue working past state pension age, but some small proprietors and others may feel that they have to continue in employment for longer than they would otherwise wish to do so. In turn, this has implications for the nature of 'transitions' from formal work to retirement, as outlined below.

Turning the focus to occupations, in the case of managers/proprietors in agriculture and services, retirement serves to increase expansion demand substantially. Secretarial and related occupations, skilled metal and electrical trades and process, plant and machine operatives are other occupations where retirement plays a crucial role in providing openings for new recruits despite an overall net reduction in the total numbers employed.

Nature of skills required

Changes in the sectoral composition of employment, along with technological change and changes in the organisation of work (occurring across all sectors and occupations to a greater or lesser extent), are altering the demand for skills. In particular sectors and occupations, different skills have been required in response to such factors as new consumer demands, regulatory developments, concerns about environmental issues, the proliferation of sub-contracting, etc. In aggregate terms, the trend is towards an increase in the level and variety of skills within most jobs (Dickerson and Green, 2002), although there remains a substantial minority of jobs for which the skill requirements are low.

Traditionally, an ageing workforce has been associated with economic stagnation. Most presumptions about the relationship between productivity and ageing imply that population ageing presents a 'problem' for maintaining the growth of economy-wide productivity, but some of the 'myths' about how potential productivity varies with age do not accord with reality (Taylor and Walker, 1998; Lindley, 1999), and generally there is as much, if not more, variation within age groups in attributes related to productivity (such as motivation and capacity for learning, intelligence and cognitive ability and physiological performance) as between age groups. Moreover, older people tend to be at an advantage over younger people in terms of social skills and awareness, which tend to increase with age and experience, and also in situations where substantial knowledge-based judgement is required. Hence, if misperceptions and discrimination can be put aside, older people need not be disadvantaged in employment. Taylor and Walker (1994), though, have shown that significant proportions of employers regard older people as difficult or slower to train, unable to adapt to new technologies and too cautious. However unfounded or generally applicable such prejudices are, they need to be set against the tendency for lower job turnover among older workers. Moreover, as the pace of change in job content increases, so the interval over which specific training is of relevance decreases. Older rural people requiring work-related training may be at a disadvantage in this respect because of the more limited range of local training opportunities available in the rural areas than in urban areas.

Conversely, employment trends placing a premium on personal service skills and communication skills at the expense of more routine non-manual and manual jobs (in which older workers in rural areas are disproportionately concentrated) may place older workers in general, and older women in particular (many of whom prefer to work on a part-time basis), at an advantage. While young people are considered by many employers as being more likely to possess the IT skills which are increasingly important across a wide range of jobs, many older women (and men) are perceived to possess the interpersonal, quality of service and other 'soft' skills also highly valued by employers. Common employer perceptions of older workers are that they represent knowledgeable, experienced, reliable and stable workers, who are thoughtful about the business, with good interpersonal and customer service skills (Kodz et al, 1999). Moreover, as the proportion of older customers increases as the population ages, there are likely to be increasing opportunities for older workers in retailing, consulting and caring activities. Some initiatives have focused specifically on recruitment of older workers (as in the case of B&Q and Tesco), whereas a policy of encouraging the workforce development of older employees is likely to be beneficial (as exemplified by the Department for Work and Pensions' 'Age Positive' campaign, the Third Age Employment Network and Age Concern's 'Workwise' programme [Hardill et al, 2004]). Yet, to date, the less qualified, part-time workers and older workers are the least likely to receive training. For older people, short courses provide a particularly cost-effective way to update and upgrade their skills. The fact that older workers tend to change jobs less often and are less geographically mobile (Dixon, 2003) serves to reinforce the importance of training of those already in work.

Other features of rural labour markets

Given the gradual drift of employment over several decades from the conurbations and major cities to smaller settlements (the so-called urban–rural shift of employment), the economies of rural areas appear strong, at least in aggregate, in quantitative terms, with employment growth in rural areas outpacing that in urban areas. However, this does not necessarily ensure that the jobs available in rural areas are the 'right kind of jobs', either to fulfil the needs and aspirations of rural residents or to ensure the sustainability of local economies (Green, 2003).

In general, rural areas display an under-representation (relative to the national average) in so-called 'knowledge' sectors and occupations – including business services and professional occupations – which are the most dynamic economic sectors of the twenty-first-century economy (Hepworth, 2003). Rural areas may be in the 'vanguard' of labour market developments in relation to flexible working (including self-employment, part-time working, temporary working, pluriactivity, etc) but in many instances this is associated with casualised employment and low wages, and with limited sustainability (Green, 1999). Traditionally, much of the employment in rural areas has been seasonal. Where this has been marked, the residents of an area may be used to a lack of consistency in employment. This, in turn, may be translated into increased insecurity, low pay and reduced opportunities for training. More generally, it has been argued that the flexibility and insecurity that were a feature of 'traditional' rural labour markets have been reproduced in many rural areas, even though the employment base has shifted away from primary sectors to services (Marsden et al, 1992).

The labour market structure of many rural areas (in terms of the industrial and occupational composition, and the size of firms) militates against an increase in investment in skills through structural change. In consequence, many rural areas have low scores on skills indicators (Hepworth and Spencer, 2003). This raises concerns that some rural areas may be particularly at risk from the entrenchment of a 'low-skill equilibrium' (ie a situation in which local employers compete in low value-added markets, and consequently demand relatively low skill levels from their employees which, ultimately, is reflected in the supply of skills).

Geographical isolation may preserve this type of feature. In more accessible rural areas such isolation is eroded by the extension of commuting journeys. Over time, commuting journeys have tended to become longer and more diverse – so leading to greater linkages between rural and urban areas. However, different sub-groups of the population have different commuting patterns. For example, full-time workers tend to commute longer distances than part-time workers, males tend to commute longer distances than female workers (Green et al, 1986), and professional workers tend to commute longer distances than semi-skilled and unskilled manual workers (Coombes et al, 1988). Commuting patterns also vary by means of transport used, with those without access to a car facing the most severe geographical constraints on employment opportunities – particularly in rural areas (Social Exclusion Unit, 2003). In rural areas, 'lack of personal transport' is a key barrier to work (Burkitt, 2000) – particularly for older women (although the growth in two-car households may offset that).

Despite these differences, for most individuals in most areas, journeys to work remain short, and so it is the availability of employment opportunities in the immediate local area that is the foremost influence on the experience and prospects of most people. In consequence, some of the more disadvantaged individuals and sub-groups may be those confined to small residual localised labour markets with low wages and poor quality jobs.

Transitions

For older people generally, there has been increased policy interest in widening the choice and scope to pursue various pathways between full-time working and retirement to suit individual circumstances and desires. These include 'flexible' ways of working (eg part-time, temporary or self-employment) or through volunteering and other opportunities for making an economic contribution (eg activities in the social economy).

It is immediately apparent from a review of the literature that those individuals with the strongest positions in the labour market are in the strongest position to proactively shape their transition to retirement. For those in a weak labour market position, there may appear to be little alternative but to react to events in the face of a variety of other (greater) constraints. Hence, the tendency is for polarisation in the labour market to be translated into polarisation in retirement. However, individuals take account of a complex range of economic and non-economic factors in deciding when, and how, to retire. Work-related factors such as 'feeling valued', autonomy, personal mission, the social environment of work and whether opportunities exist for flexible working all play a role, as do pension considerations. Non-work-related factors such as health, caring responsibilities, competing priorities and synchronisation of retirement with a partner also influence decisions (CROW, 2004b; Hirsch, 2005). Taking account of these various influences, Yeandle (2005) presents a schema of older workers encompassing 'career changers', 'downshifters', 'exit strategists', 'reluctant quitters', 'identity maintainers' and 'workers till they drop', exemplifying the great range of outlooks and experiences.

A large survey of job transitions in later life reveals that the highly qualified have greatest 'control' over both the timing and the nature of their transitions. They are more likely than those without high level qualifications both to take early retirement for positive reasons and to remain in (some form of) work after state pension age. They are also more likely to consider taking up voluntary work. They are the 'choosers', who can construct for themselves a 'package' incorporating both the benefits of work and the flexibility of retirement (Lissenburgh and Smeaton, 2003; McNair et al, 2004). Transitions of older people with no formal qualifications or in routine jobs are likely to be precipitated by factors outside their control – such as redundancy or ill health. Such people are often reluctant to stay in work, but financial considerations may prompt a return to work for some. This group comprises the 'survivors'. McNair et al (2004) also identify a third group – the 'jugglers' – mainly comprising women whose job choices (and transition to retirement options) are determined largely by domestic and caring responsibilities. If in work, members of this group are most likely to be in part-time work or in small firms, and after retirement they are more likely to consider voluntary rather than paid work. However, for some paid work may be a necessity: many older women, particularly in the context of the increasing prevalence of family breakdown, face relative poverty in later life and are likely to need to have access to some form of paid employment for longer in order to supplement meagre incomes.

These three groups were identified by McNair et al (2004) on the basis of national survey data. It would be expected that all three groups would be represented in rural areas. Based on the 2001 Census data on economic position, it seems reasonable to suggest that 'jugglers' are likely to be over-represented in rural areas relative to urban areas. This, in turn, suggests that there is likely to be a group of older people in many rural areas who are ready to consider taking up volunteering. The sectoral and occupational structure of some of the more remote and peripheral rural areas suggests that there is likely to be a preponderance of 'survivors', and fewer 'choosers' than in more accessible rural areas. The 'choosers' in these latter areas are likely to be able to select from employment and volunteering opportunities both in their immediate locality and in nearby urban areas.

In rural areas it has been recognised that there is an important link between in-migration to rural areas and self-employment, volunteering and the social economy. Pre-retirement in-movers may be self-employed, under-employed or flexibly employed, with time available to devote to voluntary service in the community. Hence, at least in some rural areas, there may be a reservoir of older people who could, or want to be, working. Volunteering may offer the opportunity to accumulate and extend social capital, to replicate aspects of work which have been lost or to provide a complete break with former employment (ie individuals have different motivations to get involved) (Davis Smith and Gay, 2005).

Social capital can also lead to the development of new forms of 'social enterprise', defined by the Department of Trade and Industry as a business with primarily social objectives whose surpluses are principally reinvested for that purpose in the business or in the community, rather than being driven by the need to maximise profits for shareholders and owners. Social enterprises/community businesses can take a number of different forms and serve different purposes. Examples include credit unions, or co-operatives; delivery of goods and services – including training, childcare, etc; and businesses operating in the private sector but owned and controlled by a community of local producer interests (eg farmers' markets). Such enterprises seek to get involved in activities that meet local needs, with any surplus of income over expenditure being reinvested to improve the range of goods and services provided, or otherwise advantage, the local community (Countryside Agency, 2003a, 2003b). Older people are crucial to the development of social enterprises (Plunkett Foundation et al, 2005). Moreover, the creation and support of social enterprises complements a range of policy themes in sustainable rural economies – and can help address difficulties faced by older (and younger) people in accessing services of various types in rural areas.

Conclusions

The limited range of job opportunities available is perhaps the key feature of many, especially the more remote and peripheral, rural areas. This implies that there are quantitatively fewer people upon whom employers can draw, and fewer jobs which potential workers can reach (within daily travelling distance). Hence, there is a limited range of job opportunities available to rural residents (Monk and Hodge, 1995). This limited range of job opportunities has both quantitative and qualitative dimensions. There is a limited mix of job opportunities to choose from and restricted opportunities for advancement. This may lead some individuals to 'trade down' and 'make do' in the labour market in order to gain employment, rather than to achieve employment in a sector/occupation that matches their skills/aspirations. This has implications for people both during their working lives and in the transition to retirement. It also has implications for recruitment of individuals (often in dual earner households) to fill employment openings resulting from the retirement of older workers. In order to attract and retain some highly qualified and specialist workers in peripheral rural areas it may be necessary to promote some of the non-economic, as well as job-related, advantages of living and working in rural areas.

A second key issue in debates on rural labour markets concerns self-employment. From the evidence presented in earlier sections of this chapter, it is clear that self-employment is relatively more important in rural areas than in urban areas, and is more prevalent among older than younger people. It is the single most important factor in explaining higher than average employment rates among older people in rural than in urban areas. Yet Monk et al (2000) suggest that often self-employment is associated with relatively low incomes and may also disguise under-employment. While for some older people in rural areas self-employment is lucrative and fulfilling, it is not always a rewarding and positive experience – but nevertheless may be one crucial component of a broader array of household income streams.

Part-time working is also more prevalent in rural than in urban areas. While some employees choose to work part-time, for others taking up part-time employment may reflect a lack of full-time job opportunities. Part-time employment is also associated, at least in some instances, with seasonal or casual labour markets that are found in some rural areas, and with low wages and a lack of investment in training. Moreover, in many rural areas there may be a significant and embedded community sector, within which many individuals – especially older females – are involved in caring activities.

Despite this emphasis on generalities, it is important to note that rural areas are themselves diverse and rural economies are heterogeneous. Economic, social and demographic drivers behave in different ways in different places, so culminating in different employment and re-tirement experiences. Likewise, among older people there is considerable heterogeneity in labour market experiences and transitions to retirement.

Looking to the future, it is easier to project trends in population than it is to forecast changes in labour market participation, and so in labour supply, as well as in labour demand. It is clear that levels of early retirement seen over the last 15 years are unsustainable in the medium and longer term: hence the policy shifts towards raising statutory pension age and ongoing debates about pensions (Ageing Population Panel, 2000) and concerns about transitions from paid work to retirement. Longitudinal data is of foremost importance in understanding such transitions, and researchers with an interest in rural areas remain frustrated with a lack of data enabling a 'rural'–'urban' as opposed to a 'regional' disaggregation. Yet such large-scale quantitative analysis would provide the essential context in which to set smaller qualitative and case study research that could provide insights into the motivations and processes under-lying the dynamics of transitions. Hence, it is important that longitudinal data on employment and the labour market is collected in such a way as to facilitate rural–urban disaggregation.

References and further reading

Ageing Population Panel (2000) *The Age Shift – Priorities for Action,* London: Foresight, Department of Trade and Industry

Barham, C. (2002) 'Patterns of economic inactivity among older men', *Labour Market Trends* 110, 301–310

Barnes, H., Parry, J. and Taylor R. (2004) *Working After State Pension Age: Qualitative Research,* Department for Work and Pensions Research Report 208, London: Department for Work and Pensions

Beatty, C. and Fothergill, S. (1999) *Labour Market Detachment in Rural England,* London: Rural Development Commission

Bryson, A. and White, M. (1997) *Moving In and Out of Self-employment,* London: Policy Studies Institute

Burkitt, N. (2000) *'Own Transport Preferred': Transport and Social Exclusion in the North East,* Newcastle upon Tyne: Low Pay Unit

Campbell, N. (1999) *The Decline in Employment among Older People in Britain,* CASE Paper 19, London: CASE, STICERD, London School of Economics

Collis, C., Green, A. and Mallier, T. (2000) 'Older female workers in Britain and its regions: millennium prospects', *Local Economy* 15, 45–58

Coombes, M.G., Green, A.E. and Owen, D.W. (1988) 'Substantive issues in the definition of localities: evidence from sub-group local labour market areas in the West Midlands', *Regional Studies* 22, 303–318

Countryside Agency (2003a) *Rural Economies: Stepping Stones to Healthier Futures,* Cheltenham: Countryside Agency

Countryside Agency (2003b) *Supporting Rural Social Enterprise,* Countryside Agency Research Notes CRN 71, Cheltenham: Countryside Agency

Countryside Agency (2004) *The State of the Countryside 2004,* Cheltenham: Countryside Agency

CROW (2004a) *Are Older Workers Different?* CROW Briefing Paper 1, Guildford: Centre for Research into the Older Workforce, University of Surrey

CROW (2004b) *Why Do People Retire When They Do?* CROW Briefing Paper 2, Guildford: Centre for Research into the Older Workforce, University of Surrey

Davis Smith, J. and Gay, P. (2005) *Active Ageing in Active Communities: Volunteering and the Transition to Retirement,* Bristol: Policy Press

Dickerson, A. and Green, F. (2002) *The Growth and Valuation of Generic Skills,* SKOPE Research Paper 26, Oxford and Coventry: Universities of Oxford and Warwick

Disney, R., Grundy, E. and Johnson, P. (1998) *The Dynamics of Retirement: Analyses of Retirement Surveys,* DSS Research Report 72, London: The Stationery Office

Dixon, S. (2003) 'Implications of population for the labour market', *Labour Market Trends* 111, 67–76

DTZ Pieda (2004) *Rural Economies of Yorkshire and the Humber. A report prepared for the Countryside Agency,* Edinburgh: DTZ Pieda Consulting

Duncan, C. (2003) 'Assessing anti-ageism to older worker re-engagement', *Work, Employment and Society* 17, 101–120

Green, A.E. (1999) 'Employment opportunities and constraints facing in-migrants to rural areas in England', *Geography* 84, 34–44

Green, A.E. (2003) 'Rural labour markets, skills and training', Presentation to Defra/Countryside Agency/ESRC seminar on 'Rural Economies', Westminster, April 2003

Green, A.E., Coombes, M.G. and Owen, D.W. (1986) 'Gender-specific local labour market areas in England and Wales', *Geoforum* 17, 339–351

Hakim, C. (2000) *Work–Lifestyle Choices in the 21st Century,* Oxford: Oxford University Press

Hardill, I., Galt, V., Higham, P. and Webb, J. (2004) *Regional Strategies and Demographic Ageing,* London: Age Concern England

Hepworth, M. (2003) *The Knowledge Economy and the Future of Rural Britain,* A Local Futures Collaboration with ACRE, London: Local Futures Group

Hepworth, M. and Spencer, G. (2003) *A Regional Perspective on the Knowledge Economy in Great Britain,* Report for the Department of Trade and Industry, London: Local Futures Group

Hirsch, D. (2005) *Sustaining Working Lives: A Framework for Policy and Practice,* York: York Publishing Services

Kodz, J., Kersley, B. and Bates, P. (1999) *The Fifties Revival,* IES Report No. 359, Brighton: Institute of Employment Studies

Lindley, R. (1999) 'Population ageing and labour force potential', *IER Bulletin* 47, Coventry: Institute for Employment Research, University of Warwick

Lissenburgh, S. and Smeaton, D. (2003) *Employment Transitions of Older Workers: The Role of Flexible Employment in Maintaining Labour Market Participation and Promoting Job Quality,* Bristol: Policy Press

Little, J. (1997) Employment marginality and women's self-identity, in P. Cloke and J. Little (eds) *Contested Countryside Cultures,* London: Routledge, 138–157

Little, J. and Austin, P. (1996) 'Women and the rural idyll', *Journal of Rural Studies* 12, 101–111

Marsden, T., Lowe, P. and Whatmore, S. (1992) *Labour and Locality: Uneven Development and the Rural Labour Process,* London: David Fulton

McNair, S., Flynn, M., Owen, L., Humphreys, C. and Woodfield, S. (2004) *Changing Work in Later Life: A Study of Job Transitions,* Guildford: Centre for Research into the Older Workforce, University of Surrey

Monk, S. and Hodge, I. (1995) 'Labour markets and employment opportunities in rural Britain', *Sociologica Ruralis* 35, 153–172

Monk, S., Hodge, I. and Dunn, J. (2000) 'Supporting rural labour markets', *Local Economy* 15, 302–311

Nickell, S. (2001) 'Fundamental changes in the UK labour market', *Oxford Bulletin of Economics and Statistics* 63 S1, 715–736

Performance and Innovation Unit (1999) *Rural Economies: Taking Stock – Trends, Opportunities and Threats,* London: Stationery Office

Plunkett Foundation, PRIME, Countryside Agency, Age Concern England (2005) *Rural Lifelines: Older People and Rural Social Enterprises: Their Role as Providers and Beneficiaries of Service Provision in Rural England,* Woodstock: Plunkett Foundation

Rural Health Forum (2005) BMA – *Recruitment and Retention of Healthcare Professionals,* available at http://www.bma.org.uk/ap.nsf/Content/healthcarerural-recruitment

Scales, J. and Scase, R. (2000) *Fit and Fifty?* Swindon: Economic and Social Research Council

Smeaton, D. and McKay, S. (2003) *Working after State Pension Age: Quantitative Analysis,* Department for Work and Pensions Research Report 182, London: Department for Work and Pensions

Social Exclusion Unit (2003) *Making the Connections: Final Report on Transport and Social Exclusion,* London: Social Exclusion Unit

Taylor, P. (2003) 'Population ageing: implications for employment and the economy in the UK regions', Paper prepared for the 'Regions for All Ages' Conference, Birmingham

Taylor, P. and Walker, A. (1994) 'The ageing workforce: employers' attitudes towards the employment of older people', *Work, Employment and Society* 8, 569–591

Taylor, P. and Walker, A. (1998) 'Employers and older workers: attitudes and employment practices', *Ageing & Society* 18, 641–658

Vickerstaff, S. (2004) 'I'd rather keep running to the end and then jump off the cliff'. Paper presented to the 'Work, Employment and Society' Conference, UMIST, Manchester

Wilson, R., Homenidou, K. and Dickerson, A. (2004) *Working Futures: National Report 2003–04,* Report for the Sector Skills Development Agency, Wath-upon-Dearne: SSDA

Yeandle, S. (2005) *Older Workers and Work–Life Balance,* York: York Publishing Services

Chapter 6

The older rural consumer

Richard Baker and Lydia Speakman

The potential importance of the older rural consumer, now and in the future, cannot be ignored by those concerned with rural policy and economic regeneration. The private choices people make about the type and source of the goods and services they buy have profound implications for the future development and sustainability of local economies and the viability of public and commercial services. In rural areas, where people aged over 50 are already 40 per cent of the population and are set to become an ever growing share, businesses and service providers need to wake up to a market which is large and expanding in both size and value. The evidence is that older consumers have not only more disposable income than in previous generations but are increasingly discerning and keen to exercise choice. Indeed the personal mobility of most older rural residents, and their increasing ability to make use of the internet to purchase goods and services, mean that rural businesses can no longer take for granted the loyalty of older customers. Therefore, it is pressing that businesses, service providers and economic development agencies become better informed of the needs and demands of this market, if its increasing potential to support more vibrant rural economies is to be realised.

Yet, while there is a significant body of research on older rural residents in relation to issues such as social exclusion, poverty, access to services, and housing, very little has been done to understand the expenditure and consumption patterns of older people in the countryside. One might argue that part of the reason for this is an inherent 'ageism' that trades on stereotypes in which age is so often seen as synonymous with poverty and failing capacity. While, sadly, that is the experience for a minority, the majority of people have a reasonable standard of living in their older age which enables them to enjoy an active later life. Indeed we present evidence to demonstrate that age alone is an increasingly poor identifier of consumer behaviour, with lifestyle, attitudes and personal health much more influential factors.

In developing this as a key issue for rural policy, this chapter highlights the existing size of the 'over 50s' market in terms of wealth, disposable income and current expenditure patterns, together with the latest projections on how these are likely to grow. The current expenditure trends of older people and the potential future impact of the more consumer-orientated 'baby boomer' generation is also beginning to have a direct impact on the purchasing decisions of the public sector. The public sector is a key employer and purchaser of goods and services on behalf of older people in rural economies. Public sector health and social care provision is seeking to be increasingly responsive to the needs of the individual, through the development of the Direct Payments scheme in which the individual is empowered to decide how to spend their personal allocation on such services. Take-up of such schemes has been relatively small to date, but the Government is very keen to see their future expansion. With an estimated annual expenditure of over £7 billion on personal social care, housing and other services for older people in England, of which a sizeable proportion will represent that spent on older rural residents, the impact of public sector purchasing on rural economies cannot be ignored and is likely to be increasingly influenced by its recipients, who are demanding quality and value for money (Department of Works and Pensions, 2005).

One of the biggest challenges in preparing this chapter is that not only is there limited data on the expenditure patterns of older people, but very little of this has been disaggregated to enable a comparison between urban and rural. The chapter therefore draws on data from the LifeForce survey (2005) undertaken on behalf of Age Concern, and a range of recent research which has looked at the importance of visitors to the countryside, of which a significant proportion are aged over 50, and their value to rural economies.

The size of the older consumer market

Until fairly recently older people were generally seen as among the poorest members of society, with little attention devoted to their consumption habits beyond basic goods and services. However, the overall financial position of older people has improved in recent years – boosted in part by the impact of private and occupational pensions, as well as growing financial and property assets. Whereas 30 years ago nearly half of retired people were below the conventional poverty line (of 60 per cent of median household income), today under a quarter of older people are below this line. The incidence of poverty among pensioners is more or less the same as among non-pensioners (Metz and Underwood, 2005). Indeed, as Gilbert, Philip and Shucksmith (Chapter 4) have highlighted, poverty in later life usually mirrors previous life and work experience.

Although a significant minority of people suffer financial hardship in retirement, at the current time most do not. Thus, while welfare benefits including the state pension account for at least half the income of 70 per cent of pensioners, for only 15 per cent of them are these benefits their sole source of income. It is a distinct possibility that over the next few decades there will be greater income and asset inequalities among older people as the shortfall in pension provision of those currently still in work begins to be felt. This is a major issue for policy makers at present. In 2004 the Pension Commission estimated that around nine million people may be under-saving, some by a small amount, some severely. The shift away from final salary schemes to defined contribution schemes is likely to cause uncertainty among future generations of older people regarding their financial security in retirement. In addition, despite the Government's new Stakeholder Pension scheme, there is a large proportion of the current workforce who, for a variety of reasons, have made insufficient contributions to a pension fund. The extent to which this will be compensated in the long term by other policy and cultural changes such as those directed at extending working lives or initiatives to promote equity release or upgrading of the state pension will be subject to much public debate and is difficult to predict.

Currently, and for the foreseeable future, however, the older person's market is not only growing in terms of numbers, but also in value as older people have increasingly larger disposable incomes than those in younger age groups. MORI identified that in 1999 the average disposable household income for people between 54 and 64 years old was £372 per week, 17 per cent higher than the average among all households, while average weekly commodity expenditure per person was £154, higher than that of any other age group, and 22 per cent higher than the average (MORI/Help the Aged, 1999). At the same time a survey by the Design Council showed that under a third of FTSE 100 companies were aware of the needs of older consumers (quoted in Population Ageing Associates, 2003, page 45). Many businesses and a large proportion of the advertising industry continue to ignore older consumers, and focus their attentions on a youth market, whose spending is often only maintained due to the frantic efforts of credit providers.

It is estimated that the ratio of average income of older people post-retirement to that of pre-retirement is around 78 per cent (Metz and Underwood, 2005). On retirement, the large majority of households have already completed mortgage repayments and will also benefit from a reduction in work-related expenses such as those incurred travelling to work. Thus most people do not experience a material fall in their living standards through the retirement transition. In consequence, consumer spending by older people is now a significant part of the economy. It is estimated that the annual expenditure of people over 50 is £200 billion. This represents about 45 per cent of total household expenditure (Office for National Statistics, 2003). With demographic ageing, that amount will rise both absolutely and proportionally, an issue which is of general interest to the national economy, as well as rural areas, but one that is under-recognised by policy makers and economists.

Wealth is even more concentrated with older age groups than income. Individual wealth is derived from accumulated savings together with inheritance, and on average this increases with age to reach a peak in the mid 60s before declining. Excluding the capital value of housing and pensions it is estimated that the total net financial wealth of people aged 50 and over is of the order of £560 billion, amounting to 85 per cent of all such wealth in the UK (Marmot et al, 2003). In 2002 the mean value of net financial wealth per family unit (single or cohabiting or married couple) was around £50,000 for people in their 60s, £38,000 for people in their 70s, and £30,000 for those in their 80s (ibid). It should be remembered that these are averages that conceal large variations between the very rich and very poor, which are even wider in rural areas than elsewhere (see Chapter 4). The above figures also do not include the value of people's homes. Sixty per cent of pensioners are owner-occupiers – a proportion expected to grow to 80 per cent as the next generation enters later life. In 1998 older homeowners in the UK held an estimated £394 billion equity (Council of Mortgage Lenders, 2001) – a figure that is set to rise with property values.

The Family Spending survey (Office for National Statistics, 2003) provides some interesting insights on the distinctive expenditure patterns of older people. Table 6.1 shows the total average weekly household expenditure by the age of the head of the household. While there is a fall in expenditure between the 50–64 age group and the 65–74 age group, this is partly a function of reduced household size. The largest reduction in expenditure is on transport, followed by miscellaneous goods and services, which includes mortgages and holidays. That would support the overall argument that there is no significant change in overall consumption patterns as people grow older and move into retirement, except for work-related travel expenses and reaching the end of mortgage payments. Older age groups above 65 do spend less on alcohol and tobacco and clothing, but relatively more on housing, fuel and power, and food.

Table 6.1 Weekly household expenditure patterns by age in 2002/03 (£)

Age group	30–49	50–64	65–74	75+
Food and non-alcoholic drinks	48.20	47.80	37.90	29.40
Alcohol, tobacco	13.00	13.40	8.50	5.10
Clothing and footwear	29.20	24.00	11.60	7.80
Housing, fuel and power	38.90	35.30	29.30	25.90
Household goods and services	35.70	36.90	22.00	14.90
Health	4.60	6.30	5.90	3.50
Transport	72.90	72.40	35.10	15.60
Communication	12.80	10.60	6.90	5.10
Recreation, culture	67.10	65.60	42.10	23.00
Education	7.40	6.94	1.00	-
Restaurants, hotels	44.00	38.50	20.10	11.50
Miscellaneous goods and services	41.20	34.70	22.22	16.90
Other goods	82.10	59.30	27.40	17.80
Total expenditure £ per week	496.90	451.40	270.90	177.20
Average no. of persons per household	3.0	2.2	1.7	1.4
Average expenditure per person	165.60	202.50	157.30	122.60

Source: Family Spending Unit, Office for National Statistics (2003)

By projecting forward the expenditure pattern of those generations currently in their 20s and 30s it is possible to forecast how population change may impact upon the age structure of demand within various market sectors over the next 40 years. Figure 6.1 presents a projection undertaken for Age Concern England by nVision, which shows that people aged over 50 account for 35–45 per cent of national expenditure on household services, alcohol, food and drink, and leisure at the current time. These shares are projected to grow over the next 40 years by at least 10 per cent such that people aged over 50 may account for the majority of expenditure in each of these sectors by 2043.

Figure 6.1 Existing and forecast spending by people aged over 50 in key sectors

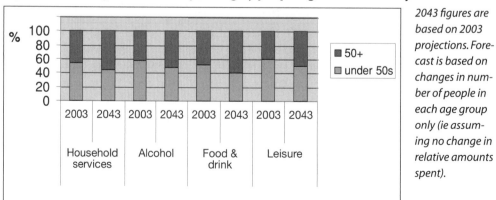

2043 figures are based on 2003 projections. Forecast is based on changes in number of people in each age group only (ie assuming no change in relative amounts spent).

Source: Family Spending Unit/Office for National Statistics/nVision

In addition to volume considerations, tomorrow's older people are likely to have different expenditure patterns compared with their parents' generation. Spending on consumer durables such as washing machines or fridges illustrates cohort-related changes in expenditure patterns already occurring. In the past people often replaced consumer durables around the time of retirement, perhaps taking advantage of a lump sum from an occupational pension. They used to do this with the expectation that the new items would last them the rest of life. However, an emerging trend, due to increased longevity and different attitudes, is that many older people are requiring subsequent replacements. Some foresighted manufacturers are becoming aware of this increasingly important market and are investing in inclusive designs for their products, which better meet those with a range of disabilities as well as age-related impairments, but still have universal appeal. The Helen Hamlyn Centre for Research at the Royal College of Art in London has been pioneering this approach. It encourages young designers to step outside their own frame of experience, and to observe older people for many months before attempting to create a product. One of the results of this approach has been a bestselling power tool for B&Q. It is shaped like a pebble so that it is easier to handle for those with less dexterity, but has also proved to be popular with the young because of its accessibility and style.

Another area where we might expect significant changes in older people's consumption behaviour in the future relates to communication technologies. The generation aged 50–65 is increasingly technology aware and able, prompted either by exposure at work, or a drive to keep in touch with children and grandchildren. A 2001 survey by MORI found that, even then, more than a million people aged over 55 were regularly communicating using mobile phone text messaging (MORI, 2001). The Age Concern LifeForce survey (2005) highlighted that 67 per cent of respondents had a mobile phone, and although use of the internet and home computer ownership was lower than in the general population, the so-called digital divide between older and younger groups was found to be much less than often perceived (see Table 6.2).

Table 6.2 Take-up of technology among people aged over 50

Technology	Percentage take-up among people aged 50+
Mobile phones	67
Home computer	39
ISP internet access	34
Telephone banking	22
Online banking	11

Source: Age Concern Life Force survey 2005

People now in their 50s are more likely than their predecessors to try new ideas and approaches in consumer products and behaviour. This after all is the outlook of the baby boom generation, which is likely to be upheld into later life as long as they retain the financial means to sustain their consumer lifestyles. In projecting the spending patterns of older people, the characteristics and values of each generation need to be considered, as successive generations actively redefine what it is to be an older person.

Changing values are also impacting on attitudes to savings. Savings are predominantly created during a person's working life to be used during retirement. The peak of surplus income over expenditure occurs for most people in their early 50s. However, people continue to save throughout their later life. Indeed, more than 80 per cent of people aged 65 and over believe it is important to save for the future (Age Concern Research Services, 2005). The predominant motivation appears to be caution about the future and a wish to have savings for whatever eventualities later life may bring – the proverbial 'rainy day'. In addition, among older generations frugal habits and attitudes inculcated through the experiences of war-time shortages and post-war rationing still linger. Some older people are also keen to leave bequests for children and grandchildren. However, recent surveys reveal an increasing reluctance to hold back expenditure in order to leave inheritable wealth. This is particularly so among the group of 'time rich' wealthier older people who want to spend their money on travel, holidays and active leisure pursuits and hobbies, including further education. It is a trend which has also been prompted by concerns over inheritance tax, as property prices put an increasingly a large number of people beyond the threshold. What is emerging is a growing divide in older people's consumption and savings behaviour between those with a more consumerist outlook who are inclined to spend while fit and able to enjoy life and those who feel they ought to keep a good reserve in hand to deal with the unexpected. It will be interesting to see whether the growing concerns over pension provision will impact on future older generations' attitudes to savings.

Characteristics of the older consumer market

The over-50 age group is not homogeneous, but is made up of different segments whose desired consumption, recreational activities and ability to purchase are very different. Many are consumers with the time to shop around and compare products, and, with years of experience as consumers, know exactly what they want. Admap research found this age group to be demanding and selective, and that they responded best to communications based on value and benefit (Parkes, 2005). Research undertaken by Campaign/Carat found 83 per cent of older people feel that ageism is a problem in the advertising and the media. Indeed there appears to be an in-built assumption by many in the marketing industry that by capturing the younger market companies can secure long-term loyalty and more lucrative business opportunities. Yet, not only do many older people have significant disposable incomes, research also shows that 90 per cent of those aged 50+ have changed one of their top ten purchases within the last 12 months (quoted in the *Guardian* 10 October 2005).

It is important to recognise that simple chronological age is not a particularly useful tool for those developing services and products and seeking to market into or provide for the older segments of the population. Policy and marketing analysts regularly use very broad age ranges such as 50–65 and 65–85 in determining their targeting. Arbitrary age cut-offs are also used by many businesses in seeking to limit their risks. It is still common practice, for example, for those aged over 70 to be routinely refused travel insurance, credit cards or car hire. However, from the point of view of the individual, age is a very weak identifier compared with other characteristics such as gender and race, or even state of health. Few people will see themselves as old, and consequently few will consume on that basis. As an indicator of preference or need, a specific age or narrow age bands are less and less likely to describe an increasingly diverse population. Therefore, while attractive because of its simplicity and precision, policy and marketing analysis which utilises chronological age as a leading feature is unlikely to be successful.

In order to understand consumption patterns in older age it is more useful to identify the key features of later life for people, and in particular a range of transitions which people experience in older age, and to overlay these transitions onto wider social and economic factors that structure people's lives. While these later-life transitions are common to many older people, they occur at increasingly divergent chronological ages and are further delineated by factors such as gender, race, class and economic circumstances, as well as personal health. Key transitions include:

- family pressures – moving through parenting, dealing with health and well-being of parents, grandparenting;

- emotional pressures – a range of positive and negative changes in outlook ranging from financial security to a sense of loss of things like work;

- changing responsibilities and attitudes to risk;

- resources and preferences;

- employment and retirement, semi-retirement, voluntary roles;

- health changes ranging from lifetime changes such as menopause through to significant loss of physical or mental capacity.

George Mochis, an American marketing academic, has suggested a segmentation of the older person's market based on health status and life events (G. Moschis, as quoted in Metz and Underwood, 2005):

MOCHIS' SEGMENTATION OF THE OLDER CONSUMER MARKET

- Health indulgers, who behave largely like younger consumers.

- Ailing 'outgoers', who experience a chronic disease or disability, so are concerned about their health but retain positive self-esteem. They constitute a prime market for consumer products and services to meet their medical needs, including health foods, functional clothing and assistive technologies, although lack of mobility may limit consumption and affect lifestyles.

- Healthy hermits, who have experienced an adverse life event such as the death of a spouse, which has triggered social withdrawal. They tend to have few consumption-related needs and are negative towards innovation.

- Frail recluses, who are experiencing both biological and social ageing and who may need support in day-to-day needs, whether in their own homes or in residential care.

Beyond these specific transitional issues, what is also identifiable is the overall generational cohort effects displayed in the differences between the general attitudes of different generations as they achieve older age. The extent to which these attitudes are individual and the extent to which they are reflective of wider political and socio-cultural pressures is difficult to discern. However, significant challenges to some of the presumed orthodoxies of older age are coming to the fore. Huber and Skidmore (2003) examined the potential impact of the 'baby boom' generation as it reaches retirement over the next 20 years and argue that, as pioneers of the consumer society, this generation has grown up in an era of affluence that has emphasised personal fulfilment through individual consumption. The future generation of older people have thus been encouraged to define themselves by the personal choices they make about what to eat, buy or watch on television. They are brand conscious and aware of the power of the consumer, for example over ethical consumption issues. This is very different from previous generations, and these trends are likely to have important consequences for the economy overall, and for the rural economy in particular.

Older rural consumers

Understanding the implications of not only demographic change but also the changing expectations of older consumers is important for those seeking to manage rural economic development and for those looking at older rural consumers as a potential market. As has been demonstrated, the older consumer market represents a huge and growing economic opportunity in general terms, with two key trends of particular importance for rural areas:

- People are living longer and healthier lives. There is an increase in the number of people who are living well into their 80s with, as this book has demonstrated, proportionally more of this age group in rural areas. They represent an increasingly dynamic market not only in terms of overall consumer spending but also spending on goods and services which enable them to continue to live independent lives as they age.

- The in-migration into rural areas of more wealthy, middle-aged professionals (who then stay on into retirement) is creating a group of people who tend to be better educated, and have higher household income and greater disposable income than longer-term residents.

While certain needs of older rural consumers are reasonably predictable, such as health care, transport and housing needs, there has been very little research undertaken of the older rural population to identify existing consumer patterns and identify potential unsatisfied needs and wants. One useful data source is the Age Concern England's LifeForce survey, which is undertaken every year and involves interviewing 1,500 respondents. The data from the 2005 survey has been analysed to enable a comparison between older urban and rural residents.

The LifeForce survey shows that levels of annual household income decline with age for rural households from an average of £16,227 for those in their 50s to £12,923 for those in their 60s, equating to a drop of 20 per cent, which reflects the move into full or partial retirement of one or more household members. In the subsequent age groups, 70–79 and those aged over 80, the data shows a further 10 per cent decline in household income for each decade. The decline is partly explained by the reduction in household size through the death of a member, but also reflects the loss in value of income from savings and pension funds. The trend is similar in urban areas, but starts at a higher average household income for those in their 50s of £19,151 and experiences a sharper decline of 27 per cent to the level for those in their 60s. (Age Concern Research Services, 2005).

Over half (55 per cent) of the rural households responding to the LifeForce survey were in receipt of the basic state pension, and 50 per cent were in receipt of various other state benefits including Income Support and Tax Credits. A total of 37 per cent derived earnings from employment, 24 per cent from savings, and a further 32 per cent had a pension from a former employer. The figures vary little from those in urban areas, apart from the percentage of those in receipt of a pension from a former employer, which is significantly higher in urban areas at 41 per cent (Age Concern Research Services, 2005).

A key dimension which shapes the purchasing habits and patterns of rural consumers is access to local shops and services, including banks and post offices. The Countryside Agency's annual State of the Countryside report has charted the availability of services to rural communities and registered a steady decline in the provision of many rural services, in particular the availability of access to banks and building societies. In sparse hamlets only 30.9 per cent and in villages 28.9 per cent of households are within 4km of a bank compared to 99.7 per cent in urban areas. Cashpoint availability has increased in recent years with 46.0 and 54.5 per cent of households within 4km of a facility (Commission for Rural Communities, 2005). It is therefore not surprising that rural LifeForce respondents were less likely to report having a current account with a bank/building society than urban respondents (75 per cent compared with 83 per cent) (Age Concern Research Services, 2005). The lack of banking or cashpoint facilities has proved to have a direct impact on the shopping habits of rural residents, to the detriment of local shops, leading to a range of initiatives to provide cashpoint facilities in post offices and local shops or even rural pubs (Defra, 2002).

Table 6.3 shows the proportions of different types of purchases that rural residents make locally. The retired have the greatest propensity to shop locally, while commuters make most of their purchases outside the locality. By and large also, those who are relatively new to an area are less reliant on local shops. For example, 93 per cent of retired incomers do their weekly shop outside the locality, compared with 78 per cent of retired long-term residents. The purchasing patterns of retired incomers may relate to the fact that they are more likely to have a higher income and have access to a car. In Chapter 8 Bevan and Croucher highlight the importance of access to the car in enabling older people to use a choice of shops and facilities.

Table 6.3 Local purchasing patterns of rural residents (percentage spend)

Purchases of	Incomers			Long-term residents		
	Work locally	Commuters	Retired	Work locally	Commuters	Retired
Weekly shopping	10	5	7	21	0	22
Petrol	36	32	35	48	25	23
Milk	46	42	51	76	62	74
Newspapers	73	47	75	62	50	76

Source: Migration Impacts in Rural England, Countryside Agency (1999)

The LifeForce survey found that 80 per cent of rural respondents use supermarkets to do their food shopping, 35 per cent additionally or instead use local independent shops, and 5 per cent make use of the internet to purchase food. Such figures support research findings on the changing role of rural settlements as service centres that emphasise the high level of mobility and dispersed activity of rural residents. For example, while market towns play a key role fulfilling the service needs of their own residents, village and dispersed countryside residents are more likely to travel greater distances to other urban centres (Countryside Agency, 2004b).

The mobility of modern rural living and the high level of car ownership (70 per cent of rural LifeForce households have a car) mean that it is not surprising that, like the rest of the population, most older rural consumers have fairly peripatetic consumption patterns. However, a significant share of household spending is undertaken with local retailers, with older people – especially the retired – having a much higher propensity to shop locally than younger people. It should not be ignored that 30 per cent of rural LifeForce households do not have access to a car and this group is much more reliant on local shops.

For those concerned with the future sustainability of rural communities therefore, the continuation of a thriving retail sector is important not simply to support the poor and the disadvantaged but also to cater for the needs and preferences of older residents. The older rural consumer market is very significant and is expanding, but for its potential to be fully realised local organisations such as Chambers of Commerce and Economic Development Agencies should support local businesses to identify how to target and service this market better, in particular focusing on quality and customer service. For example, locally sourced food products is a segment which both taps into growing concern about healthy lifestyles and loyalty to the local area and has been shown to have considerable potential through the Farmers' Market movement. In some areas also, rural retailers have not been afraid to innovate to retain and extend their customer base through expanding the range of products and services they offer, the use of mobile shops, door-to-door delivery schemes and internet ordering.

A trip to the country – older people's contribution

An important dimension to the consumer patterns of older people and their impact on rural economies is tourism. Tourism for many rural economies is an increasingly important sector, supporting a range of businesses and acting as a major employer. For example in the North East of England, tourism (including day visitors) in the Northumberland Coast Area of Outstanding Natural Beauty results in an annual expenditure in the locality of over £72 million per annum (SQW, 2004). Likewise, it is estimated that the South West Coastal Path brings into the region an annual visitor spend of £300 million (South West Tourism and Tourism Associates, 2003).

The Great Britain Day Visit Survey (GBDVS) revealed that 62 per cent of adults in England took at least one leisure day visit to the countryside in 2002/03, totalling 1,126 million visits. People over 55 years old account for around a third of all visits to the countryside. The survey also demonstrated that residents of rural settlements are likely to make more countryside visits than urban residents, although the absolute number of urban visitors is larger (Countryside Agency, 2004a).

Figure 6.2 Number of countryside leisure day trips taken in the last 12 months by those aged over 55

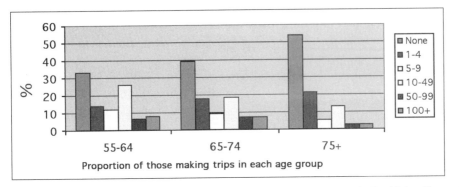

Source: Based on data from the Great Britain Day Visitor Survey (2002/03)
supplied by the Countryside Agency

Figure 6.2 demonstrates the frequency of visits to the countryside by older people, with 66.7 per cent of all those aged 55 to 64 visiting the countryside at least once a year and 40.5 per cent visiting once a month or more. The figures for the 65–74 age group are 60.5 per cent visit at least once a year or more and 33.6 per cent once a month or more. GBDVS identified that the average spend per leisure day trip in 2002/03 was £13.50; this suggests that the value of day trips to rural areas by older people could be somewhat in excess of £5 billion. This figure excludes expenditure by older people taking short breaks or holidays, which is also a signifi-cant market. A survey by nVision found that half (51 per cent) of people aged over 50 have a holiday in the UK of four nights or longer and half (51 per cent) have a short break of between one and three nights (quoted in Age Concern Research Services, 2005). Older leisure consum-ers unconstrained by commitments such as children's schooling are much more likely to visit countryside attractions off-peak, including mid week and in the shoulder months of the year, and are therefore an important target market for those promoting countryside destinations.

Interest in countryside recreation remains high among older age groups. The Ramblers' Association (2003) estimated that 528 million walking trips are made annually, resulting in a direct spend of £6 billion, and supporting around 200,000 full-time jobs. Most of this expendi-ture is generated by people aged over 50. In a recent survey looking at participation rates in sport and leisure activities, walking was the most popular activity, with 35 per cent of adults having participated in walking in the 4 weeks prior to being interviewed. The peak participa-tion rate was those in the age groups 45–59 at 40 per cent, with 37 per cent of those aged 60 to 69 having been on a walk within the previous month, and 22 per cent of those over 70 (Office for National Statistics, 2004). The Age Concern LifeForce survey found that 61 per cent of older people go for short walks regularly, with rural residents doing this more frequently than urban residents (Age Concern Research Services, 2005).

The trends for participation in countryside recreation among older people remain buoyant, despite the growing levels of physical inactivity within the general population. The Govern-ment is keen to promote regular moderate exercise, as a means of reducing the risk of coro-nary disease, cancer, osteoporosis and obesity (Department of Health, 2004). A range of or-ganisations such as the Countryside Agency, Sport England and the British Heart Foundation through schemes such as the Walking the Way to Health initiative have been actively working with health professionals and voluntary organisations to promote walking to improve overall health. It is not surprising, therefore, that there is a growing number of 'active' older people who are engaged in low impact physical activity such as walking for the benefit of both their physical and mental health. Rural areas offer not only an attractive destination for these older 'activity seekers', but also have everything to gain in ensuring they provide appropriate facilities and services to encourage these visitors to spend money in the local economy.

Conclusions

Those who are interested in the regeneration of rural economies cannot afford to stereotype the ageing population as a symptom or cause of rural economic decline. The ageing population is not only growing but also accounts for a growing proportion of national expenditure and wealth. What this chapter has demonstrated is that older people potentially have an important and increasing contribution to make to rural economies as both residents and visitors to the countryside. It is also clear that older people are becoming increasingly consumer focused in their outlook, and the demand for customer choice and quality is already influencing other aspects of their lives including their expectations of public services and health care.

Quite apart from the consumer patterns of individual older people explored in this chapter, there is also the considerable purchasing undertaken by the public and private sector on behalf of older people. It is estimated that around 10 per cent of the rural workforce are employed in health and social services (Commission for Rural Communities, 2005). The strength of the older rural consumer at an individual level, and cumulatively through the purchases made on their behalf by the public sector, was demonstrated during the foot and mouth crisis which had major impacts on both agriculture and tourism. The £1 billion pension income that flows into households in the county ensured a continued level of consumer spending and helped bolster the rural economy (Countryside Agency, 2003).

There is no doubt that the contribution of older people to rural economies merits much further research and analysis to better inform policy makers and businesses on how best to maximise the potential of older consumers to rural economies and on how to realise the potential value of expenditure on older people's services in rural areas; sound business and services planning demands nothing less. That is especially so within the context of an ageing population which is increasingly healthy and whose members seek to be active consumers exercising choice and control over the provision of the services they use.

References and further reading

Age Concern Research Services (2005) *Analysis of LifeForce 2004/5 Data – Urban/Rural Split* (unpublished)

Commission for Rural Communities (2005) *The State of the Countryside Report 2005*

Council of Mortgage Lenders (2001) *The Market for Equity Release Schemes,* London: Council of Mortgage Lenders

Countryside Agency (1999) *Migration Impacts in Rural England,* CAX19, Cheltenham: Countryside Agency

Countryside Agency (2003) *Rural Economies: Stepping Stones to Healthier Futures,* Cheltenham: Countryside Agency

Countryside Agency (2004a) *Great Britain Day Visitor Survey,* Cheltenham: Countryside Agency

Countryside Agency (2004b) *The Role of Settlements as Service Centres,* Research Note CRN 83, Cheltenham: Countryside Agency

Defra (2002) *Shops, Pubs and Post Offices,* Department for Environment, Food and Rural Affairs Factsheet

Defra (2004) *Social and Economic Change and Diversity in Rural England,* Rural Evidence Research Centre, Birkbeck College

Department of Health (2004) *Choosing Health: Making Healthier Choices Easier,* London: The Stationery Office

Department for Work and Pensions (2005) *Opportunity Age – Opportunity and Security Throughout Life,* London: HMSO

DTZ Pieda (2004) *Rural Economies of Yorkshire and the Humber,* a report prepared for the Countryside Agency

Huber, J. and Skidmore, P. (2003) *The New Old. Why the Baby Boomers Won't be Pensioned Off,* London: Desmos

Le Mesurier, N. (2003) *The Hidden Store – Older People's Contribution to Rural Communities,* London: Age Concern England

Marmot, M., Banks J., Blundell, R. et al (eds) (2003) *Health, Wealth and Lifestyles of the Older Population in England: The 2002 English Longitudinal Study of Ageing,* London: Institute of Fiscal Studies

Meadows, P. (2004) *The Economic Contribution of Older People: Report for Age Concern England,* London: Age Concern England

Metz, D. and Underwood, M. (2005) *Older Richer Fitter – Identifying the Customer Needs of Britain's Ageing Population,* London: Age Concern England

MORI (2001) *Embracing Technology,* The EGG report (December 2001)

MORI/Help the Aged (1999) *Grey Power, Booming Baby Boomers*

Office for National Statistics (2003) *Family Spending 2002,* London: HSMO

Office for National Statistics (2004) Social Trends in Sport and Leisure

Parkes, G. (Harper-Adams) (2005) *Action Plan for Rural Development Group to More Fully Utilize the Latent Economic Market Potential of Seniors in the Rural Areas,* West Midlands Business Council, available at http://www.wmbusinesscouncil.org.uk/ruralactionplan.html

Pension Commission (2004) *Pension Challenges and Choices; The First Report of the Pension Commission,* London: The Stationery Office

Plunkett Foundation (2005) *Rural Lifelines: Older People and Rural Social Enterprises*

Population Ageing Associates (2003) *The Implications of an Ageing Population for the Sustainable Development of the East of England*

Ramblers' Association (2003) *The Economic and Social Value of Walking in England*

Regeneris Consulting, Lydia Speakman Associates and Douglas Tourism Associates (2005) *Economic and Social Benefits of Countryside Access Routes in the North East* (unpublished report for the Countryside Agency)

Royal Commission on Long-term Care (1999) *With Respect to Old Age,* London: HMSO

South West Tourism and Tourism Associates (2003) *The Economic Value of the South West Coast Path*

SQW (2004) *The Economic Value of Protected Landscapes in the North East of England* (unpublished report for One North East and the Countryside Agency)

Wanless, D. (2002) *Securing Our Future Health, Taking a Long-Term View,* London: HMSO

Warnes, T. and McInerney, B. (2004) *The English Regions and Population Ageing,* Age Concern Reports

Chapter 7

The contributions of older people to rural community and citizenship

Nick Le Mesurier

Introduction

Rural policy assumes and increasingly relies upon cohesive and active communities in rural areas. In policy documents, 'Vital Villages' and 'community vibrancy' are presented as means and ends of both good governance and effective service delivery in rural areas (DETR/MAFF, 2000). Defra's Policy Paper on community capacity building and the voluntary sector specifically identifies the importance of 'social capital and of voluntary and community activity to the well-being of rural areas' (Defra, 2003, 2004).

What is rarely acknowledged in such documents is the key contribution of older people to the maintenance of a healthy civic society in rural areas through voluntary work, informal care and active involvement in a wide range of community groups. Retirement from paid employment and the end of rearing children bring opportunities of time, releasing people to offer skills and experience gained over many years and to engage in a wider variety of networks. Yet, where older people do feature in policy documents, it is often only in the context of their 'needs', their active contributions overshadowed by ageist stereotypes of dependency and decrepitude. The consequence is that the most vital source of social capital in the English countryside is little understood and somewhat overlooked.

The National Survey of Voluntary Activity (Office for National Statistics, 1997) found that 40 per cent of people aged 55–64, 45 per cent of those aged 65–74 and 35 per cent of those aged over 75 years old had undertaken some form of organised voluntary work during the previous year. Older people are also involved in a wide range of informal support activity, including caring for grandchildren and assistance to neighbours, as well as a range of collective leisure and recreational activities, from rambling clubs to the University of the Third Age. In rural areas they are more likely to be involved in voluntary groups, particularly pensioner and women's groups such as Age Concern or the Women's Institute (WI), or in church groups, all of which provide informal reciprocal contact and support (Wenger, 2001). Older people are also more likely to participate in and see themselves as part of a localised community. Many community institutions – from parish councils to local environmental schemes, from the provision of day care for other older people to Neighbourhood Watch schemes – rely heavily on their contributions. A study of the experience of ageing in place has identified 'the enormous commitment to and capacity for involvement in community' on the part of older people, and suggests that this 'outward and other centred approach to life' is a 'potential resource that can be built upon within localities to support and sustain healthy communities' (Godfrey et al, 2004).

The capacity to build and maintain community links and other social networks is often understood and interpreted through the concept of social capital, and that is the approach adopted in this chapter. Social capital takes a variety of forms, often termed bonding, bridging and linking social capital. The chapter will look at these three forms of social capital in more detail to help tease out why a sense of belonging and community participation are so important and what they mean for the lived experience of rural residents. In particular it will look at the ways in which older people participate in voluntary groups and organisations, and how those contributions bring both individual and group benefits to the quality of life and help to maintain the essential 'glue' of rural society. It will also identify social and cultural changes which are impacting on the social capital of rural communities, and the implications for policy.

The concept of 'social capital'

The term social capital, which characterises relationships of reciprocity, is largely associated with the work of the American political scientist Robert Putnam. In his article 'Bowling alone: America's declining social capital', Putnam explains social capital by analogy with:

> '... notions of physical capital and human capital – tools and training that enhance individual productivity – "social capital" refers to features of social organisations such as networks, norms, and social trust that facilitate co-ordination and co-operation for mutual benefit.'

(Putnam, 1995)

The central premise of social capital is that social networks have value. Who people know and what they do for each other result in levels of trust, reciprocity and co-operation. Social capital is to some extent a quite tangible phenomenon, manifest in exchanges of information, in collective actions and in identification with groups – a 'we' mentality rather than an 'I' mentality. In a pivotal study of the performance of local governments in Italy after their introduction in 1970, Putnam concluded that 'the stock of social capital in a region – for example as measured by the density of citizens' participation in community organisations (choral societies, soccer leagues, Rotary clubs and the like) turned out to be the best predictor of local government performance' (Kawachi and Kennedy, 1997). This performance was measured in terms of the presence of civic institutions and services, such as 'day care programmes and job-training centres, promoting investment and economic development, pioneering environmental standards and family clinics'. Those regions where citizens were traditionally engaged by public issues, where social and political networks were organised horizontally, not hierarchically, and where social issues were perceived to be everybody's business, not just the responsibility of those in power, were found to correlate strongly with higher local levels of community participation and trust than those where these were thought to be somebody else's problem (Putnam, 1993).

Social capital is a fragile thing, however, and the processes by which it is damaged or enhanced are complex and often indirect. Factors such as the decrease in membership of community groups and the increasing tendency towards individualised and private consumption, such as watching television, are seen by many as diminishing the stock of social capital available to a community. Migration, to some extent, can also affect the quality of social capital. Wenger (1995) identified a correlation between community stability and the quality of informal support networks of older people which somewhat belied the myth that rural communities are necessarily closer and more supportive. Many rural communities have become so-called 'dormitory villages', serving as locations from which people commute out in the day and return to in the evening. Without the presence of certain institutions that help promote social capital these can be lonely places indeed, even for those with the means to escape to other locations, either physically or virtually by means of the internet and other media.

Almost by definition, voluntary and community groups and organisations draw upon and contribute to networks and resources that are already there. Many activities go on day after day contributing to a community's social capital. Neighbourhood Watch schemes are a formal example of social capital in action; instances of neighbours 'popping in' to see if someone is 'all right' are a less formal example. Collective efforts to raise funds for a school or to protest against a development scheme help to form social capital. Friendship networks, clubs and societies also help to form social capital. An information and advice service is a mechanism to help promote social capital. Volunteering itself is a direct means of promoting social capital. In different ways they each involve relationships of trust, engagement and reciprocity.

Different forms of social capital

In their reviews of social capital and the voluntary sector, Jochum (2002) and Yates and Jochum (2003) draw upon Putnam's work to describe two types of social capital, and on Woolcock (2001) for a third:

'Bonding social capital *involves closed networks and describes strong ties within homogeneous groups, primarily among family members, close friends and neighbours.*

'Bridging social capital … *involves overlapping networks where (members) of one group access the resources of another group through overlapping membership. It describes weaker, more diffuse ties with, for instance, distant friends or work colleagues, and other communities.*

'Linking social capital *relates to the connections between individuals and groups in hierarchical or power-based relationships. It describes social relationships with those in authority and relates specifically to the capacity to leverage resources, ideas and information from formal institutions beyond the community.'*

Each of these types of social capital has implications for the way the involvement of older people in the English countryside is understood. This chapter looks at each type in turn and considers some of the ways they work in practice, and what the implications for policy are. These forms of social capital do not operate as discrete entities, however, and in practice are often mediated via close and shifting networks of relationships between individuals, groups, agencies and institutions. Thus a group of people may draw upon bonding social capital to meet some purposes, and bridging or linking social capital for others, often at the same time.

Bonding social capital – the lived reality

Bonding social capital is associated with high levels of personalised reciprocity and trust. It is the 'glue' that binds people together. It is made up of 'horizontal' connections between individuals such as family, friendship or neighbourly ties that give a shared sense of identity and help people get along with each other. Through such ties individuals may have access to a variety of resources, including practical, material and financial help, emotional support, advice, information and personal validation.

Many community groups and local voluntary services depend upon bonding social capital for their very existence. Bonding social capital helps people to identify with their neighbours and to recognise shared endeavours and goals. It can also help to address feelings of isolation and promote self-confidence. While it tends to be strongest among homogeneous groups in which there is a sense of shared identity, that identity can be extended by the activities of the group to include the whole community.

An example of a complex institution that lives by and through social capital in many forms, but is particularly dependent upon a sense of shared identity and social responsibility, is the rural church. Anglican and other churches are present in almost every settlement in the country. At an individual level, faith affiliation is, along with age and social class, one of the strongest predictors of social engagement (Francis, 2003, cited in Langrish, 2005). The inclusiveness of church communities means that they often comprise members who otherwise would be vulnerable or isolated, as well as those who are better connected. Of note, in this context, is that the rural church has a disproportionate number of older people within its congregations; nationally the Church of England estimates that over two-thirds of church-goers are aged over 50, but in dioceses such as York, which covers a large rural hinterland, three-quarters of church-goers are over 50 (Church Life Profile, 2001).

The rural church is closely linked with a wide range of arts and cultural events, fêtes, fairs and festivals, as well as the ongoing social and spiritual ministry to the community, providing a focus that is felt at every level. Church resources provide physical capital, in the form of buildings that can be used for things like mother and toddler groups, school visits, exhibitions, educational activities and social care services. They also provide human capital in the form of skills and experience, and financial capital in the form of monies raised for local initiatives and other charitable causes. The Church can speak up, too, for those who are disadvantaged, and can act flexibly and in accordance with local needs and facilities in ways that statutory agencies cannot. Rural churches are deeply connected to a whole range of groups and institutions within the community, but are also present in relationships outside the local community, thereby strengthening bridging and linking social capital too.

SHEEPY MAGNA POST OFFICE

The post office in Sheepy Magna, Leicestershire, closed in 2003 leaving a vacuum in a village where there are many older people and/or people who lack transport. The vicar and Parochial Church Council offered All Saints' vestry as a replacement space. Following approval from the Post Office, the Borough Council and Church authorities, 12 modest grants were obtained to set up a satellite post office, and provide a disabled WC and a community help desk. It now opens two mornings a week, and is used by 40–50 people weekly. The community help desk, staffed by the Borough Council, advises on everything from planning permission to recycling; a pensions advice service is being added.

(The Archbishops' Council, 2004)

Voluntary self-help groups are a secular example of bonding social capital in action. As the Rural Lifelines report which surveyed a sample of such groups found, not only are the management boards dominated by people over 50, but the majority of volunteers are in their 60s and 70s (Plunkett Foundation et al, 2005). One example is the Northern Fells Group based in Cumbria, which covers eight remote parishes. The group runs volunteer-led services such as community transport, a luncheon club and a 'lend-a-hand' scheme offering neighbourly support to those incapacitated in any way. As one volunteer explained:

> 'An underlying principle of all that we do is no one ever feels that they are accepting charity or being patronised by do-gooders.'
>
> (Volunteer, quoted in Age Concern 2005)

TALTON VILLAGE SHOP

In 1993 the village of Talton in Devon was told that its post office and shop was due to close. With support from the Village Retail Service Association a steering group of villagers was formed, and funding secured to open the shop in 1994 as a community-owned enterprise. The shop currently has a turnover of £50,000 per year. The whole community benefits from the shop, but particularly older people. The shop is run and staffed mainly by older people acting as volunteers. There are over 30 volunteers. The majority of them are over 60 years old and originally met through the Women's Institute. The shop now recruits new volunteers through door-to-door approaches, particularly to involve newcomers and occupiers of holiday cottages.

(Plunkett Foundation et al, 2005)

The contribution of social capital to health

There is increasing empirical evidence that social capital is a significant contributor to people's ability to maintain health into and throughout later life. Put simply, people who are socially integrated live longer (Berkman and Syme, 1979; House et al, 1988; Kawachi et al, 1996). Socially isolated people are more likely to suffer illness and premature mortality, presumably reflecting a lack of forms of support, whether emotional or instrumental (eg financial aid) (Kawachi and Kennedy, 1997). However, the causal mechanisms relating social isolation – and its converse, social engagement – to health are far from understood. One possible explanation is that many social activities encourage a certain amount of physical activity, although that is not their explicit purpose. It therefore often goes unrecognised and unrecorded, but nevertheless has beneficial effects that reduce the risk of functional decline. This in turn reduces health and social care costs (Everard et al, 2000).

An example of the use that health bodies have made of social capital to promote health and well-being is the partnership created by the Central Cornwall Primary Care Trust and the Women's Institute to raise awareness of falls prevention and osteoporosis using peer-led heath education. The Ageing Well programme provided by Age Concern is another practical example (Age Concern England, 2002). It recruits and trains local volunteers aged over 50 to become Senior Health Mentors. They then make contact with isolated people and community groups, providing vital links to health services and opportunities. Such volunteers, as 'normal everyday people', act as positive role models in overcoming the common perception that health is linked only to medical services. Indeed, Ageing Well provides advice on a range of issues, including diet/nutrition, physical activity and falls prevention. In County Durham the programme works in partnership with local health providers and has become an important means of promoting health improvement programmes locally to older residents (Le Mesurier, 2003).

At a more abstract level, there have been some attempts to measure the association between social activity, through which social capital may emerge, and health. A study by Glass et al (1999) measured the association between social and productive activities (such as participation in social groups or playing games, and gardening, shopping, or volunteering) and mortality over a 13-year period with a cohort of 2,761 older Americans. The results indicated a link between survival and social activities even when these involved little or no physical exertion (though many involved some physical activity) (Riddoch, 2000). This may be due in part to reduced levels of psychological stress, the promotion of self-efficacy, a sense of purpose in life, and enhanced social networks, all of which have been linked to survival in a number of studies. One well-known example examined the association between social and community ties and mortality in a random sample of almost 7,000 adults over 9 years in California. A strong association was found between a lack of social contact and an increased risk of mortality (Berkman and Syme, 1979). The findings were reported as independent of self-reported physical health, socio-economic status, and a wide range of common health-related behaviours such as excessive eating, alcohol consumption and smoking.

Furthermore, the strength of an older person's social and support networks has been shown to directly relate to their ability to cope with increasing frailty. A study in Israel explored the relationship between social network type and morale in over 2,000 older people (Letwin, 2001). Those with broad networks that included a wide range of friends as well as family reported higher levels of morale than those with more restricted or exclusively family networks. Broad and supportive networks were found to be second only to freedom from disability in predicting morale – a finding which further reinforces the value placed by many older people on friendships and relationships, as well as family (Langan et al, 1996).

The activities of many voluntary organisations – such as community transport, or luncheon clubs or walking groups – can therefore have indirect 'mental' health benefits that are likely to go unrecognised and are certainly not acknowledged in the labels they attract in public policies and strategies, such as 'support services' or 'leisure activities'. Their value goes beyond the facilitation of individual welfare, by strengthening the capacity of whole communities to access essential resources and wider social networks through which people have greater opportunities to flourish. In rural areas, where distance and limited infrastructure may further diminish the opportunities for disadvantaged and socially excluded people to participate, the work done by voluntary and community groups and organisations is often crucial.

Policies that seek to support the health of older people in the countryside need to recognise that health benefits cannot always be measured quantitatively, and that quality of life, including contentment and self-respect, can do much to promote well-being and independence (Clark et al, 1998).

Bridging social capital – the contribution of the voluntary sector

As well as providing innumerable opportunities for people to get together and work for the good of the local community, voluntary organisations also facilitate joint working and partnerships with other organisations and groups, many of which are informal and are mediated through individual relationships. Voluntary and community groups in the countryside depend upon a grass-roots approach, working closely with local people, often to a precise local mission. Increasingly, Government policy looks to those voluntary sector organisations that can provide the bridging social capital to give a denser infrastructure in the countryside. Services that can provide a 'one-stop shop' are good examples of how bridging and bonding social capital can be enhanced.

Yates and Jochum (2003) describe a Healthy Living Centre Partnership that operates in a large village and is run on the basis of a cross-sectoral partnership led by a voluntary sector provider. The centre has links to a range of other local clubs and community institutions, such as the local school, gardening and other activity groups. Its primary aim is to provide health benefits through an integrated package of services to those who are particularly vulnerable, such as people with mental health problems, the unemployed and those who are socially isolated (many of whom may be older people), but it also provides a range of opportunities for local people to volunteer.

For agencies involved in the provision of social services in the countryside, one of the many challenges is to match those services to local needs, and here the role of local contacts and volunteers may be crucial. Local and individual needs are not always apparent on the surface, and the response to them must be diverse and flexible enough to be both personal and sensitive to changing circumstances and requirements. Bringing services to people in sparsely populated areas requires innovative responses which, if they are to reflect local needs and draw upon local support, depend upon a thorough understanding of the way particular communities are structured and perceive themselves.

Services that are grounded in the communities they serve can have an advantage in that they are 'owned' by those communities and are less restricted by procedural regulation imposed from above. In this sense, voluntary sector organisations have an advantage in that they function on the strength of local support and integration. They also have a degree of flexibility in their working procedures, which accords with the need for providers to disseminate responsibility to a variety of locations in order to respond sensitively to a range of local circumstances and changing local needs. The role of management in such an organisation is thus concerned less with procedural regulation than the promotion and maintenance of quality, the volume of output and the facilitation of local outposts (Cumella and Le Mesurier, 1999).

If a service is to become part of the fabric of the community it must be seen to belong to that community. Relationships of trust take time to develop, and grow on the basis of personal contact and reputation. In both the development and maintenance of rural voluntary services it is important to identify and include key people and to be aware that in rural areas such people are more likely to perform multiple, often unpaid, roles. In this sense, reliance on a small number of well-connected people is both necessary and useful, as links can quickly be made through personal contact. Local people possess the information required to ensure that a service is used and maintained.

If local networks are used well, not only do people take ownership of a service, but flexible planning, in which the minutiae of parochial differences are recognised, can be reflected in the outcome. Small details, such as knowledge of the local bus times or other events, can make or mar an initiative's chances of success, and recruiting support through local networks helps to ensure that the service remains congruent, reflecting local need over time. The danger of a service closing for lack of support by volunteers or information about need or availability of resources is reduced if local links are maintained. Ideally the service should act as a focal point for the community to which other services may be added when required, thus enriching local infrastructure.

AGE CONCERN MOBILE DAY CENTRE

The Mobile Day Centre (MDC) provided by Age Concern Leominster & District offers regular day services for older people in surrounding rural parishes. Funded jointly by the local authority and other funders, it aims to reduce social isolation by providing accessible day care to older people who live too far away from day centre services in the county. Meetings can be held in many different locations, including village and church halls, sheltered housing schemes and school halls. Transport and a hot meal are provided, and there is access to hairdressing, foot-care and counselling services.

Assessments are made by Age Concern staff, and referrals come from social workers and health professionals as well as members themselves or their friends or families. The range of needs is wide, as there are few if any alternative provisions available locally. Members tend to stay with the service for a long time; often, older people begin their association as volunteers, and in time become members as their needs change. In practice it is often difficult to tell who is who.

Significantly, the MDC acts as a gateway through which members can access other agencies and services, such as the Citizens' Advice Bureau, Benefits Agency and Age Concern's own local information service. It can thus be seen to provide bridging as well as bonding social capital, not only to the older people who use it but also to the community, including family members and local businesses and institutions who provide facilities or services to it.

(Le Mesurier and Duncan, 2002)

Linking social capital – the role of partnerships and the recruitment of older volunteers

The changing nature of rural governance means that few local organisations can afford to operate without links to larger, often public, organisations or ignore pressures to adopt standards and formal procedures if they are to access additional sources of funding. At the same time public bodies seek to connect with voluntary organisations to get a better understanding of the needs of rural residents and to improve the delivery of services.

Partnerships are increasingly the way by which Government initiatives are mediated, and are especially important in the countryside where joined-up working and integration is providing the key to delivering a range of services to dispersed rural communities. The aim of partnerships is to 'offer a blending of resources from the public, private and voluntary sectors which adds up to more than the sum of its parts' (Goodwin, 2003). Effective partnerships allow local voices to be heard and foster a sense of shared objectives and a common commitment to local development. In recent years the Government has promoted partnerships as a cornerstone of rural policy, calling for 'strong partnerships between county, district and town and parish councils, supporting and encouraging rural communities on matters which local councils can manage themselves, and working in partnership on wider local services' (DETR/MAFF, 2000).

Such partnerships take a variety of forms and include formal structures such as Older People's Forums, Local Strategic Partnerships and Rural Transport Partnerships, as well as more informal partnerships with bodies such as the Rural Community Council or local authorities who are in a position to help access funding and resources. Woods et al (2003) note the high level of community governance present in the countryside:

> '... leadership activity in rural communities is vibrant, diverse in format, and often successful in drawing down resources from external bodies to the community. Rural areas generate more applications for support from the Lottery Funds per head of population than urban areas, and have a higher success rate in turning applications into grants. Rural areas also have a greater number of voluntary sector community groups registered with national and regional associations per head of population than urban areas, providing more opportunities for participation. And there are nearly 80,000 people across England and Wales engaged in service as town, parish and community councillors, directly involved in the governance of their communities.'

Older people, already at the heart of voluntary bodies in rural areas and active in community leadership, often occupy positions of responsibility in local partnerships representing their community.

Such is the extent of partnership working in the countryside that one might conclude that it has become an industry in its own right, complete with its own professional class. Edwards et al (2000) enumerated over 150 partnerships operating in three counties solely in the area of rural regeneration. Most of these were only a few years old, and had been formed in response to policy changes that imposed a requirement that partnerships be formed in order to access resources.

Perhaps, inevitably, it is the larger voluntary groups, often with a professional structure or members that come from a professional background, that are best equipped to engage directly in formal partnerships.

> '... active participation in local partnerships requires an inordinate amount of time, much of it spent in meetings. The people who typically emerge as community leaders and who end up as the community representatives on partnership bodies are often dynamic individuals who have developed skills in mobilising their communities, developing community networks and articulating the needs and demands of their communities'
>
> (cited in Goodwin, 2003)

In any scramble for resources it is the strong that are likely to succeed over the weak. Not only is there disparity between the ability of different voluntary organisations and local interests in their ability to attract resources but also, as Goodwin (2003) notes, the ideal of equal representation from public, private and voluntary sectors via partnership is rarely met in practice. Moreover, a distinct hierarchy can be observed, with the public sector retaining the greatest influence in strategic discussion and decision making, and the private and voluntary sectors engaged at a more local level in partnerships focused on issues of service delivery. Factors such as time, professional expertise, confidence and resources, as well as forms of discourse that belong to paid public sector officials rather than the locations and communities in which people live, can serve to militate against genuine community engagement.

Maintaining and supporting the voluntary sector

For all the contributions to social capital that older people make to local communities through volunteering, it might be argued that there are risks inherent in too great a reliance upon what is, often, an ageing corps of people willing to devote time, energy and commitment to serving others in their community. Many organisations operating in the countryside recognise that they depend on older people who have the time as well as the personal association with the place in which they live. English Nature, for example, manages sites for nature conservation across the countryside and in doing so relies heavily on the assistance of local volunteers. Half its volunteer workforce is aged over 50, and almost 1 in 10 is over 70. Older people are seen as bringing experience, skills and time to the work of the organisation, and it is often older volunteers who take on the daily work involved with being a site warden. Loyalty to the organisation is strong, and recent negotiations have extended the insurance cover available to allow volunteers to participate after their 80th birthday, a move which was made in part to retain the skills and dedication of its ageing volunteers, but also to recognise the value of older volunteers to the organisation more generally (Le Mesurier, 2004). As with other agencies that are equally reliant on volunteers, English Nature will also need to consider how to present itself to attract fresh generations of older people.

The general ageing of experienced volunteers in many voluntary bodies represents a diminishing resource which must be continuously refreshed. However, the willingness of people to volunteer is coming under severe pressure from a number of factors, including more individualised and market-oriented lifestyles, migration and family break-up. Many of the larger voluntary bodies have therefore recognised the need to adopt new ways of organising, recruiting and retaining volunteers, promoting in some cases a new 'career' in voluntary work and offering a variety of experiences and access to training and recognition of skills. Indeed there are plenty of examples where older people now work in a paid capacity for a voluntary organisation or social enterprise.

Some organisations actively seek to recruit volunteers from large employers, targeting those who are about to retire, inviting older workers to see the opportunities available to them and presenting volunteering in a positive light. Leaders of the voluntary sector argue for Government support for employers to release staff for voluntary activities, particularly for more time-consuming roles such as serving as a board member or trustee. Such a scheme is currently in place for members of the voluntary fire services, the Territorial Army and the National Lifeboat Association (Le Mesurier, 2004).

The need to maintain a strong voluntary sector thus demands an increasingly creative approach not only by individual organisations themselves, but, given the recognition of their value to the community, within public policy as well, particularly to address certain generic challenges. For example, by general experience, recruitment of volunteers has been found to be more difficult in some parts of the country than in others (Le Mesurier, 2004), which may call for some very targeted encouragement if a decided patchiness in volunteering activity is to be avoided (see Chapter 8). In addition, specific help may be needed for smaller and more localised voluntary groups to adopt the more professional and systematic approaches to the recruitment and retention of volunteers pursued already by some of the larger voluntary organisations.

In valuing the social capital and vibrancy of communities, partners also need to recognise that the changes in regulation governing service provision, and an increasing emphasis on training to national standards for volunteers as well as staff, sometimes as a precondition of grant awards, places heavy burdens on small organisations. Many voluntary bodies operate, to a certain extent, on good will and sense of duty to the local community from its members, and there is often a delicate balance between sensible regulation and enabling grass-roots organisations to flourish and grow in an organic way that reflects the needs and values of their community.

Conclusions

Social capital is an important measure of the health of communities. It is defined as the extent and means to which people co-operate with and help each other, often through informal relationships, but also through membership of groups and organisations and participation in community roles. Social capital cannot be imposed on or created for people. Community based organisations can, however, provide the means by which people, including a large proportion of older people living in rural communities, enhance their own and others' social capital.

The extent to which older people are active in rural communities, and the holding of office within community institutions such as the Parish Council, the Women's Institute, the local church or local Age Concern groups, belies stereotypes of dependency and age. Groups run by and for older people are an important part of the rural infrastructure, offering activities and social support, as well as part of the fabric of rural life providing indirect benefits in terms of personal health and social cohesion.

As the rural baby boomers grow older they too will bring with them a vast range of skills, knowledge, energy and interests that can help to make the countryside a worthwhile place to live in. However, as Baker and Speakman demonstrate in Chapter 6, they are likely to be more consumerist in their expectations of service delivery, and the impact of more and potentially wealthier in-migrants will also shape the future of rural social capital. While it is unlikely that the countryside will see a significant decline of social capital, the institutional and cultural structures through which it is developed and maintained will change to meet the needs of these new generations. There is no doubt that in a rural society with an increasingly wealthy older population social capital could accrue to those with already substantial financial and human capital resources, further disenfranchising the disadvantaged. For the larger voluntary organisations and statutory authorities, which have duties to ensure equal access to services and resources, this means that there is a duty to ask whose social capital shall be enhanced as a consequence of their activities. For the downside of social capital – particularly bonding social capital – is exclusiveness, as members are recruited who share similar profiles to those already established. In embracing social capital rural policy makers need to be sure that they do not create a rural landscape of the haves and the have-nots.

References and further reading

Age Concern England (2002) *Ageing Well UK*, available at http://www.ageconcern.org.uk/AgeConcern/staying_64.htm

Age Concern England (2005) *Delivering for Older People in Rural Areas – A Good Practice Guide*

The Archbishops' Commission on Rural Areas (ACORA) (1990) *Faith in the Countryside: A Report Presented to the Archbishops of Canterbury and York,* Stoneleigh Park, Warwickshire: ACORA

The Archbishops' Council (2004) *Building Faith in Our Future,* London: Church House Publishing

Berkman, L.F. and Syme, S.L. (1979) 'Social networks, host resistance and mortality: a nine-year follow-up study of Alameda County residents', *American Journal of Epidemiology* 109, 186–204

Blackmore, A., Bush, H. and Bhutta, M. (2005) *The Reform of Public Services: The Role of the Voluntary Sector,* London: National Council for Voluntary Organisations

Church Life Profile (2001) *Churches Information for Mission*

Clark, H. et al (1998) *That Bit of Help: The High Value of Low Level Preventative Services for Older People,* Bristol: The Policy Press

Cooper, H., Arber, S., Fee, L. and Ginn, J. (1999) *The Influence of Social Support and Social Capital on Health: A Review and Analysis of British Data,* London: Health Education Authority

Countryside Agency (2002) *The State of the Countryside 2002,* Cheltenham: Countryside Agency

Countryside Agency (2004) *The State of the Countryside 2004,* Cheltenham: Countryside Agency

Cumella, S. and Le Mesurier, N. (1999) *Re-designing Health and Social Care for Older People: Multi-Skill Case Teams in Primary Care,* Managing Community Care, Brighton: Pavilion

Defra (2003) *Community Capacity Building and Voluntary Sector Infrastructure in Rural England,* London

Defra (2004) *The Rural Strategy,* London: The Stationery Office

DETR/MAFF (Department of Environment, Transport and the Regions/Ministry of Agriculture, Fisheries and Food) (2000) *Our Countryside: the Future – A Fair Deal for Rural England,* London: The Stationery Office

Dunn, J., Hodge, I., Monk, S. and Kiddle, C. (1998) *Developing Indicators of Rural Disadvantage,* Salisbury: The Rural Development Commission

Edwards, B., Goodwin, M., Pemberton, S. and Woods, M. (2000) *Partnership Working in Rural Regeneration,* Bristol: Policy Press

England Marketing (2004) *National Volunteer Survey 2003: Report For English Nature*

Everard, K.M., Lach, H.W., Fisher, E.B. and Baum, M.C. (2000) 'Relationship of activity and social support to the functional health of older adults', *The Journals of Gerontology Series B: Psychological and Social Sciences* 55, S208–S212

Francis, L.J. (2003) Religion and social capital: the flaw in the 2001 census in England and Wales, in P. Avis (ed) *Public Faith: The State of Religious Belief and Practice in Britain,* London: SPCK

Glass, T.A., de Leon, C.M., Marottoli, R.A. and Berkman, L.F. (1999) 'Population based study of social and productive indicators of survival among elderly Americans', *British Medical Journal* 319, 478–483

Godfrey, M., Townsend, J. and Denby, T. (2004) *Building a Good Life for Older People in Local Communities: The Experience of Ageing in Time and Place,* York: Joseph Rowntree Foundation

Goodwin M. (2003) *Rural Governance: A Review of Relevant Literature,* a paper prepared for ESRC, Countryside Agency and Defra, available at http://www.defra.gov.uk/rural/pdfs/research/governance_lit_review.pdf

Hall, P.A. (1999) 'Social capital in Britain', *British Journal of Political Science* 29, 417–459

House, J.S., Landis, K.R. and Umberson, D. (1988) 'Social relationships and health', *Science* 214, 540–545

James, G.R. (2005) Parish governance: has Dibley a future? in J. Martineau, L.J. Francis and P. Francis (eds) *Changing Rural Life: A Christian Response to Key Rural Issues,* Norwich: Canterbury Press

Jochum, V. (2002) *Social Capital and the Voluntary Sector in Britain,* London: National Council for Voluntary Organisations

Kawachi, I. and Kennedy, B.P. (1997) 'Health and social cohesion: Why care about income inequality?', *British Medical Journal* 314, 1037–1040

Kawachi, I., Colditz, G.A., Ascherio, A., Rimm, E.B., Giovannucci, E., Stampfer, M.J. et al. (1996) 'A prospective study of social networks in relation to total mortality and cardiovascular disease in men in the US'. *Journal of Epidemiology and Community Health* 50, 245–251

Langan, J., Means, R. and Rolfe, S. (1996) *Maintaining Independence in Later Life: Older People Speaking,* Kidlington, Oxfordshire: Anchor Trust

Langrish, M.L. (2005) Dynamics of community, in J. Martineau, L.J. Francis and P. Francis (eds) *Changing Rural Life: A Christian Response to Key Rural Issues,* Norwich: Canterbury Press

Le Mesurier, N. (2003) *The Hidden Store: Older People's Contributions to Rural Communities,* London: Age Concern England

Le Mesurier, N. (2004) A telephone survey of rural voluntary organisations (unpublished)

Le Mesurier, N. and Duncan, G. (2000) *Over the Hills and Far Away – Providing Accessible Day Care Services for Older People in Rural Areas,* Managing Community Care, Brighton: Pavilion Publishing

Letwin, H. (2001) 'Social network type and morale in old age', *The Gerontologist* 41, 516–524

Leveson Foundation (2004) *Working with Older People: A Resource Directory for Churches,* available at http://rps.gn.apc.org/leveson/index.htm

McLaughlin, B. (1986) 'The rhetoric and reality of rural deprivation', *Journal of Rural Studies* 2 (4), 291–307

Murphy, D. (2001) 'Working with older volunteers', speech to the National Volunteer Managers Forum, 'Diversity and Social Exclusion', available at http://www.csv.org.uk/Volunteer/Senior+Volunteers/RSVP+Directors+speech+2001.htm

Office for National Statistics (1997) *The National Survey of Voluntary Activity,* London: The Stationery Office

Office of the Deputy Prime Minister (2003) *The Quality Parish and Town Council Scheme,* available at http://www.odpm.gov.uk/stellent/groups/odpm_localgov/documents/page/odpm_locgov_022517.hcsp

Plunkett Foundation, PRIME, Cambridge Interdisciplinary Research Centre on Ageing (2005) *Rural Lifelines,* Plunkett Foundation

Putnam, R. (1993) 'The prosperous community: social capital and public life', *The American Prospect* 4 (13), 21 March

Putnam, R. (1995) 'Bowling alone: America's declining social capital', *Journal of Democracy* 6 (1), 65–78

Putnam, R. (1996) 'The strange disappearance of civic America', *The American Prospect* 7 (24)

Riddoch, C. (2000) 'Activities have been confused' (letter), *British Medical Journal,* 320, 184

Shucksmith, M. (2000) *Exclusive Countryside? Social Exclusion and Regeneration in Rural Areas,* London: Joseph Rowntree Foundation

Shucksmith, M., Roberts, D., Chapman, P. and Conway, E. (1996) *Disadvantage in Rural Areas,* Salisbury: Rural Development Commission

Wenger, G.C. (1995) 'A comparison of urban with rural support networks: Liverpool and North Wales', *Ageing & Society* 15, 59–81

Wenger, G.C. (2001) 'Myths and realities of ageing in rural Britain', *Ageing & Society* 21 (1), 117–130

Woolcock, M. (2001) 'The place of social capital in understanding social and economic outcomes', *Isuma* 2 (1), 11–17, available at http://www.isuma.net/v02n01/woolcock/woolcock_e.pdf

Woods, M., Edwards, B., Anderson, J. and Gardner, G. (2003) *Participation, Power and Rural Community Governance in England and Wales: Full Report of Research Activities and Results,* available at http://www.aber.ac.uk/communitygovernance/esrcsummary.pdf

World Health Organisation (1947) 'The constitution of the World Health Organisation', *WHO Chronicle 1*

Wuthnow, R. (1994) *Sharing The Journey: Support Groups and America's New Quest for Community,* New York: The Free Press

Yates, H. (2002) *Supporting Rural Voluntary Action,* London: NCVO, The Countryside Agency

Yates, H. and Jochum, V. (2003) *It's Who You Know that Counts: The Role of the Voluntary Sector in the Development of Social Capital in Rural Areas,* London: NCVO Publications

Chapter 8

Delivering services for older people in rural areas

Mark Bevan and Karen Croucher

Introduction

This chapter looks at how 'rurality' influences the services older people receive in rural areas. In particular it focuses on the impact of the relative remoteness of communities from main service centres, the growing centralisation of services and the dispersed pattern of rural settlements on the lives of older residents. It also looks at the issues to be addressed by those commissioning and providing services if they are to meet the needs of an ageing population.

The Government's publication *Opportunity Age* (Department for Work and Pensions, 2005) sets out the objective to promote well-being, independence and accessibility, with older people as active consumers of public services – exercising control and choice about the way services are designed and delivered – rather than as passive recipients. This vision offers the potential to improve the quality of life for older people, particularly those who are more vulnerable, but, if the vision is to be realised, the implications for local service delivery will be profound. The proportion of people aged over 60 in most rural districts is already more than a quarter of the population, and this is forecast in many areas to increase to around half over the next two decades (see Chapter 2). All services in local authorities – and not just those dedicated to the care of older citizens – will have to adjust to reflect the changing profile of the local population. That calls for a holistic approach to older people's lives embracing a wide range of service usage including transport, leisure and planning, rather than the pigeonholing of older people's interests within social services departments. However, if greater equity of access is to be achieved, then the poor mobility and isolation of many older rural residents will require imaginative and innovative approaches to service delivery.

This chapter builds on the existing evidence concerning the provision of services to older people by drawing on the experience and attitudes of older rural residents themselves, as well as the outlook of those involved in designing and delivering appropriate services to meet their needs. The chapter identifies a number of key issues to be addressed not only by local service commissioners and providers in the future but also by national and regional policy makers, particularly in relation to resource allocation and planning.

The chapter draws on the findings of a research project undertaken for the Countryside Agency and the Housing Corporation that examined the housing and support needs of older people aged 55 and over in rural areas. The project involved detailed interviews with over 70 older people and a further 57 interviews with officials of provider agencies in both the statutory and voluntary sectors. The older people who were invited to participate in the research were selected to reflect a diverse range of ages and also circumstances in rural areas, including people living in the private and public rented sectors, and homeowners. Some respondents had lived in the same village or settlement all their lives, others were local to their area of residence, and others had retired or moved in later life to live in the countryside. Most of the older participants lived alone, and many of these had cared for a partner who had since died. Others lived with their partners or other family members. Some people enjoyed good health, and others did not. The younger participants were usually in paid employment. Many undertook some type of voluntary activity. The research was undertaken in five rural districts: Scarborough in North Yorkshire, Bromsgrove in Worcestershire, North Dorset, Pendle in Lancashire and Waveney in Suffolk. Apart from providing a good regional spread these districts were chosen to cover a variety of rural areas including remote, coastal, traditional retirement and mixed urban/rural areas.

Older people's concerns

The interviews with older residents and provider agencies yielded insights into the realities of rural living and highlighted the main issues that concerned older people in rural areas. These included:

- transport;
- isolation;
- support for independent living.

Transport

In all the interviews a dominant theme was the inadequacy of transport services in rural areas. The significance of the means of access to services for older people cannot be underestimated. The location of their home in relation to the services, facilities and transport they used was often of greater concern to people than the type of accommodation they were living in. The cost of transport – whether private car ownership or other means of getting about – was seen to make living in the countryside relatively more expensive than elsewhere. National data confirms that people living in rural areas do spend the most on transport and furthermore transport was identified as a key priority during consultation by the newly formed Countryside Agency in 1999 and has remained a constant theme in subsequent consultations and research (Countryside Agency, 2000, page 12; Countryside Agency 2005, page 59).

While many younger residents take for granted the mobility of rural living, older people increasingly recognise their own transport dependency. As one respondent remarked, whatever service or activity is being planned or provided, transport has to be considered from the outset. In particular, the ability to drive was seen to be a key factor in independent living in the countryside. Ease of access to friends or family, to shops, to services and to clinics depended upon the car. Those people who could drive realised that they might not always be able to do so, and there were fears that their lives would then be both more difficult and greatly diminished:

'We all dread the day we aren't allowed to drive anymore. Hang onto that as long as possible.'

(Single female resident, aged 79)

Indeed, some felt that if they or their spouse became unable to drive they would have little choice but to move, otherwise the lack of easily accessible facilities locally would make them too reliant on lifts from family, friends or neighbours. Other people were resigned to organising their lives differently without a car, and making do with the services and facilities that were available locally. For those who could no longer drive or who had lost their driver partner, the lack of transport had been a factor in their housing choice, and had certainly curtailed their lifestyle.

A minority of those interviewed thought they were reasonably well served by public transport, but most did not. However, it was recognised that, with most people using cars, the viability of rural bus services was undermined. For those in remote locations or smaller villages there was often no bus service at all, or a very infrequent service. Those without access to a car were either dependent on neighbours and friends for lifts, or made use of any voluntary or community transport services available such as Dial-A-Ride. Inevitably opportunities to go out were limited:

'More buses should be provided. My life was absolutely ruined 'cos of the buses not running. I lost my chance to get up and go, you have to swallow your pride and ask people for a lift.'

(Single female resident, aged 82)

However, many people remarked on the willingness of neighbours to assist, particularly at difficult times, and many respondents themselves regularly offered lifts to others.

'Well, we give people lifts. I have three people on Mondays, Wednesdays and Saturdays. I am their bus.'

(Single male resident, aged 79)

Public transport, usually bus services, was thought to be improving in some places, but was still inadequate to meet the needs of older people. This was in part because of the infrequency of services, or service timetabling that left people with either too little or too much time at their destination. The most commonly expressed complaint was that people were unable to walk to a bus stop. Half of rural residents in settlements of 3,000 people or fewer live further than 13 minutes' walk from a bus stop with a service at least once an hour (Countryside Agency, 2005, pages 57–59). Such walking distances were too far for those who felt frail or suffered from physical or sensory impairment; an indication of the numbers this may affect is reflected in the 2.9 per cent of the overall rural population who currently claim Disability Living Allowance (Countryside Agency, 2005). With services thought to be unreliable and few bus shelters, a long wait in the cold and wet was not an attractive prospect.

'The parish council are trying to get a shelter for the buses otherwise you have to stand in the rain.'

(Female resident, couple, aged 69)

Private taxis were considered to be very expensive, and beyond the budget of most older people. In any case, taxis from nearby towns were often reluctant to travel long distances to collect a fare, especially for short journeys. It was also reported that some taxis were reluctant to take travel vouchers issued to older people by social services as they could not be readily cashed in.

In contrast, community transport services offered a more affordable option for older people although they could be quite limited. Journeys usually had to be booked in advance, and most voluntary services only covered fairly local destinations. Some services were only intended to take people for specific reasons such as hospital or doctors' appointments, and would not take people to social events, or vice versa. Where services were dependent on volunteer drivers, this usually constrained outings to weekdays and daytime, as volunteers were less likely to be available at weekends and evenings. Some people also remarked on the patchy nature of voluntary sector services – they could be excellent in some places, and non-existent in others. Nevertheless, community transport services were highly valued by respondents and, limitations notwithstanding, offered the flexible response to transport needs that were required in rural areas. In addition, a couple of respondents commented on the additional benefits of this kind of service such as the opportunity for meeting and making friends.

Personal mobility was also a concern. For those unable to walk any distance the only transport services that were of much use were door-to-door services such as taxis, lifts from friends and neighbours or voluntary transport schemes which picked people up from their homes. For this group, transport provision was essential for even the shortest journeys. The point is well illustrated by the experience in one village, where the local GP surgery had moved to the neighbouring village and, in recognition of the expected difficulties that this might cause, the Primary Care Trust had contracted with a local voluntary transport service to bring older and disabled patients to appointments at the surgery. In the event, this outcome was actually preferred by the older people, even though the surgery was further away, because they had not been able to walk to the former surgery despite its relative proximity.

Given the greater reliance of older people on public transport, respondents universally approved of schemes that enabled older people to travel more cheaply on buses and trains. Some felt that all older people should be able to travel free on public transport. In one area when a county council planned to reduce its transport subsidies to older people, the police had to be called to the council meeting to quell the vociferous protests of older people's groups from across the county.

Isolation

Respondents often referred to isolation as a pervasive but complex feature of rural living. Physical isolation could be due to living in remote locations, or arise from limited personal mobility. Social isolation could be a consequence of being physically isolated, but not necessarily so. While it was recognised that some people preferred to keep themselves to themselves, in the main social isolation was viewed by respondents as a significant factor that diminished the overall well-being of older residents in rural areas, contributing to loneliness and depression.

The British Household Panel Survey does show that the extent to which urban or rural residents communicate with their neighbours tends to reduce as settlement size diminishes, and residents of villages, hamlets and isolated dwellings are least likely to have regular local social contact. Over 20 per cent of residents over the age of 55 do not have contact with neighbours more than once or twice a month (Countryside Agency, 2005, pages 62–63). For older people social isolation may come about from feeling an outsider, from being distant from friends and family, from their own declining mobility or from the loss of a partner or close neighbour. One respondent reflected on this issue while commenting on her ideal form of accommodation for older people:

> '*I think we all like our own home. But we also like a bit of company and you can get very lonely. Proper sheltered accommodation where you can do your own thing but if you want help you can pull a bell. Or if you want to go and have a meal in their restaurant, or sit in their community room you can, or sit on your own. It gives you your dignity and privacy. That's very important as one gets older. You may be a bit old and frail and maybe can't do what you'd like to do, but we've still got our dignity.'*
>
> (Female, single, aged 82)

Respondents saw the potential for increasing isolation in current trends in service delivery and in broader social changes. For example, people retiring to the countryside were having to establish new networks distant from families, and more and more older people had to cope with being on their own. Established residents might have to face similar challenges either with bereavement or as their adult children moved away in pursuit of work or afford- able housing. Making new friends and contacts as one got older was not an easy task. One respondent noted:

> '*What is so rare is to commission someone to get you integrated into the community, go to the local community centre, the local church, to maintain your contacts with other human beings outside your house, and I think that's terribly important and terribly missed.'*
>
> (Male, couple, aged 68)

In some case study areas (North Yorkshire, Dorset and parts of Suffolk), second homes were seen as contributing to the isolation of the permanent residents, with some settlements with very high levels (20 per cent or more) of second home ownership being described as 'virtually dead' in the winter months. More generally it was felt that there was an overall reduction in the opportunity for social contact because of the decline of local services and facilities such as shops and public transport, the growing emphasis on telephone and internet-based services, and the withdrawal of on-site wardens from retirement and sheltered housing complexes.

Certain facilities such as post offices and shops were valued specifically as hubs for the main- tenance of community support and social interaction in rural communities. Respondents were particularly concerned about the closure of post offices: not only was this facility im- portant for older people without a car to access benefits and financial services, but also for its contribution to the vitality of the community. Likewise, transport provision in rural areas may not just provide access to services but may also help combat social isolation. A number of respondents commented on the positive social benefits ascribed to projects whose primary objective was transport provision.

Emotional support from frequent informal social contact was considered crucial in enabling older people to sustain their quality of life, but all too often it did not figure in calculations about the rationalisation of service delivery. This view was also echoed in some of the discus- sions with service providers. One practitioner commented on attitudes towards delivering services to older people compared with other groups in society:

'If we look at younger people with physical disabilities, we concentrate far more on their quality of life and emotional well-being. For older people, quality of life tends to be ignored. Emotional well-being tends to be ignored.'

(Practitioner, Social Services)

However, the consequences from the loss of opportunities for local social contact went beyond people's sense of well-being. Social isolation was viewed as a barrier to uncovering hidden needs in rural areas, not least because so many agencies relied on word of mouth to inform people of the services available.

Support for independent living

Older people value their independence, but to remain independent they may rely on a variety of formal and informal supporting services. Informal help from neighbours, friends and family was frequently reported as the main form of support. For those who needed assistance with small household tasks, shopping or transport, this came mainly from friends and neighbours, as family were usually too far away to be able to offer much in the way of day-to-day support:

'There's one person whose husband has gone to a care home, and people take her every day up to the care home so she can see her husband. That kind of thing goes on voluntarily without any kind of organisation. You get that in a village which is closely knit. Not necessarily family, but friends or neighbours.'

(Female, single, aged 78)

Many respondents remarked on the preference of older people in rural areas, particularly those who had always lived in relatively isolated communities where self-sufficiency was the norm, to accept informal assistance rather than engage with external organisations which were perceived as bureaucratic and interfering:

'There's a feeling that it's OK if it's a friend or a neighbour, and a feeling of not wanting to engage with authority and to go through all the bureaucracy ...'

(Male, single, aged 72)

Much of the 'formal' community support in the case study areas was provided by voluntary sector agencies (often with funding from the statutory sector), and many of the volunteers were themselves above retirement age. A variety of schemes addressing diverse needs were operating, including befriending, handyman schemes, shopping, social/lunch clubs, day centres, and exercise and activity groups (such as Walk Out Well in North Yorkshire). Such services may benefit from their informality and local responsiveness, but may also be quite variable. If a local voluntary group is very active in a particular location, then services will be in place, but in another location there will not be the same level of activity. Local authorities also have different attitudes towards the voluntary sector, some being more supportive than others. The consequence is a patchiness in voluntary sector services with some areas better served than others. Among those interviewed, voluntary sector support services were valued, but were clearly seen as only one element in people's support networks.

In addition, many people paid for assistance with odd jobs, gardening and cleaning when they could afford such services, and indeed find people who would do them:

'My daughter said to me, "Have you thought about getting a woman to come and clean once a week?", but I said "Who would I get? The days are done when your mum used to do this. Up and coming generation – you wouldn't do a Mrs Mop, would you?" No, it's a changing world.'

(Female, single, aged 83)

Finding reputable and trustworthy tradespeople was consistently noted as a difficulty. Assistance with small domestic repairs, heavier gardening tasks, lifts to the doctor, hospital appointments and fetching shopping were all greatly valued, and indeed were essential for many older people. Such services do not usually fall within the ambit of statutory sector responsibilities, even though they provide crucial support. When asked what types of services or support made a real difference in enabling older people to remain independent in the countryside, people usually talked about these low level preventative services. However, one agency official commented ruefully:

'Everybody knows that if money can be put into prevention, money can be saved later on, but the world doesn't work like that and so the resources that are there tend to go into crisis and end of the scale needs.'

The challenge of providing services for rural communities

In all the interviews with service providers and commissioners, respondents were asked what the greatest challenges were for delivering services in rural areas. A number of themes consistently emerged relating to the practical and organisational difficulties of working in a rural area:

● serving dispersed populations;

● identifying need;

● land use and planning requirements;

● organisational challenges, staffing and funding.

Serving dispersed populations

Service commissioners and providers struggled with the question of how and where to cluster services to ensure access to all their catchment population, particularly for those living in smaller settlements. The dispersed nature of rural populations reduces the opportunities for economies of scale. This applies to all types of services, from sheltered housing developments, to day care services, to advice and information, to voluntary befriending and visiting schemes, to out-of-hours emergency GP services.

Service providers were well aware of the notion of delivering services to people in their own homes. Indeed, facilitating housing choice in the countryside must be about promoting solutions for people to stay in their homes just as much as it is about providing a variety of alternative 'bespoke' types of accommodation to meet the diverse range of needs that people experience. However, successfully translating this strategic aim into a shift in direction away from predominantly accommodation-based services must be backed by sufficient resources, particularly to cope with growing demand in rural areas in the future. One practitioner remarked:

> 'People feel there should be a lot more prevention stuff. There's a feeling that social services are only interested in you if you are on your last legs. There's a lot of talk as well because we as a department do not help with things like housework and cleaning. The agency cost around here is about £8 per hour, and most older people around can't or won't pay £8 for somebody to wash their curtains, or clean their house, and then their house becomes a mess. They become depressed, and it's a downward spiral really. There's a feeling that nobody really cares about them.'

(Practitioner, Social Services)

When services were delivered in the home, or on an outreach basis, travel distances increased the costs of service provision both in terms of travelling costs (for fuel, travel allowances and so forth) and the staff time required to make the journey. Many agencies reported that these additional costs reduced their capacity to meet the demands for their services, and some were reluctantly forced to restrict home visits in remoter locations. Some local authorities – such as East Sussex – had introduced a rural premium, which recognised the additional costs of providing such services as domiciliary care in rural areas (Bainbridge and Ricketts, 2003).

An alternative approach pursued by some service providers was to locate in larger population centres and expect clients scattered across surrounding rural areas to come in for the service. Some respondents maintained that certain specialist provision (such as day care for dementia sufferers) was difficult to provide on an outreach or mobile basis. However, it was felt that many older people simply could not be bothered with the inconvenience and discomfort of travelling long distances or making complicated journeys, and thus did not take up services which could have been beneficial to them such as physiotherapy, chiropody, day care and respite care. A compromise solution seemed to be offered by some of the accommodation schemes in larger villages which, while offering extra care to their residents, were being used additionally as a base from which outreach services could be delivered to non-residents who lived locally.

Respondents frequently noted the difficulties in ensuring people in rural settlements got the information they might need about services. Various methods were used or had been tried. Most agencies produced publicity leaflets about their services, for display in council offices and information points, GP surgeries, post offices, local libraries and other public venues. There was concern that older people most in need, particularly those who were isolated or housebound, might not get a chance to see these (Brown, 1999). Some councils produced regular newsletters delivered to all homes in their areas, giving broad information about services and highlighting new service developments. Information about services was sometimes included with Council Tax bills. One local authority promoted any vacancies in sheltered housing schemes in this way. Many respondents felt that word of mouth was the most effective way of promoting services, but this could not be relied on exclusively because of the physical and social isolation that many older people experience. A number of agencies were developing services to respond to the need for effective advice and information in rural areas, including, for example, Care and Repair England, which has developed two rural pilots of the 'Should I stay or should I go' project. These pilots were intended to test the practicality of providing specialist housing advice services to older people in the countryside.

There were examples of mobile services that visited different locations on different days, using local village halls or pubs as a venue. However, many agencies reported that mobile advice and information services had been withdrawn because they had aroused little response. It seems that people in small communities do not want to be seen using certain services. One practitioner commented:

> 'Communities, particularly isolated communities, are furiously independent and won't engage with services. We've had the benefits van and whatnot in the middle of the market town, but people won't go. They wouldn't want to be seen going in and asking for help and advice.'
>
> (Practitioner, Home Improvement Agency)

Likewise 'special days' organised jointly by housing, health and social care agencies had generated limited interest in smaller communities despite publicity: again it was thought people did not want to be seen seeking advice so publicly. Conversely, piggybacking advice or information sessions onto an existing social gathering such as a regular lunch or social club appeared to be effective, as no one had to identify themselves as being in need of a particular service.

Such efforts were thought to be vital to ensure that people who required a certain type of assistance or support were aware of the services available before they reached a crisis. There was frustration therefore that Social Care and Health departments were so resource constrained that they could increasingly only cater for people with critical needs. Even day centres that used to provide services primarily to help overcome isolation were now having to cope with individuals with much more intensive care needs. A further challenge for services in some rural areas is the growth in numbers of older people resulting not only from an ageing population that has been resident in the area for many years but also from people migrating into these areas to retire. As one practitioner noted:

> 'About 5 years ago about 5 per cent of people supported by social services were self-funders who had run out of money. But now about 25–30 per cent of the purchasing budget for nursing and residential care is for self-funders who have run out of money. So there is not only a rise in population of older people, but [the county] is also an importer, and people are running out of money.'
>
> (Practitioner, Social Services)

Identifying need

The needs of rural communities are not homogeneous, and can vary from village to village reflecting differences in social composition, location, local facilities, transport links, existing community groups, and so forth. Agencies claimed that they had a good understanding about the diversity and specifity of needs, but often found it difficult to quantify them. In particular, needs assessment methods were lacking. As a result, agencies were hard pressed to make a case to justify the provision of resources for particular services or groups, although there was a consensus that there were considerable unmet needs for a range of services.

There was concern that widely used indicators of need inadequately captured the experience of rural residents, including the Index of Multiple Deprivation (Noble and Wright, 2000) and measures of housing need and affordability. A characteristic of rural areas is the way that, unlike in many urban areas, households on low incomes are dispersed geographically with rich and poor often living in close proximity, so area-based measures aggregate extremes of income, and thus tend not only to mask households on low incomes but also to gloss over local inequalities. The criticism has been extended to other measures of need. For example, it has been argued that traditional indices of health based on urban models give a false impression of the health of rural populations (North Dorset Primary Care Trust, 2003).

Large-scale surveys are useful at the strategic level, but are quite blunt instruments for identifying rural needs. Respondents noted that district-wide housing needs surveys provided a helpful overall assessment of need, but could not be disaggregated to the level of individual rural settlements.

One feature of prevailing needs assessments is the extent to which they are demand-led, recording numbers of people coming forward for services or from referrals. However, Oldman (2002) has emphasised the extent to which needs in rural areas remain stubbornly hidden. A reason highlighted in the case study areas by agencies was that older people in rural communities were disinclined to seek help and were more likely to make do, or struggle on. In part, it was felt that such stoicism reflected the attitude of an older generation that did not expect help from statutory services, and that accepted, or at least was used to, a way of life without services and facilities that others took for granted. Among established elements of rural communities, such as farmers, there was also a culture of independence and of not asking for outside help. More generally, there was a stigma associated with being seen to be taking up welfare, and people were concerned to retain their dignity and privacy. The twin dangers are that needs remain hidden and unrecorded, and that providers are unresponsive or insensitive.

Consequently, there is a certain wariness towards social services departments, linked with the perception that once social services are involved a person's independence will be compromised. In part, this view may stem from the feeling that, having expressed a need, someone may lose control over the decision-making process and, since housing options are so limited in rural areas, may be steered towards accommodation that they do not really want, such as residential care some distance from their home. In this context, Home Improvement Agencies and voluntary organisations had an important role to play as honest brokers and in raising awareness of the range of options available to older people. In Suffolk a pilot project called Helping Hands, which aims to provide care and support services specifically for older people in rural areas, has been set up as a co-operative social enterprise to enable the full participation of customers in the way services are delivered and in the running of the organisation.

Other reasons for not articulating need are because people lack knowledge about the services that are available, or do not expect certain services to be available. An example of the latter is social rented accommodation: re-lets or new build are so rare in rural settlements that people do not bother applying (ACC, 1989). There is concern therefore about the value of waiting lists as an indicator of need because they reflect too much the pattern of existing supply, rather than unmet need. The tendency for households to come forward in villages wherever a vacancy occurs does reveal hidden need for accommodation. In consequence, in considering proposals for the development of affordable housing under the special rural programme for settlements below 3,000 population, the Housing Corporation expect evidence to be drawn from small-scale surveys of housing needs. This highlights the significance of parish councils, community groups and Rural Housing Enablers in identifying those in housing need in local areas. As one practitioner commented: 'The more rural you get, the more important it is to get the bottom tier right'.

However, while sensitive, community-based processes for assessing need are now institutionally accepted, organisational priorities and constraints may still prevail. For example, the Housing Corporation's rural programme has focused overwhelmingly on family-sized units (Housing Corporation, 2001). Similarly, one of the Rural Housing Enablers noted the preference of a local social housing provider for the development of multi-storey properties and a consequent resistance to building bungalows. Thus, even though needs may be clearly delineated, it is not guaranteed that local or national agencies will respond to them. Of course, providers do have to juggle competing claims against limited resources. For Waveney District, Suffolk, the emphasis was on family housing as this group was seen to present the most pressing need for housing in the area. In Dorset, claims for resources for different groups had to be balanced against the specific and immediate needs of homeless households.

Land use and planning requirements

The development of specialised accommodation for older people in rural areas – whether sheltered housing schemes, retirement complexes, or accommodation units designated for older people – was considered to be particularly problematic. Not only could it be difficult to identify a critical mass of people in a locality requiring such accommodation, but the process of planning and developing it could be so lengthy that the original intended beneficiaries might no longer need it. In addition, the cost of land for building is usually very high because so few sites within the development limits of villages come onto the market, and these are highly sought after by private developers to build executive homes.

Suitable sites for development of social housing of any sort are difficult to find. There are stringent planning restrictions in National Parks, green belt areas, conservation areas and Areas of Outstanding Natural Beauty. Unit building costs tended to be higher in rural areas because of the smaller scale of schemes. Additional costs were encountered in more remote settlements, in places inaccessible to vehicles, where equipment and materials had to be carried on site by hand, and where planning requirements stipulated that new building should use traditional methods and materials. Housing Associations were reluctant to take on smaller developments because the unit costs were so high:

> 'It just isn't easy building in rural areas. Anyone who says it is isn't being honest. It just isn't easy, even if you're building on a brown field site. The land is expensive, the lead-in time is a problem and people are nervous about signing agreements about only letting to people born and bred in the parish …'

Private developers of older people's housing schemes were also reported as encountering difficulty in finding suitable sites that met their requirements for being near to the centre of market towns and within easy and level access of a range of facilities.

Organisational challenges, staffing and funding

All service providers remarked on the considerable difficulties they experienced recruiting and retaining staff. Although the shortage of social care staff was most frequently mentioned, difficulties in recruiting occupational therapists, speech therapists, social workers and nursing staff were also highlighted. For social care staff, low rates of pay, lack of career development, the low status of caring, and other, more attractive, employment opportunities (eg in hotels and catering, or in supermarkets) were all blamed for causing a growing shortage and high turnover of staff. Not only did this cause day-to-day problems in maintaining services but it was also not conducive to staff training and development.

Indeed, it was felt that necessary improvements in care standards could not be attained with a workforce paid the minimum wage and with many staff caught in the benefits trap. It was recognised that the requirement for staff to be better trained and qualified to meet national care standards would inevitably increase costs, partly because trained staff had greater expectations of better wages and promotion, and partly due to the expense of the training itself. In this regard, it was felt that the resources available through the Training Organisation for Personal Social Services (TOPSS) were woefully inadequate – 'a drop in the ocean'. It was also felt that making training opportunities more available locally might encourage people to take up caring who would not otherwise have considered taking on this type of work.

Unfortunately, the severe shortage of affordable housing – whether for sale or for rent – in most rural areas was forcing the younger and less well paid workers to move to areas where housing was cheaper. In all the case study areas, house prices in rural areas and villages were high, and well beyond the reach of those working in the local service economy. Any new developments tended to be of costly executive homes, and the social housing stock had been greatly reduced by the Right to Buy.

The severe shortage of affordable housing in rural areas was exacerbating staffing shortages. In one case study area (Dorset) it was reported that sometimes no provider agency could be found who would deliver domiciliary care to people in remote areas of the county. In another case study area (North Yorkshire), independent sector care providers were bussing care staff in from neighbouring counties on a daily basis. The strategic intention to support and maintain more older people in their own homes is thus severely testing the ability of agencies to recruit and retain sufficient numbers of suitably trained and qualified staff to realise the strategy.

Service commissioners and providers were responding in different ways to the staffing difficulties they faced. Social services commissioners were increasingly using block contracting (purchasing a total number of hours of care from a care provider) instead of spot purchasing, thereby allowing agencies to offer more secure work opportunities to their care staff, and to undertake better recruitment and service planning. Block contracts also allowed cover for rural and urban areas to be included in one contract to ensure coverage across both areas and to allow agencies to recruit staff over a wider geographical area. Employers were also increasingly offering incentives such as cheap mobile phones, interest-free loans for car repairs and maintenance, and other small perks to make their employment packages more attractive. Looking to the future, some respondents were interested in the possibility of having more generic care staff trained to cover a range of tasks and able to make referrals to more specialist staff if required. This could reduce the number of staff from different agencies visiting the same client – to do 'health' or 'rehabilitation' or 'social care' tasks – and cut down on the amount of travelling.

A different set of possibilities were seen to be opened up by the Disabled Living Allowance. Those receiving the allowance may employ their own carers. For example, someone living in a rural area could recruit a neighbour who might be particularly well placed to help. The informality and responsiveness of such personalised arrangements could offer so much more support than funding an agency-employed carer to travel some distance for brief, periodic visits. There were concerns however about the lack of regulation of personal carers. There is no requirement to be registered (unlike, for example, child minders), and there was some anecdotal evidence of people dismissed by care agencies becoming personal carers and working independently for a number of clients. There were also concerns that problems of staff recruitment and retention were being passed on to clients and their families.

It might be thought that voluntary sector organisations would avoid the recruitment problems of private and statutory agencies, but this is not necessarily so. They usually rely on a core of paid staff. Moreover, all the voluntary sector organisations interviewed remarked that recruitment of volunteers was a constant concern and a time-consuming activity. One difficulty highlighted was the impact of work pressures on volunteering. For example, a voluntary agency noted that people were retiring later in life and also that couples with children of school age now both tended to be out at work, whereas this form of household used to be a good source of volunteers. An emerging issue also noted by another agency was felt to be the impact of a 'blame' culture developing within society and an increasing reluctance by individuals to place themselves in situations as volunteers where they may get sued. The majority of volunteers were people aged 55 and over, and mainly women. Men were more likely to volunteer for services that involved driving, or offered small-scale repairs and maintenance in the home. The significant contribution made by older people within communities was highlighted by a respondent from a voluntary agency, who commented:

'Older people are our resource. The mainstay of the organisation and support systems.'
(Voluntary agency)

Respondents agreed that partnership working was crucial if the various needs of older people were to be met. In rural areas partnership working can be a complex activity. Unlike urban areas where there is likely to be one unitary authority, in a rural county served by a county council there may be many agencies involved. These may include a number of district councils, possibly several Primary Care Trusts usually with boundaries that are not coterminous with district council boundaries, a patchwork of different voluntary sector agencies serving different areas, some Home Improvement Agencies, various Housing Associations, maybe a National Park, and various acute hospital trusts serving populations within and across district and county boundaries, as well as Strategic Health Authorities and Regional Housing Boards. Linking all these agencies together to produce district- or county-wide strategic plans and partnerships is a complex and resource-hungry task. Different agencies have different priorities and statutory duties, with varying levels of funding available and different degrees of flexibility in how they can deploy it. District councils and other agencies in rural areas are usually small organisations whose professional staff often find themselves fully stretched by the consultation and co-ordination requirements of the various partnerships and separate strategies of the private, statutory and voluntary organisations that provide the range of services for older people. Nevertheless, the necessity for a joint approach to take forwards an effective response to the needs of older people in the countryside was recognised in most of the case study areas, as it is in many other rural localities. A number of housing departments in Dorset, Suffolk and Lancashire were developing Older Persons' Housing Strategies with other agencies such as Social Care and Health, Primary Care Trusts and Registered Social Landlords.

Undeniably, the characteristic features of rural areas affect the provision of services, not least the fact that the cost of supplying services is higher per capita in rural than in urban areas. However, in England (but not Wales and Scotland) resource allocation systems in areas such as health care do not compensate for the additional costs arising from rurality (Asthana et al, 2003). Social care services also tend to be focused towards provision in urban areas. For example, a study by Cumbria County Council found that twice the population of those aged over 65 received home care services in urban compared with remoter areas (Asthana et al, 2002). There is a potential for double discrimination; certain needs are concentrated in rural areas – such as those associated with an ageing population – where the costs of supporting those needs is intrinsically higher, but these greater needs and costs are not acknowledged in resource allocation (Gordon et al, 2004). There is an additional difficulty when planning in a situation where new needs are arising, because the formulae that Government uses in distributing funds to local authorities are retrospective. The Barker Review highlighted the detrimental effect that additional housing growth could have on local authority finances because of the failure of the funding formulae to allocate sufficient funds to areas experiencing rapid population growth (Barker, 2004). The Review made particular reference to the resources required in areas where sheltered housing schemes were being developed.

All public sector services in rural and urban areas face funding shortfalls, or would develop and expand services if additional funding were provided. Perhaps the main difference between rural and urban areas is that rural areas rarely score highly enough on deprivation indices to attract certain types of regeneration funding. Many rural councils are traditionally low spending authorities, and are reluctant to increase local taxes. Craig and Manthorpe (2000) found that rural authorities traditionally spent less on social care services and direct provision. A number of respondents criticised the withdrawal of the Local Authority Social Housing Grant (LASHG) as having a particularly detrimental impact on rural authorities. It was felt that this removed a key source of flexible local funding for rural areas, which do not attract considerable mainstream funding via the Approved Development Programme.

Respondents from voluntary sector agencies reported funding to be their biggest challenge. It appeared to be much easier to get funding for new and apparently innovative services than for sustaining existing services. This was a cause of much frustration. Various respondents reported on schemes that had disappeared due to funding restraints despite being used and valued, and serving a number of agendas. An example was a Hospital Discharge scheme where volunteers would visit people as soon as they were discharged from hospital offering practical assistance and support to ensure they were managing their return home.

Conclusions

The older people who were spoken to as part of the research on which this chapter is based discussed their views and experiences of living in rural areas. As part of these discussions, the majority of older people were keen to stress the positive aspects of living in rural areas, as well as highlighting some of the difficulties that they faced. This chapter has emphasised some of the problems about living in rural areas that older people described and also some of the challenges that agencies faced as they developed and provided services to respond to these issues.

Various studies have investigated older people's preferences for housing in later life (see, for example, Wilson et al, 1995; Appleton, 2002; Clough et al, 2003; Croucher et al, 2003). These studies reiterated the views expressed in this research that the concerns that older people have about their housing are not just limited to the home itself (although heating, security, size and quality of accommodation, aids and adaptations, and level access are consistently raised as issues within the home) but are also closely linked to location, access to a range of services, and particularly transport. Other research has also demonstrated the high value placed by older people on low level preventative services that assist them with small tasks in the home, and enable them to socialise and get out of their homes (see, for example, Clark et al, 1998; Raynes et al, 2001). Previous studies have not had a primarily rural focus. However, work recently carried out with older people by Care and Repair England in rural Devon at a series of Listening Events[1] also clearly echoes our findings that people do not see their housing in isolation, but are also concerned particularly about transport, support services and other types of infrastructure that facilitate independence.

An implication for policy is that spending on features such as transport and low level support may well indirectly help to facilitate and support the housing choices and preferences of older people in the countryside. An imperative for the development of 'whole system' approaches for strategies in rural areas is the links between agencies and services which help people to draw together these diverse aspects of daily living. One consideration here is the extent to which there is a shared understanding between practitioners of the contribution that housing can make to meeting objectives in relation to health and vice versa. The rural dimension of regional and sub-regional housing strategies also needs to be further developed: there is evidence of rural proofing, but clearly greater consideration of the needs and aspirations of older people at regional level is required.

Limited housing options and poor access to transport services mean that low level support and preventative services play a particularly crucial role in rural areas. The development of a national strategy for preventative services or a national preventative service framework would appear to be one way in which services might achieve a greater consistency across England and a more stable funding base. The National Service Framework for Older People, Best Value reviews and performance indicators have driven the development of health and social care services. However, there are no similar incentives to drive the development of preventative services, and there is no national programme or standard that indicates what older

---

1   Further information available from Care and Repair England: http://www.carenandrepair-england.org.uk.

people should expect as a minimum. This is perhaps not surprising. Defining what 'preventative' services are or should be is problematic. Clearly, Falls Prevention Programmes, support following hospital discharge, intermediate care and other services with a health focus can be seen as preventative services. However, the net could be cast much wider to encompass services that broadly speaking promote independence and well-being. Community transport services, handy person schemes, lunch clubs, carers' support and so forth could also be described as preventative. There is no getting away from the fact that delivering preventative services in rural areas comes at a price because of the distances that services need to cover to reach older people. However, the costs of delivering preventative services in rural areas need to be considered against the social and economic costs of individuals having to give up their own home, or spend more time in other settings such as hospitals. Voluntary agencies make a crucial contribution to the delivery of preventative services, but find they are hampered by uncertain and insecure funding. A particular frustration highlighted by voluntary agencies in this research was the way that established and valued services were sometimes cut in favour of 'new' and 'exciting' projects.

The importance of transport in allowing people to sustain successful ageing in place also points to the necessity for strong links between agencies at local level in the preparation of joint strategies, and the relationship between housing strategies for older people and the Local Strategic Partnership and Community Plan. This issue also highlights the need for better integration at regional level between Regional Housing Strategies and Regional Transport Strategies (the latter as an integral part of Regional Spatial Strategies) to adequately reflect both the rural dimension and the needs of older people.

Although housing markets are high on the Government agenda at national, regional and local levels, little notice has been paid to date of older people in this debate, despite the fact that we have an ageing population and the proportion of older people who are homeowners is increasing. The rural dimension is particularly important since the level of home ownership by older people is higher in rural areas than urban areas. However, the proportion of the population who can take advantage of new properties in the countryside is very limited. A difficulty here is the low amount of new development in rural areas, with the consequent limited ability for policy to significantly influence the balance of property types into the future. The efficacy of planning policy with respect to a circumscribed supply of housing in rural areas is not the issue here. The point is that, since the amount of new build in and around most villages is so limited, the dwellings that are developed have a proportionately more significant role to play in helping to broaden choice in rural communities. In the context of an ageing society it is essential to ensure that new build – both in the private and public sector – can meet the needs and aspirations of older people in the future. Beyond accessibility, consideration needs to be given to space standards to allow opportunities in the future for adaptation and installation of equipment.

Finally, the way that providers and policy makers engage and work in partnership with older people is a necessary component of any policy or service development that touches on the concerns of older people themselves. It is essential that the views of older people living in the countryside are part of this process and that the development of engagement models includes the potential for incorporating a rural dimension.

References and further reading

ACC (1989) *Homes We Can Afford.* London: Association of County Councils

Appleton, N. (2002) *Planning for the Majority: The Needs and Aspirations of Older People in General Housing.* York: York Publishing Services

Asthana, S., Halliday, J., Brigham, P. and Gibson, A. (2002) *Rural Deprivation and Service Need: A Review of the Literature and an Assessment of Indicators of Service Planning, South West Public Health Observatory,* available via http://www.swpho.org.uk

Asthana, S., Gibson, A., Moon, G. and Brigham, P. (2003) 'Allocating resources for health and social care: the significance of rurality', *Health and Social Care in the Community* 11 (6), 486–493

Bainbridge, I. and Ricketts, A. (2003) *Improving Older People's Services: An Overview of Performance,* London: Department of Health

Barker, K. (2004) *Delivering Stability: Securing Our Future Housing Needs,* London: HM Treasury

Brown, D. (1999) *Care in the Country – Inspection of Community Care in Rural Communities.* London: Department of Health

Clark, H., Dyer, S. and Horwood, J. (1998) *'That Bit Of Help': The High Value of Low Level Preventative Services for Older People,* Bristol/York: The Policy Press/Joseph Rowntree Foundation

Clough, R., Leamy, M., Bright, L. et al (2003) *Homing in on Housing: A Study of Housing Decisions of People Aged Over 60,* Lancaster: Eskrigg Social Research

Countryside Agency (2000) *Tomorrow's Countryside – 2020 Vision,* Cheltenham: Countryside Agency

Countryside Agency (2005) *The State of the Countryside 2005,* Cheltenham: Countryside Agency

Craig, G. and Manthorpe, J. (2000) *Fresh Fields. Rural Social Care: Research, Policy and Practice Agendas,* York: York Publishing Services

Croucher, K., Pleace, N. and Bevan, M. (2003) *Living at Hartrigg Oaks: Residents' Views of the UK's First Continuing Care Retirement Community,* York: Joseph Rowntree Foundation

Department for Work and Pensions (2005) *Opportunity Age – Opportunity and Security Throughout Life,* London: HMSO

Gordon, D., Kay, A., Kelly, M., Nandy, S., Senior, M. and Shaw, M. (2004) *Targeting Poor Health: Review of Rural and Urban Factors Affecting the Costs of Health Services and Other Implementation Issues,* Cardiff: National Assembly for Wales

Housing Corporation (2001) *Rural Strategy,* London: Housing Corporation

Noble, M. and Wright, G. (2000) 'Identifying poverty in rural England', *Policy and Politics* 28 (3), 293–308

North Dorset Primary Care Trust (2003) *Public Health Report,* Dorchester: North Dorset Primary Care Trust

Oldman, C. (2002) *Support and Housing in the Countryside: Innovation and Choice,* Wetherby: The Countryside Agency

Raynes, N., Temple, B., Glenister, C. and Coulthard, L. (2001) *Quality at Home for Older People: Involving Service Users in Defining Home Care Specifications,* Bristol/York: The Policy Press/ Joseph Rowntree Foundation

Wilson, D., Aspinall, P. and Murie, A. (1995) *Factors Influencing the Housing Satisfaction of Older People,* Birmingham: Centre for Urban and Rural Studies, University of Birmingham

About Age Concern

Age Concern is the UK's largest organisation working for and with older people to enable them to make more of life. We are a federation of over 400 independent charities which share the same name, values and standards.

We believe that ageing is a normal part of life, and that later life should be fulfilling, enjoyable and productive. We enable older people by providing services and grants, researching their needs and opinions, influencing government and media, and through other innovative and dynamic projects.

Every day we provide vital services, information and support to thousands of older people of all ages and backgrounds.

Age Concern also works with many older people from disadvantaged or marginalised groups, such as those living in rural areas or black and minority ethnic elders.

Age Concern is dependent on donations, covenants and legacies.

Age Concern England
1268 London Road
London SW16 4ER
Tel: 020 8765 7200
Fax: 020 8765 7211
Website:
www.ageconcern.org.uk

Age Concern Cymru
Ty John Pathy
Units 13 and 14 Neptune Court
Vanguard Way
Cardiff CF24 5PJ
Tel: 029 2043 1555
Fax: 029 2047 1418
Website:
www.accymru.org.uk

Age Concern Scotland
113 Rose Street
Edinburgh EH2 3DT
Tel: 0131 220 3345
Fax: 0131 220 2779
Website:
www.ageconcernscotland.org.uk

Age Concern Northern Ireland
3 Lower Crescent
Belfast BT7 1NR
Tel: 028 9024 5729
Fax: 028 9023 5497
Website:
www.ageconcernni.org

Publications from Age Concern Books

Age Concern Books publishes over 65 books, training packs and learning resources aimed at older people, their families, friends and carers, as well as professionals working with and for older people. Publications include:

Your Rights: A guide to money benefits for older people

Sally West

Your Rights has established itself as ***the*** money benefits guide for older people. Updated annually, and written in clear, jargon-free language, it ensures that older people – and their advisers – can easily understand the complexities of state benefits and discover the full range of financial support available to them.

£5.99: For more information, please telephone 0870 44 22 120.

To order from Age Concern Books

Call our **hotline: 0870 44 22 120** (for orders or a free books catalogue)

Opening hours 9am-7pm Monday to Friday, 9am-5pm Saturday and Sunday

Books can also be ordered from our secure on-line bookshop: **www.ageconcern.org.uk/shop**

Alternatively, you can write to Age Concern Books, Units 5 and 6 Industrial Estate, Brecon, Powys LD3 8LA. Fax: 0870 8000 100. Please enclose a cheque or money order for the appropriate amount plus p&p made payable to Age Concern England. Credit card orders may be made on the order hotline.

Our **postage and packing** costs are as follows: mainland UK and Northern Ireland: £1.99 for the first book, 75p for each additional book up to a maximum of £7.50. For customers ordering from outside the mainland UK and NI: credit card payment only; please telephone for international postage rates or email sales@ageconcernbooks.co.uk

Bulk order discounts

Age Concern Books is pleased to offer a discount on orders totalling 50 or more copies of the same title. For details, please contact Age Concern Books on 0870 44 22 120.

Customised editions

Age Concern Books is pleased to offer a free 'customisation' service for anyone wishing to purchase 500 or more copies of most titles. This gives you the option to have a unique front cover design featuring your organisation's logo and corporate colours, or adding your logo to the current cover design. You can also insert an additional four pages of text for a small additional fee. Existing clients include many prominent names in British industry, retailing and finance, the trade union movement, educational establishments, public, private and voluntary sectors, and welfare associations. For full details, please contact Sue Henning, Age Concern Books, Astral House, 1268 London Road, London SW16 4ER. Fax: 020 8765 7211. Email: sue.henning@ace.org.uk

Age Concern Information Line/Factsheets subscription

Age Concern produces 45 comprehensive factsheets designed to answer many of the questions older people (or those advising them) may have. These include money and benefits, health, community care, leisure and education, and housing. For up to five free factsheets, telephone 0800 00 99 66 (8am-7pm, seven days a week, every week of the year). Alternatively you may prefer to write to Age Concern, FREEPOST (SWB 30375), ASHBURTON, Devon TQ13 7ZZ.

For professionals working with older people, the factsheets are available on an annual subscription service, which includes updates throughout the year. For further details and costs of the subscription, please contact Age Concern at the above Freepost address.

We hope that this publication has been useful to you. If so, we would very much like to hear from you. Alternatively, if you feel that we could add or change anything, then please write and tell us, using the following Freepost address: Age Concern, FREEPOST CN1794, London SW16 4BR.

Index

(Numbers in italics refer to figures and tables)